本书由东南大学教务处教材建设项目资助

高校英语选修课系列教材

美国文学与文化

American Literature:
A Cultural Perspective

主 编 朱丽田

编 者 梁文艳 圣小利

南京大学出版社

前　言

《美国文学与文化》是一本文学作品和文化背景紧密结合的教材，适用于英语专业学生、具有较高英语水平的非英语专业学生和英语爱好者。文学作品选读的范围上溯到15世纪哥伦布发现新大陆，下延至美国当代文学名著。教材共选编了美国文学中的24位作家的主要作品，按年代和文本体裁分成19章。每一章分成两大部分：文学作品聚焦和文化背景知识。文学作品聚焦分为作者简介、作品选读和文学术语，其中作品选读前提供一段关于作品内容的中文简介，选文中加上了一些必要的生词注释，选文后列出思考题供学生讨论；文化背景知识主要选取与前面选文联系密切的历史知识短文，通过一系列的练习使学生理解作品的文化背景知识。总体看来，本教程具备以下主要特色：

1. 突出文学作品本身的重要性。对作家进行简单扼要的介绍，为了帮助学生更好地理解作品，将文学作品的内容和相关文学术语放在教程中加以具体阐述；

2. 注重文学作品的文化内涵。由于文学与文化密不可分，对美国社会、历史等文化的了解有助于理解作品，因此专门设计文化背景知识部分，把文化置于非常重要的地位，以期加深对作品的掌握；

3. 设计新颖的教学板块。尤其是每一章的第二部分主体内容包括 Before You Read，Start to Read，After You Read 三大板块，包括课前热身、主题阅读、课后练习等。教材在结构上确立了学生的主体地位，而且系统的安排也方便教师借助教材有条不紊地安排教学活动。

4. 推荐有趣的多媒体学习材料。在每一单元的最后是 For Fun 环节，它是对教学内容的延伸和拓展。编者向学生推荐了根据文学作品改编的电影或与作品相关的影视作品和网站等学习资源。这不仅有益于学生开阔视野，也使教材具有开放性，方便不同水平学生的使用。这些环节的设置使课堂教学得以延展，也最大程度地激发学生的学习兴趣和热情。

《美国文学与文化》的问世离不开东南大学教务处及外国语学院领导的关心和支持，更要感谢南京大学出版社，尤其是本书的责任编辑董颖女士的辛勤付出。在此，我代表编者向他们表示诚挚的谢意。

本教程由东南大学外国语学院朱丽田主编，东南大学梁文艳和南通大学圣小利两位老师参加了编写工作。具体分工如下：朱丽田负责全书策划、统稿、校改，并编写了第1—8章、第19章；梁文艳编写第9—13章；圣小利编写第14—18章。另外，张晓、刘琚、倪梦蕾、高君实和汪琳等也参加了后期的统稿和校改工作。本教程编写者参考了有关的美国文学选集和教材，并参考了一些公共网站文献进行改写编撰。由于对作家作品的了解、认识和研究不一，加上编者水平有限，我们的观点和对作家作品的选择可能与研究美国文学的专家学者意见有出入，欢迎广大读者提出宝贵意见和建议，以期不断完善教材。

编　者

2015年9月于南京

Contents

Chapter 1	Christopher Columbus (1451–1506)	1
Chapter 2	Benjamin Franklin (1706–1790)	6
Chapter 3	Ralph Waldo Emerson (1803–1882)	17
Chapter 4	Nathaniel Hawthorne (1804–1864)	24
Chapter 5	Edgar Allan Poe (1809–1849)	32
Chapter 6	Henry David Thoreau (1817–1862)	45
Chapter 7	Herman Melville (1819–1891)	53
Chapter 8	The Nineteenth Century American Poets	64
	Walt Whitman (1819–1892)	64
	Emily Dickinson (1830–1886)	71
Chapter 9	Mark Twain (1835–1910)	77
Chapter 10	Jack London (1876–1916)	86
Chapter 11	F·Scott Fitzgerald (1896–1940)	95
Chapter 12	William Faulkner (1897–1962)	111
Chapter 13	Ernest Miller Hemingway (1899–1961)	124
Chapter 14	The Twentieth Century American Poets (Ⅰ)	132
	Ezra Pound (1885–1972)	132
	Robert Frost (1874–1963)	136
Chapter 15	The Twentieth Century American Drama	143
	Eugene Glastone O'Neill (1888–1953)	143
	Tennessee Williams (1911–1983)	153
	Arthur Miller (1915–2005)	170
Chapter 16	Joseph Heller (1923–1999)	187
Chapter 17	The Twentieth Century American Poets (Ⅱ)	209
	Allen Ginsberg (1926–1997)	209
	Sylvia Plath (1932–1963)	215
Chapter 18	Toni Morrison (1931–)	224
Chapter 19	John Updike (1932–2009)	246
参考文献		256

Chapter 1

Christopher Columbus (1451-1506)
克里斯托弗·哥伦布

Section A Literary Focus

作者简介(About the Author)

Christopher Columbus (1451-1506)

【生平】 克里斯托弗·哥伦布(Christopher Columbus),探险家、殖民者、航海家,出生于中世纪的热那亚共和国(今意大利西北部)。在西班牙的天主教君主的赞助下,他在1492年到1502年间四次横渡大西洋,并且成功到达美洲。他使得普通欧洲人知道了美洲。他的这些航行,以及在伊斯帕尼奥拉岛建立永久居民点的努力,拉开了西班牙殖民美洲的序幕,同时也是欧洲殖民后来所谓"新大陆"的先驱。

【主要作品】 《航海日志》(*Journal of the First Voyage to America*)(1493)

作品选读(Selected Writings)

Journal of the First Voyage to America

《航海日志》记述了哥伦布第一次西航时的艰辛以及沿途所遇到的困难,他们首次登上美洲大陆时所见到的旖旎动人的风光,大陆的主人——印第安人健美的体格,以及他们热情淳朴的品质等等。《航海日志》还暴露了哥伦布一行对黄金的贪欲,以及为掠取黄金在交易中对天真淳朴的印第安人的欺哄诈骗。这是欧洲第一部记述新大陆情况和欧洲人在新大陆活动的作品。哥伦布发现美洲之举在当时的欧洲成为街谈巷议的话题,人们对那里所发生的一切都大感新奇,因此,《航海日志》一经问世,便在欧洲引起巨大反响,随即被译成欧洲各主要文字。此日记对研究美洲历史,尤其印第安人历史和早期殖民史提供了丰富的第一手资料。这是一部研究美洲历史不可多得的重要文献。

This account begins in the days after Columbus landed on San Salvador.

SUNDAY, Oct. 21st [1492]. At 10 o'clock, we arrived at a cape of the island, and anchored, the other vessels in company. After having dispatched a meal, I went ashore, and found no habitation save a single house, and that without an occupant; we had no doubt that the people had fled in terror at our approach, as the house was completely furnished. I suffered nothing to be touched, and went with my captains and some of the crew to view the country. This island even exceeds the others in beauty and fertility①. Groves of lofty and flourishing trees are abundant, as also large lakes, surrounded and overhung by the foliage②, in a most enchanting manner. Everything looked as green as in April in Andalusia. The melody of the birds was so exquisite that one was never willing to part from the spot, and the flocks of parrots obscured the heavens. The diversity in the appearance of the feathered tribe from those of our country is extremely curious. A thousand different sorts of trees, with their fruit were to be met with, and of a wonderfully delicious odor. It was a great affliction to me to be ignorant of their natures, for I am very certain they are all valuable; specimens of them and of the plants I have preserved. Going round one of these lakes, I saw a snake, whither we killed, and I have kept the skin for your Highness; upon being discovered he took to the water, whither we followed him, as it was not deep, and dispatched him with our lances; he was seven spans in length; I think there are many more such about here. I discovered also the aloe tree, and am determined to take on board the ship tomorrow, ten quintals③ of it, as I am told it is valuable. While we were in search of some good water we came upon a village of the natives about half a league④ from the place where the ships lay; the inhabitants on discovering us abandoned their houses, mad took to flight, carrying off their goods to the mountain. I ordered that nothing which they had left should be taken, not even the value of a pin. Presently we saw several of the natives advancing towards our party, and one of them came up to us, to whom we gave some hawk's bells and glass beads, with which he was delighted. We asked him in return, for water, and after I had gone on board the ship, the natives came down to the shore with their calabashes⑤ full, and showed great pleasure in presenting us with it. I ordered more glass beads to be given them, and they promised to return the next day. It is my wish to flu all the water casks⑥ of the ships at this place, which being executed, I shall depart immediately, if the weather serve, auld sail round the island, till I succeed in meeting with the king, in order to see if I can acquire any of the gold, which I hear he possesses. Afterwards I shall set sail for another very large island which I believe to be Cipango, according to the indications I receive from the Indians on board. They call the Islauad Colba, and say there are many large ships, and sailor there. This other island they name Bosio and

---

① fertility: 肥沃
② foliage: 树叶
③ quintals: 公担（公制重量单位，=100 公斤）
④ league: 里格（长度单位，1 里格约等于 3 英里）
⑤ calabash: 葫芦
⑥ cask: 桶

inform me that it is very large; the others which lie in our course, I shall examine on the passage, and according as I find gold or spices in abundance, I shall determine what to do; at all events I am determined to proceed on to the continent, and visit the city of Guisay where I shall deliver the letters of your Highnesses to the Great Can, and demand an answer, with which I shall return.

Questions for discussion
1. What is Columbus' impression after his seeing the scenery of the island?
2. According to Columbus' narration, why were the houses empty when he and his men went ashore?
3. How long was Columbus to stay on this island? What did he intend to do later?

文学术语(Definition of Terms)

A **journal** is an individual's day-by-day account of events. It provides details of events and the writer's personal idea about the events.

Section B Cultural Notes

Before You Read

1. Try to search on the Internet or in the library about more information about the Mayflower Compact.
2. Who signed on the Mayflower Compact?
3. Why did they agree to sign the compact?

Start to Read

During the 1500s, King Henry VIII made a Protestant Reformation to encourage establishing of the Church of England. At this time, many puritans, who didn't think it is possible to change the Church of England and abandoned Anglicanism, called "Separatists", didn't support the official English church. It's normal that the Separatists were persecuted by the king's soldiers, so the Separatists determined to secure religious freedom, boarded the Mayflower and set sail for America's shores.

The 102 passengers who undertook the long, perilous journey on the Mayflower were not all Separatists (later called Pilgrims). These Separatists had originally left England for the Netherlands to escape religious persecution but believed the New World, discovered by Christopher Columbus in 1492, was a better option. The Separatists had obtained a land patent from the London Virginia Company allowing them to settle at the mouth of the Hudson River. To raise money for the voyage they were financed by the Merchant Adventurers who were looking to make a profit. The Pilgrims agreed to repay their backers.

Only 41 of them were Separatists. The passengers were split into two groups—the Separatists (Pilgrims) and the rest of the passengers, who were called "strangers" by the Pilgrims. The two groups are referred to as the "Strangers" and the "Saints". And the Saints were the Separatists, a close society, whose primary motivation in making the journey was the establishment of a colony in which they could have religious freedom, and were not unified by religion, they were not close family units, and they were described as "common people"; the Strangers were not motivated by the prospect of religious freedom—they wanted to make money and the Strangers were tradesmen, craftsmen, skilled workers, laborers and indentured servants and several young orphans. The "Saints" were a less than tolerant community because they did not welcome other groups or different points of view. There were major differences between the two groups of "Saints" and "Strangers" in terms of levels of education, religion, social structure, political views, aspirations and beliefs, at the same time they knew nothing about the New World, so the differences between the two groups were dangerous and could threaten their very survival in the New World. Therefore the two groups realized that if they didn't work as a group, they could all die in the wilderness. There was no room for their differences to be of paramount importance when their lives were at stake. The two groups had to come to an agreement in order for them to survive. The idea of the Mayflower Compact was born.

The significance of the Mayflower Compact

The Mayflower Compact was written by the colonists before landing at Plymouth Rock and was the first governing document of Plymouth Colony under the sovereignty of James I of England. The Mayflower Compact specified basic laws and social rules for the new colony and served as a foundation for the democratic structure of the settlers. The significance of the Mayflower Compact is that it contains extremely important concepts that helped to shape the History of America. The Mayflower Compact document established a social contract within the community of colonists and formed a government based upon the consent of the people. ① The Mayflower Compact set a precedent and was an influential document for the Founding Fathers as they created the US Constitution. The Mayflower Compact made a significant contribution to the creation of a new democratic nation which would become the United States of America. ②

---

① http://en.wikipedia.org/wiki/Mayflower_Compact
② http://www.landofthebrave.info/mayflower-compact.htm

After You Read

I. Questions for discussion
1. Who are "the Strangers" and who are "the Saints"?
2. What are the major differences between the Strangers and the Saints?
3. How does the idea of the Mayflower Compact come into being?
4. What role does the Mayflower Compact play in American history?

II. True or false
1. The Puritans made a Protestant Reformation to encourage establishing of the Church of England. (　)
2. These Separatists had originally left England for the Netherlands to escape religious persecution. (　)
3. The Strangers were motivated by the prospect of religious freedom. (　)
4. The Strangers were tradesmen, craftsmen, skilled workers, laborers and indentured servants and several young orphans. (　)
5. The Mayflower Compact document established a social contract within the community of colonists and formed a government based upon the consent of the people and King Henry VIII. (　)
6. The Mayflower Compact was an influential document for the Founding Fathers as they created the US Constitution. (　)

For Fun

I. Movies to see
The Mayflower (2006): *The Mayflower* is a historical non-fiction movie. It is about the Puritans' journey on the ship Mayflower in the 17th century. It is directed by American director Lisa Wolfinger and produced in 2006.

II. Websites to visit
http://en.wikipedia.org/wiki/Mayflower_Compact
http://www.landofthebrave.info/mayflower-compact.htm

III. Writing
Imagine you were one of the sailors with Columbus, and rewrite the journal about 250 words from your point of view. Maybe you can discover something different from his narration about the Indians.

Chapter 2

Benjamin Franklin（1706-1790）
本杰明·富兰克林

Section A Literary Focus

作者简介（About the Author）

【生平】 本杰明·富兰克林是18世纪美国的作家、科学家、社会活动家、实业家、思想家，他参与了《独立宣言》(The Declaration of Independence)和美国宪法等重要文件的草拟，积极主张废除奴隶制度，曾出任美国驻法国大使，成功取得法国对美国独立的支持，因而深受美国人民的崇敬。

富兰克林在文学和出版业方面也获得了巨大成功。他发表了《穷理查年鉴》（又译《格言历书》）(Poor Richard's Almanac, 1732-1758)，多年来富兰克林一直在年鉴的每一页空白处记录下自己创作的成语、插图和寓言。"穷理查"教导人们勤奋工作、诚实守信，同时对事物持有健康的怀疑态度。当时美国人正在摆脱过去的清规戒律，"穷理查"代表了他们的精神特质，宣告了美国人共同的价值观。

【主要作品】《穷理查年鉴》（又译《格言历书》Poor Richard's Almanac，1732-1758）；《自传》(The Autobiography of Benjamin Franklin)。

作品选读（Selected Writings）

The Autobiography of Benjamin Franklin

富兰克林的著作《自传》叙述了他具有传奇色彩的一生，介绍了他创业、奋斗、成功的历程和为人处世的原则，影响了一代又一代的美国人。《自传》由四部分组成，第一部分讲述了富兰克林一生前25年的经历，如短暂的学校生活、印刷厂的学徒经历、做报纸的匿名撰稿人以及后来在印刷业获得成功后结婚成家。第二部分写于巴黎，主要描写作者科学研究方面的工作和成就；第三和第四部分写于家乡费城，主要讲述25岁以后作者在欧洲和美国政界及外交界的经历和成就。《自传》的意义和价值在于重点突出了作者道德品性的塑造过程和清教主义的勤奋、务实和积极进取的精神。作品展示了18世纪美国社会及启蒙时代的精神风貌,塑造了一个全新的美国人形象,在一定程度上开始扭转欧洲人对美国人的蔑视和偏见,这一人物形象对于美国民族个性的形成起到了重要而深远的影响。

Dear son,

  I have ever had pleasure in obtaining any little anecdotes① of my ancestors. You may remember the inquiries I made among the remains of my relations when you were with me in England, and the journey I undertook for that purpose.

  Imagining it may be equally agreeable to you to know the circumstances of my life, many of which you are yet unacquainted with, and expecting the enjoyment of a week's uninterrupted leisure in my present country retirement, I sit down to write them for you. To which I have besides some other inducements②. Having emerged from the poverty and obscurity in which I was born and bred, to a state of affluence and some degree of reputation in the world, and having gone so far through life with a considerable share of felicity③, the conducing means I made use of, which with the blessing of God so well succeeded, my posterity may like to know, as they may find some of them suitable to their own situations, and therefore fit to be imitated.

  That felicity, when I reflected on it, has induced me sometimes to say, that were it offered to my choice, I should have no objection to a repetition of the same life from its beginning, only asking the advantages authors have in a second edition to correct some faults of the first. So I might, besides correcting the faults, change some sinister accidents and events of it for others more favorable. But though this were denied, I should still accept the offer. Since such a repetition④ is not to be expected, the next thing most like living one's life over again seems to be a recollection⑤ of that life, and to make that recollection as durable as possible by putting it down in writing.

  Hereby, too, I shall indulge the inclination so natural in old men, to be talking of themselves and their own past actions; and I shall indulge it without being tiresome to others, who, through respect to age, might conceive themselves obliged to give me a hearing, since this may be read or not as any one pleases. And, lastly (I may as well confess⑥ it, since my denial of it will be believed by nobody), perhaps I shall a good deal gratify my own vanity. Indeed, I scarce ever heard or saw the introductory words, "Without vanity⑦ I may say," etc., but some vain thing immediately followed. Most people dislike vanity in others, whatever share they have of it themselves; but I give it fair quarter wherever I meet with it, being persuaded that it is often productive of good

---

① anecdote:奇闻轶事
② inducement:动机
③ felicity:幸运
④ repetition:重复,重演
⑤ recollection:回忆
⑥ confess:承认
⑦ vanity:浮华,空虚

to the possessor, and to others that are within his sphere of action; and therefore, in many cases, it would not be altogether absurd if a man were to thank God for his vanity among the other comforts of life.

And now I speak of thanking God, I desire with all humility to acknowledge that I owe the mentioned happiness of my past life to His kind providence, which lead me to the means I used and gave them success. My belief of this induces me to hope, though I must not presume①, that the same goodness will still be exercised toward me, in continuing that happiness, or enabling me to bear a fatal reverse, which I may experience as others have done: the complexion of my future fortune being known to Him only in whose power it is to bless to us even our afflictions②.

The notes one of my uncles (who had the same kind of curiosity in collecting family anecdotes) once put into my hands, furnished me with several particulars relating to our ancestors. From these notes I learned that the family had lived in the same village, Ecton, in Northamptonshire, for three hundred years, and how much longer he knew not (perhaps from the time when the name of Franklin, that before was the name of an order of people, was assumed by them as a surname when others took surnames all over the kingdom), on a freehold③ of about thirty acres, aided by the smith's business, which had continued in the family till his time, the eldest son being always bred to that business; a custom which he and my father followed as to their eldest sons. When I searched the registers at Ecton, I found an account of their births, marriages and burials from the year 1555 only, there being no registers kept in that parish at any time preceding. By that register I perceived that I was the youngest son of the youngest son for five generations back. My grandfather Thomas, who was born in 1598, lived at Ecton till he grew too old to follow business longer, when he went to live with his son John, a dyer at Banbury, in Oxfordshire, with whom my father served an apprenticeship④. There my grandfather died and lies buried. We saw his gravestone in 1758. His eldest son Thomas lived in the house at Ecton, and left it with the land to his only child, a daughter, who, with her husband, one Fisher, of Wellingborough, sold it to Mr. Isted, now lord of the manor there. My grandfather had four sons that grew up, viz.: Thomas, John, Benjamin and Josiah. I will give you what account I can of them, at this distance from my papers, and if these are not lost in my absence, you will among them find many more particulars⑤.

Thomas was bred a smith under his father; but, being ingenious, and encouraged in learning (as all my brothers were) by an Esquire Palmer, then the principal gentleman in

---

① presume: 臆断，推测
② affliction: 苦难
③ freehold: 自由领地
④ apprenticeship: 学徒
⑤ particulars: 材料

that parish, he qualified himself for the business of scrivener①; became a considerable man in the county; was a chief mover of all public-spirited undertakings for the county or town of Northampton, and his own village, of which many instances were related of him; and much taken notice of and patronized by the then Lord Halifax. He died in 1702, January 6, old style, just four years to a day before I was born. The account we received of his life and character from some old people at Ecton, I remember, struck you as something extraordinary, from its similarity to what you knew of mine.

"Had he died on the same day," you said, "one might have supposed a transmigration②."

John was bred a dyer, I believe of woolens. Benjamin was bred a silk dyer, serving an apprenticeship at London. He was an ingenious man. I remember him well, for when I was a boy he came over to my father in Boston, and lived in the house with us some years. He lived to a great age. His grandson, Samuel Franklin, now lives in Boston. He left behind him two quarto volumes, MS., of his own poetry, consisting of little occasional pieces addressed to his friends and relations, of which the following, sent to me, is a specimen. He had formed a short-hand of his own, which he taught me, but, never practicing it, I have now forgotten it. I was named after this uncle, there being a particular affection between him and my father. He was very pious, a great attender of sermons of the best preachers, which he took down in his short-hand, and had with him many volumes of them. He was also much of a politician; too much, perhaps, for his station. There fell lately into my hands, in London, a collection he had made of all the principal pamphlets, relating to public affairs, from 1641 to 1717; many of the volumes are wanting as appears by the numbering, but there still remain eight volumes in folio, and twenty-four in quarto and in octavo. A dealer in old books met with them, and knowing me by my sometimes buying of him, he brought them to me. It seems my uncle must have left them here, when he went to America, which was about fifty years since. There are many of his notes in the margins③.

It was about this time I conceived④ the bold and arduous⑤ project of arriving at moral perfection. I wished to live without committing any fault at any time, and to conquer all that either natural inclination⑥, custom, or company might lead me into. As I knew, or thought I knew, what was right and wrong, I did not see why I might not always do the one and avoid the other. But I soon found I had undertaken a task of more difficulty than I had imagined. While my care was employed in guarding against one fault, I was often surprised by another; habit took the advantage of inattention;

---

① scrivener：书记官，公证人
② transmigration：灵魂转世，轮回
③ margin：页边的空白，边缘，书边上
④ conceive：构思，考虑
⑤ arduous：费力的
⑥ inclination：倾向，爱好

inclination was sometimes too strong for reason. I concluded, at length, that the mere speculative① conviction that it was our interest to be completely virtuous, was not sufficient to prevent our slipping; and that the contrary habits must be broken, and good ones acquired and established, before we can have any dependence on a steady, uniform rectitude② of conduct. For this purpose I therefore tried the following method.

In the various enumerations③ of the moral virtues I had met with in my reading. I found the catalogue more or less numerous, as different writers included more or fewer ideas under the same name. Temperance④, for example, was by some confined to eating and drinking, while by others it was extended to mean the moderating every other pleasure, appetite, inclination, or passion, bodily or mental, even to our avarice and ambition. I proposed to myself, for the sake of clearness, to use rather more names, with fewer ideas annexed to each, than a few names with more ideas; and I included under thirteen names of virtues all that at that time occurred to me as necessary or desirable, and annexed to each a short precept, which fully expressed the extent I gave to its meaning. These names of virtues, with their precepts, were:

1. TEMPERENCE.

Eat not to dullness; drink not to elevation.

2. SILENCE.

Speak not but what may benefit others or yourself; avoid trifling⑤ conversation.

3. ORDER.

Let all your things have their places; let each part of your business have its time.

4. RESOLUTION⑥.

Resolve to perform what you ought; perform without fail what you resolve.

5. FRUGALITY⑦.

Make no expense but to do good to others or yourself; that is, waste nothing.

6. INDUSTRY.

Lose no time; be always employed in something useful; cut off all unnecessary actions.

7. SINCERITY.

Use no hurtful deceit; think innocently and justly; and if you speak, speak accordingly.

8. JUSTICE.

Wrong none by doing injuries, or omitting the benefits that are your duty.

---

① speculative: 推测的,思索的
② rectitude: 公正,诚实
③ enumeration: 列举,计算
④ temperance: 节制,温和
⑤ trifling: 微不足道的
⑥ resolution: 决心
⑦ frugality: 节俭

9. MODERATION.

Avoid extremes; forbear① resenting injuries so much as you think they deserve.

10. CLEANLINESS.

Tolerate no uncleanliness in body, clothes, or habitation.

11. TRANQUILITY②.

Be not disturbed at trifles, or at accidents common or unavoidable.

12. CHASTITY③.

Rarely use venery but for health or offspring, never to dullness, weakness, or the injury of your own another's peace or reputation.

13. HUMILITY.

Imitate Jesus and Socrates④.

My intention being to acquire the habitude of all these virtues, I judged it would be well not to distract my attention by attempting the whole at once, but to fix it on one of them at a time; and, when I should be master of that, then to proceed to another, and so on, till I should have gone through the thirteen; and, as the previous of acquisition of some might facilitate the acquisition of certain others, I arranged them with that view, as they stand above. Temperance first, as it tends to procure⑤ that coolness and clearness of head, which is so necessary where constant vigilance⑥ was to be kept up, and a guard maintained against the unremitting attraction of ancient habits, and the force of perpetual⑦ temptations. This being acquired and established, Silence would be more easy; and my desire being to gain knowledge at the same time that I improved in virtue, and considering that in conversation it was obtained rather by the use of the ear than of the tongue, and therefore wishing to break a habit I was getting into of prattling, punning, and jesting, which only made me acceptable to trifling company, I gave Silence the second place. This and the next, Order, I expected would allow me more time for attending to my project and my studies. Resolution, once become habitual, would keep me firm in my endeavors to obtain all the subsequent virtues; Frugality and Industry relieving me from my remaining debt, and producing affluence and independence, would make more easy the practice of Sincerity and Justice, etc., etc. Conceiving then, that, agreeably to the advice of Pythagoras⑧ in his *Golden Verses*⑨, daily examination would be necessary, I contrived the following method for

---

① forebear：忍耐，克制
② tranquility：宁静，平静
③ chastity：贞洁，纯洁
④ Socrates：苏格拉底(古希腊哲学家)
⑤ procure：获得，取得
⑥ vigilance：警觉
⑦ perpetual：永久的，不断的
⑧ Pythagoras：毕达哥拉斯，古希腊哲学家，数学家
⑨ *Golden Verses*：《金科玉律》，由毕达哥拉斯所著的关于道德方面的劝告，共71条

conducting that examination.

I made a little book, in which I allotted① a page for each of the virtues. I ruled each page with red ink, so as to have seven columns, one for each day of the week, marking each column with a letter for the day. I crossed these columns with thirteen red lines, marking the beginning of each line with the first letter of one of the virtues, on which line and in its proper column I might mark, by a little black spot, every fault I found upon examination to have been committed respecting that virtue upon that day.

I determined to give a week's strict attention to each of the virtues successively②. Thus, in the first week, my great guard was to avoid every the least offense against Temperance, leaving the other virtues to their ordinary chance, only marking every evening the faults of the day. Thus, if in the first week I could keep my first line, marked T. clear of spots, I supposed the habit of that virtue so much strengthened, and its opposite weakened, that I might venture extending my attention to include the next, and for the following week keep both lines clear of spots. Proceeding thus to the last, I could go through a course complete in thirteen weeks and four courses in a year. And like him who, having a garden to weed, does not attempt to eradicate③ all the bad herbs at once, which would exceed his reach and his strength, but works on one of the beds at a time, and, having accomplished the first, proceeds to a second, so I should have, I hoped, the encouraging pleasure of seeing on my pages the progress I made in virtue, by clearing successively my lines of their spots, till in the end, by a number of courses, I should be happy in viewing a clean book, after a thirteen weeks' daily examination ...

The precept④ of Order requiring that every part of my business should have its allotted time, one page in my little book contained the following scheme of employment for the twenty-four hours of a natural day.

MORNING	5	Rise, wash, and address Powerful Goodness!
Question:	6	Contrive⑤ day's business, and take the resolution of the day; prosecute⑥ the present study, and breakfast.
What good shall I do this day?		
	7	
	8	
	9	Work.
	10	
	11	

---

① allot: 分配,拨出
② successively: 相继地,接连着地
③ eradicate: 根除,消灭
④ precept: 规则,训诫
⑤ contrive: 谋划,设计
⑥ prosecute: 从事,依法进行

NOON	12	Read, or overlook my accounts, and dine.
	1	
	3	Work.
	4	
EVENING	6	Put things in their places. Supper. Music or diversion, or conversation.
Question: What good have I done today?		
	7	Examination of the day.
	8	
	9	
	10	
	11	
	12	
NIGHT	1	Sleep.
	2	
	3	
	4	

I entered upon the execution of this plan for self-examination, and continued it with occasional intermissions① for some time. I was surprised to find myself so much fuller of faults than I had imagined; but I had the satisfaction of seeing them diminish. To avoid the trouble of renewing now and then my little book, which, by scraping out② the marks on the paper of old faults to make room for new ones in a new course, became full of holes, I transferred my tables and precepts to the ivory leaves of a memorandum③ book, on which the lines I marked my faults with a black-lead pencil, which marks I could easily wipe out with a wet sponge. After a while I went through one course only in a year, and afterward only one in several years, till at length I omitted them entirely, being employed in voyage and business abroad, with a multiplicity of affairs that interfered; but I always carried my little book with me.

Questions for discussion
1. What do you think makes Benjamin Franklin write this autobiography?
2. What the family anecdotes does he collect? Do you also like to collect something?
3. People living during the American Revolution wanted to create a new American way of life. The Autobiography shows his desire of self-improvement. What is your plan of improving yourself in the college or university?
4. List the experiences you would choose to write about if you were preparing an

---

① intermission: 幕间休息，暂停
② scrape out: 擦去，挖空
③ memorandum: 备忘录

autobiography.

文学术语(Definition of Literary Terms)

An **autobiography** is an account of the life of a person, written by himself or herself.

Section B Cultural Notes

Before You Read

1. Try to search on the Internet or in the library about more information about Benjamin Franklin. What impression does the greatest Benjamin Franklin leave on you?
2. How do you see Franklin as a national fighter?
3. What role does Franklin play in American history? Why is he regarded as one of the Founding Fathers?

Start to Read

Spirit of Nationalism

Benjamin Franklin's extraordinary energy and varied talents made him successful as a writer, humorist, statesman, diplomat, businessman, and scientist. The tale of his rise from humble beginnings through hard work and virtue has become a familiar lesson in the American dream. So exemplary is Franklin's story that his *Autobiography* is often considered, in literary critic Sacvan Bercovitch's term, an auto-American-biography. That is, it functions as a narrative that displays a kind of ideal American citizen, even conflating Franklin's personal history with the founding of the nation.

Born the youngest son in a family of fifteen, Franklin rebelled at an early age against the narrow constraints① of life in Puritan Boston. As a teenager, he rejected his family's pious Puritanism in favor of Deism, a persuasion that privileges reason over faith and rejects traditional religious tenets in favor of a general belief in a benevolent creator. He also rebelled against his lengthy apprenticeship in his brother's Boston print shop. After mastering the printing trade, Franklin violated his contract of indenture② to his brother and ran away to Philadelphia, where he found another position as a printer's assistant. On his own in a new city, Franklin learned to look out for his own best interests, though he also was taken advantage of on occasion. Notably, he found himself

---

① constraint: 约束
② indenture: 契约

in trouble in England after gullibly① accepting a fake offer of assistance. Always one to turn adversity to his advantage, Franklin soon found work in England and acquired new printing skills.

Franklin returned to Philadelphia in 1726, convinced that virtue and hard work were the keys to success. Crucially, for Franklin, an *appearance* of virtue and industry was almost as important as actually possessing these qualities. He took pains to cultivate a reputation for hard work, carrying his own paper through the streets in a wheelbarrow and keeping his light burning late to ensure that others would notice his dedication to his business. Franklin prospered following this formula, and by 1732 he was operating his own print shop, publishing the *Pennsylvania Gazette*, and composing the best-selling *Poor Richard's Almanac*. As his wealth and stature increased, Franklin involved himself in a variety of benevolent② social projects, including the formation of the first American lending library and the first American fire department. In the mid-1740s he began serious work on the scientific experiments that would win him international recognition. Building on ideals of Enlightenment rationalism in his scientific inquiries, Franklin discovered the theory of electricity that still serves as the basis for our use of electric energy.

Franklin devoted the remaining years of his life primarily to politics, diplomacy, and writing. As a leading member of the Pennsylvania Assembly, he was sent to England in 1757 to present the colony's grievances against the Crown. Despite his best diplomatic efforts, he eventually resigned himself to the idea that American independence from British rule was necessary. In 1771, Franklin began composing his *Autobiography*, only to put the project on hold when the Revolution necessitated his return to America. He was selected as a Pennsylvania delegate to the Second Continental Congress and served on the committee that helped Thomas Jefferson draft the *Declaration of Independence*. Franklin then spent much of the war as America's minister to France, using his charm to ensure French support and eventually reach a peace accord with the Great Britain. His last official public duty was his service at the Constitutional Convention of 1787.

After You Read

I. Questions for discussion
1. How do you understand Sacvan Bercovitch's term, "an auto-American-biography"?
2. What kind of person is Franklin at an early age? Could you provide some examples?
3. For Franklin, "an *appearance* of virtue and industry was almost as important as actually possessing these qualities," do you agree? Why and why not?
4. What does "formula" refer to in the text?

---

① gullibly: 轻信地
② benevolent: 仁慈的

5. What are the benevolent social projects did Franklin involve himself in?
6. Why was he sent to England in 1757?
7. Why did Franklin begin to compose his *Autobiography* in 1771?

II. True or false

1. Benjamin Franklin is a successful writer, humorist, statesman, diplomat, businessman and scientist. ( )
2. Franklin is not the youngest in his family. ( )
3. Franklin couldn't find the way out when he found himself stranded in England after gullibly accepting a spurious offer of assistance. ( )
4. The theory of electricity serves as the basis for our use of electric energy. ( )
5. Franklin devoted all his life to politics, diplomacy, and writing. ( )
6. Thomas Jefferson drafted the *Declaration of Independence* together with Benjamin Franklin. ( )
7. Franklin, as America's minister to France, used his charm and charisma to ensure French support and finally reached peace with the Great Britain. ( )
8. Franklin did not belong to the Pennsylvania Assembly. ( )

For Fun

I. Movies to see

Franklin (2005): It is a historical non-fiction movie. It is about the life of Benjamin Franklin, one of the Founding Fathers in American history.

II. Websites to visit

1. http://www.ushistory.org/franklin/info/index.htm
2. http://www.biography.com/people/benjamin-franklin-9301234
3. http://www.learner.org/amerpass/unit04/authors-5.html

III. Writing

Imagine you are going to further your study in an American university and write a personal statement to impress your future supervisor. Your personal statement is your introduction to a committee. It determines whether you are invited to have an interview. If you are selected as a finalist, interview questions will be based on the material. Try to figure out the shining points to make your personal statement impressive.

Chapter 3

Ralph Waldo Emerson（1803—1882）
拉尔夫·沃尔多·爱默生

Section A　Literary Focus

作者简介（About the Author）

【生平】　拉尔夫·沃尔多·爱默生,美国思想家、文学家,是确立美国文化精神的代表人物。美国前总统林肯称他为"美国的孔子"、"美国文明之父"。1835 年 9 月,爱默生和一些志趣相投的知识分子创立了"超验俱乐部",直到 1840 年 7 月,爱默生用化名出版了他在 1836 年 9 月创作的第一本小品文《论自然》(Nature)。1840 年爱默生任超验主义刊物《日晷》(The Dial)的主编,进一步宣扬超验主义思想。后来他把自己的演讲汇编成书,这就是著名的《论文集》。《论文集》第一集于 1841 年发表,包括《论自助》(Self-Reliance)、《论超灵》(The Over-Soul)、《论补偿》(Compensation)等 12 篇论文。三年后,《论文集》(Collected Essays)第二集也出版。这部著作为爱默生赢得了巨大的声誉,他的思想被称为超验主义的核心,他本人则被冠以"美国的文艺复兴领袖"之美誉。

【主要作品】　《英国人的性格》(English Traits,1856);《论文集》(Collected Essays,1841)。

作品选读（Selected Writings）

Nature

《论自然》是爱默生的第一部重要哲学著作,最初发表于 1836 年。它虽非作者成熟之作,但却集超验主义思想之大成,有新英格兰超验主义宣言的美称。全书由《前言》和《自然》等 8 章组成。在表达自然神秘的统一性时,爱默生提出了"超验"的概念。超验为人所用,每个人的思想都存在于超验中,人以直觉观能同它交流。爱默生赞美人的发展潜力无限,推崇人的至高无上,提出"人就是一切,世界为人而存在,人决定自己的命运,人要自信、自尊、自助"。人有神性,只要潜心修养,洁身自好,便可成为完人;而个人的完善则是世界进步的基础。

爱默生的《论自然》发展了美国民族精神和自立精神。从他的《论自然》可以看到，人在自然中是平等的，无阶级之分，也无尊卑意识，我们只是大自然中的一分子。爱默生强调人性的精神性，认为人的精神可以超越物质世界、感性世界及经验世界的种种限制。生活就是为了发掘自我，表达自我，充实自我。

Chapter I Nature

1

To go into solitude①, a man needs to retire as much from his chamber② as from society. I am not solitary whilst I read and write, though nobody is with me. But if a man would be alone, let him look at the stars. The rays that come from those heavenly worlds, will separate between him and what he touches. One might think the atmosphere was made transparent③ with this design, to give man, in the heavenly bodies, the perpetual④ presence of the sublime. Seen in the streets of cities, how great they are! If the stars should appear one night in a thousand years, how would men believe and adore; and preserve for many generations the remembrance of the city of God which had been shown! But every night come out these envoys of beauty, and light the universe with their admonishing smile.

2

The stars awaken a certain reverence⑤, because though always present, they are inaccessible; but all natural objects make a kindred impression, when the mind is open to their influence. Nature never wears a mean appearance. Neither does the wisest man extort⑥ her secret, and lose his curiosity by finding out all her perfection. Nature never became a toy to a wise spirit. The flowers, the animals, the mountains, reflected the wisdom of his best hour, as much as they had delighted the simplicity of his childhood.

3

When we speak of nature in this manner, we have a distinct but most poetical sense in the mind. We mean the integrity⑦ of impression made by manifold natural objects. It is this which distinguishes the stick of timber of the wood-cutter, from the tree of the poet. The charming landscape which I saw this morning, is indubitably⑧ made up of some twenty or thirty farms. Miller owns this field, Locke that, and Manning the woodland beyond. But none of them owns the landscape. There is a property in the horizon which no man has but he whose eye can integrate all the parts, that is, the poet.

---

① solitude：孤独
② chamber：房间
③ transparent：透明的
④ perpetual：永久的
⑤ reverence：敬畏，尊敬
⑥ extort：侵占，强求
⑦ integrity：完整
⑧ indubitably：无疑地，不容置疑地

This is the best part of these men's farms, yet to this their warranty-deeds give no title. To speak truly, few adult persons can see nature. Most persons do not see the sun. At least they have a very superficial seeing. The sun illuminates only the eye of the man, but shines into the eye and the heart of the child. The lover of nature is he whose inward and outward senses are still truly adjusted to each other; who has retained the spirit of infancy even into the era of manhood. His intercourse① with heaven and earth, becomes part of his daily food. In the presence of nature, a wild delight runs through the man, in spite of real sorrows. Nature says,—he is my creature, and maugre② all his impertinent griefs, he shall be glad with me. Not the sun or the summer alone, but every hour and season yields its tribute of delight; for every hour and change corresponds to and authorizes a different state of the mind, from breathless noon to grimmest midnight. Nature is a setting that fits equally well a comic or a mourning piece. In good health, the air is a cordial of incredible virtue. Crossing a bare common, in snow puddles, at twilight, under a clouded sky, without having in my thoughts any occurrence of special good fortune, I have enjoyed a perfect exhilaration. I am glad to the brink of fear. In the woods too, a man casts off his years, as the snake his slough③, and at what period soever of life, is always a child. In the woods, is perpetual youth. Within these plantations of God, a decorum and sanctity reign, a perennial festival is dressed, and the guest sees not how he should tire of them in a thousand years. In the woods, we return to reason and faith. There I feel that nothing can befall me in life,—no disgrace, no calamity, (leaving me my eyes,) which nature cannot repair. Standing on the bare ground,—my head bathed by the blithe air, and uplifted into infinite space,—all mean egotism vanishes. I become a transparent eye-ball; I am nothing; I see all; the currents of the Universal Being circulate through me; I am part or particle of God. The name of the nearest friend sounds then foreign and accidental: to be brothers, to be acquaintances,—master or servant, is then a trifle and a disturbance. I am the lover of uncontained and immortal beauty. In the wilderness, I find something more dear and connate than in streets or villages. In the tranquil landscape, and especially in the distant line of the horizon, man beholds somewhat as beautiful as his own nature.

4

The greatest delight which the fields and woods minister, is the suggestion of an occult④ relation between man and the vegetable. I am not alone and unacknowledged. They nod to me, and I to them. The waving of the boughs in the storm, is new to me and old. It takes me by surprise, and yet is not unknown. Its effect is like that of a higher thought or a better emotion coming over me, when I deemed I was thinking justly

---

① intercourse: 交流
② maugre: 不管
③ slough: 蜕皮
④ occult: 神秘的

or doing right.

5

Yet it is certain that the power to produce this delight, does not reside in nature, but in man, or in a harmony of both. It is necessary to use these pleasures with great temperance. For, nature is not always tricked in holiday attire, but the same scene which yesterday breathed perfume and glittered as for the frolic① of the nymphs②, is overspread with melancholy today. Nature always wears the colors of the spirit. To a man laboring under calamity, the heat of his own fire hath sadness in it. Then, there is a kind of contempt of the landscape felt by him who has just lost by death a dear friend. The sky is less grand as it shuts down over less worth in the population.

Questions for discussion

1. How do you understand Emerson's description of nature?
2. What's the favorable relationship between humans and nature in your mind? What are the possible ways to attain that goal?
3. Do you have any experiences to come close to nature? Please share with your partners about your unique and unforgettable feelings.
4. How is transcendentalisim reflected in Emerson's thinking?

文学术语(Definition of Literary Terms)

1. **Transcendentalism** is a, philosophical and literary movement that flourished in New England from about 1836 to 1860. It is the summit of American Romanticism. The beliefs that God is imminent in each person and in nature and that individual intuition is the highest source of knowledge led to an optimistic emphasis on individualism, self-reliance, and rejection of traditional authority.
2. **Essay** is a short literary composition on a single subject, usually presenting the personal view of the author.

Section B Cultural Notes

Before You Read

1. Search for more information about transcendentalism and its representative figures.
2. How are the ideas of transcendentalism reflected in Emerson's works, such as *Nature* and *Self-Reliance*?

---

① frolic：嬉戏
② nymphs：山林仙女

3. What is your comment on transcendentalism?

Start to Read

Transcendentalism

Transcendentalism is an American literary, political, and philosophical movement of the early nineteenth century, centered around Ralph Waldo Emerson. Other important transcendentalists were Henry David Thoreau, Margaret Fuller, Amos Bronson Alcott, Frederic Henry Hedge, and Theodore Parker. Stimulated by English and German Romanticism, the Biblical criticism of Herder and Schleiermacher, and the skepticism of Hume, the transcendentalists operated with the sense that a new era was at hand. They were critics of their contemporary society for its unthinking conformity, and urged that each person find, in Emerson's words, "an original relation to the universe" (O, 3). Emerson and Thoreau sought this relation in solitude amidst nature, and in their writing. By the 1840s they, along with other transcendentalists, were engaged in the social experiments of Brook Farm, Fruitlands, and Walden; and, by the 1850s in an increasingly urgent critique of American slavery. Origins and Character what we now know as transcendentalism first arose among the liberal New England Congregationalists, who departed from orthodox Calvinism in two respects: they believed in the importance and efficacy of human striving, as opposed to the bleaker Puritan picture of complete and inescapable human depravity; and they emphasized the unity rather than the "Trinity" of God (hence the term "Unitarian"① originally a term of abuse that they came to adopt). Most of the Unitarians held that Jesus was in some way inferior to God the Father but still greater than human beings; a few followed the English Unitarian Joseph Priestley (1733-1804) in holding that Jesus was thoroughly human, although endowed with special authority. The Unitarians' leading preacher, William Ellery Channing (1780-1842), portrayed orthodox Congregationalism as a religion of fear, and maintained that Jesus saved human beings from sin, not just from punishment. His sermon "Unitarian Christianity" (1819) denounced "the conspiracy of ages against the liberty of Christians" (P, 336) and helped give the Unitarian movement its name. In "Likeness to God" (1828) he proposed that human beings "partake" of Divinity and that they may achieve "a growing likeness to the Supreme Being" (T, 4). The Unitarians were "modern." They attempted to reconcile Locke's empiricism with Christianity by maintaining that the accounts of miracles in the Bible provide overwhelming evidence for the truth of religion. It was precisely on this ground, however, that the transcendentalists found fault with Unitarianism. For although they admired Channing's idea that human beings can become more like God, they were persuaded by Hume that no empirical proof of religion could be satisfactory. In letters

---

① Unitarian: 一位论派

written in his freshman year at Harvard (1817), Emerson tried out Hume's skeptical arguments on his devout and respected aunt Mary Moody Emerson, and in his journals of the early 1820's he discusses with approval Hume's *Dialogues on Natural Religion* and his underlying critique of necessary connection. "We have no experience of a Creator," Emerson writes, and therefore we "know of none" (JMN 2, 161). Skepticism about religion was also engendered by the publication of an English translation of F. D. E. Schleiermacher's *Critical Essay Upon the Gospel of St. Luke* (1825), which introduced the idea that the Bible was a product of human history and culture. Equally important was the publication in 1833—some fifty years after its initial appearance in Germany—of James Marsh's translation of Johann Gottfried van Herder's *Spirit of Hebrew Poetry* (1782). Herder blurred the lines between religious texts and humanly-produced poetry, casting doubt on the authority of the Bible, but also suggesting that texts with equal authority could still be written. It was against this background that Emerson asked in 1836, in the first paragraph of *Nature*: "Why should we not have a poetry and philosophy of insight and not of tradition, and a religion by revelation to us, and not the history of theirs" (O, 5). The individual's "revelation"—or "intuition," as Emerson was later to speak of it—was to be the counter both to Unitarian empiricism and Human skepticism.

After You Read

I. Questions for discussion

1. How do you understand the expression "a new era was at hand"? (line 6, paragraph 1)
2. What is the relation between the ideas of transcendentalism and American slavery?
3. What are the opinions of the liberal New England Congregationalists?
4. Why were the Unitarians "modern"?
5. What fault did the transcendentalists find with Unitarianism?
6. How do the empiricism and skepticism reconcile with each other?
7. What is the meaning of "revelation" when Emerson uses this word?
8. What does "theirs" refer to in the sentence "why should we not have a poetry and philosophy of insight and not of tradition, and a religion by revelation to us, and not the history of theirs"?

II. True or false

1. The transcendentalists criticized their contemporary society for its unthinking conformity. ( )
2. Transcendentalism arose from the skepticism, empiricism and the contrast between the Trinity and Unitarianism. ( )
3. *Walden* was written in the 1840s. ( )

4. Schleiermacher's *Critical Essay Upon the Gospel of St. Luke* strongly threatened the skepticism.   (   )
5. Transcendentalism is closely related to religion.   (   )

For Fun

I. Websites to visit

1. http://emersoncentral.com/texts.htm
2. http://plato.stanford.edu/contents.html
3. http://www.thefreedictionary.com/Transcendentalism
4. http://www.emersoncentral.com/selfreliance.htm
5. http://plato.stanford.edu/entries/transcendentalism/

II. Writing

   Nature is regarded as the friend of human beings. What is your idea about nature? Write an essay about your understanding of Nature.

Chapter 4

Nathaniel Hawthorne（1804-1864）
纳撒尼尔·霍桑

Section A　Literary Focus

作者简介（About the Author）

【生平】　纳撒尼尔·霍桑是19世纪前半期美国最伟大的小说家。他出生于一个没落的世家，大学毕业后即从事写作。曾两度在海关任职。霍桑采取了浪漫主义（Romanticism）小说的创作形式。他认为只有这样，作者才能以自己选择的方式构思和创作，而又不必拘泥于细节的真实，才能在"真实的世界"和"仙境"之间找到现实与想象相结合的"中间地带"。霍桑的伟大在于他能以表面温和而实质犀利的笔锋暴露黑暗、讽刺邪恶、揭示真理。

描写社会和人性的阴暗面是霍桑作品的突出特点，这与加尔文教关于人的"原罪"和"内在堕落"的理论的影响是分不开的。霍桑是心理小说（psychological novel）的开创者。他着重探讨道德和罪恶的问题，主张通过善行和自忏来洗刷罪恶、净化心灵，从而得到拯救。然而霍桑并非全写黑暗，他在揭露社会罪恶和人的劣根性的同时，对许多善良的主人公寄予极大的同情。霍桑的作品想象丰富，结构严谨。他除了进行心理分析与描写外，还运用了象征主义（symbolism）手法。构思精巧的意象为他的作品增添了浪漫色彩，加深了寓意。

【主要作品】　短篇小说集《古宅青苔》（*Mosses from an Old Manse*，1846）、《重讲一遍的故事》（*Twice-Told Tales*，1837）等，长篇小说《红字》（*The Scarlet Letter*，1850）、《带七个尖顶的阁楼》（*The House of the Seven Gables*，1851）、《福谷传奇》（*The Blithedale Romance*，1852）、《玉石人像》（*The Marble Faun*, Or, *The Romance of Monte Beni*，1860）等。

作品选读（Selected Writings）

The Scarlet Letter

霍桑的代表作《红字》一经问世，便引起了巨大轰动，在时隔一个半世纪后的今日仍是不朽的经典名著。小说以17世纪殖民地时期的美洲为背景，讲述了发生在北美殖民地的恋爱悲剧。女主人公海丝特·白兰嫁给了医生奇灵渥斯,他们之间却没有爱情。在孤独中白兰与牧师丁梅斯代尔相恋并生下女儿珠儿。白兰被当众惩罚,戴上标志"通奸"的红色 A 字示众。然而白兰坚贞不屈,拒不说出孩子的父亲。小说用象征手法,人物、情节和语言都颇具主观想象色彩,在描写中又常把人的心理活动和直觉放在首位。因此,它不仅是美国浪漫主义小说的代表作,同时也被称美国心理分析小说的开创篇。

Chapter 2　THE MARKET-PLACE

　　THE grass-plot before the jail, in Prison Lane, on a certain summer morning, not less than two centuries ago, was occupied by a pretty large number of the inhabitants of Boston; all with their eyes intently fastened on the iron-clamped oaken door. Amongst any other population, or at a later period in the history of New England, the grim rigidity that petrified① the bearded physiognomies② of these good people would have augured some awful business in hand. It could have betokened③ nothing short of the anticipated execution of some noted culprit, on whom the sentence of a legal tribunal had but confirmed the verdict of public sentiment. But, in that early severity of the Puritan character, an inference of this kind could not so indubitably④ be drawn. It might be, that a sluggish bond-servant, or an undutiful child, whom his parents had given over to the civil authority, was to be corrected at the whipping-post. It might be, that an Antinomian, a Quaker, or other heterodox religionist, was to be scourged⑤ out of the town, or an idle and vagrant⑥ Indian, whom the white man's fire-water had made riotous about the streets, was to be driven with stripes into the shadow of the forest. It might be, too, that a witch, like old Mistress Hibbins, the bitter-tempered widow of the magistrate, was to die upon the gallows⑦. In either case, there was very much the same solemnity of demeanour on the part of the spectators; as befitted a people amongst whom religion and law were almost identical, and in whose character both were so thoroughly interfused, that the mildest and the severest acts of public discipline were alike made venerable and awful. Meagre, indeed, and cold, was the sympathy that a transgressor might look for, from such bystanders, at the scaffold. On the other hand, a penalty which, in our days, would infer a degree of mocking infamy and ridicule, might then be invested with almost as stern a dignity as the punishment of death itself.

　　It was a circumstance to be noted, on the summer morning when our story begins its course, that the women, of whom there were several in the crowd, appeared to take a peculiar interest in whatever penal infliction might be expected to ensue. The age had

---

① petrified: 惊呆的
② physiognomy: 外貌
③ betoken: 预示
④ indubitably: 无疑地,不容置疑地
⑤ scourge: 鞭打
⑥ vagrant: 漂泊的
⑦ gallows: 绞刑架

not so much refinement, that any sense of impropriety restrained the wearers of petticoat and farthingale from stepping forth into the public ways, and wedging their not unsubstantial persons, if occasion were, into the throng nearest to the scaffold at an execution. Morally, as well as materially, there was a coarser fibre in those wives and maidens of old English birth and breeding, than in their fair descendants, separated from them by a series of six or seven generations; for, throughout that chain of ancestry, every successive mother has transmitted to her child a fainter bloom, a more delicate and briefer beauty, and a slighter physical frame, if not a character of less force and solidity, than her own. The women who were now standing about the prison-door stood within less than half a century of the period when the man-like Elizabeth had been the not altogether unsuitable representative of the sex. They were her country-women; and the beef and ale of their native land, with a moral diet not a whit more refined, entered largely into their composition. The bright morning sun, therefore, shone on broad shoulders and well-developed busts, and on round and ruddy cheeks, that had ripened in the far-off island, and had hardly yet grown paler or thinner in the atmosphere of New England. There was, moreover, a boldness and rotundity① of speech among these matrons, as most of them seemed to be, that would startle us at the present day, whether in respect to its purport or its volume of tone.

"Goodwives," said a hard-featured dame of fifty, "I'll tell ye a piece of my mind. It would be greatly for the public behoof, if we women, being of mature age and church-members in good repute, should have the handling of such malefactresses as this Hester Prynne. What think ye, gossips? If the hussy stood up for judgment before us five, that are now here in a knot together, would she come off with such a sentence as the worshipful magistrates have awarded? Marry, I trow② not!"

"People say," said another, "that the Reverend Master Dimmesdale, her godly pastor, takes it very grievously to heart that such a scandal should have come upon his congregation."

"The magistrates are God-fearing gentlemen, but merciful overmuch-that is a truth," added a third autumnal matron. "At the very least, they should have put the brand of a hot iron on Hester Prynne's forehead. Madam Hester would have winced at that, I warrant me. But she—the naughty baggage—little will she care what they put upon the bodice of her gown! Why, look you, she may cover it with a brooch, or such like heathenish adornment, and so walk the streets as brave as ever!"

"Ah, but," interposed, more softly, a young wife, holding a child by the hand, "Let her cover the mark as she will, the pang of it will be always in her heart."

"What do we talk of marks and brands, whether on the bodice of her gown, or the flesh of her forehead?" cried another female, the ugliest as well as the most pitiless of

---

① rotundity: (声音等)洪亮
② trow: (古)相信,以为

these self-constituted judges. "This woman has brought shame upon us all, and ought to die. Is there not law for it? Truly there is, both in the Scripture and the statute-book. Then let the magistrates, who have made it of no effect, thank themselves if their own wives and daughters go astray!"

"Mercy on us, goodwife," exclaimed a man in the crowd, "is there no virtue in woman, save what springs from a wholesome fear of the gallows? That is the hardest word yet! Hush, now, gossips! For the lock is turning in the prison-door, and here comes Mistress Prynne herself."

The door of the jail being flung open from within, there appeared, in the first place, like a black shadow emerging into sunshine, the grim and grisly① presence of the town-beadle, with a sword by his side, and his staff of office in his hand. This personage prefigured and represented in his aspect the whole dismal severity of the Puritanic code of law, which it was his business to administer in its final and closest application to the offender. Stretching forth the official staff in his left hand, he laid his right upon the shoulder of a young woman, whom he thus drew forward; until, on the threshold② of the prison-door, she repelled him, by an action marked with natural dignity and force of character, and stepped into the open air, as if by her own free will. She bore in her arms a child, a baby of some three months old, who winked and turned aside its little face from the too vivid light of day; because its existence, heretofore, had brought it acquainted only with the grey twilight of a dungeon③, or other darksome apartment of the prison.

When the young woman—the mother of this child-stood fully revealed before the crowd, it seemed to be her first impulse to clasp the infant closely to her bosom; not so much by an impulse of motherly affection, as that she might thereby conceal a certain token, which was wrought or fastened into her dress. In a moment, however, wisely judging that one token of her shame would but poorly serve to hide another, she took the baby on her arm, and, with a burning blush, and yet a haughty④ smile, and a glance that would not be abashed, looked around at her townspeople and neighbours. On the breast of her gown, in fine red cloth, surrounded with an elaborate embroidery and fantastic flourishes of gold thread, appeared the letter A. It was so artistically done, and with so much fertility and gorgeous luxuriance of fancy, that it had all the effect of a last and fitting decoration to the apparel which she wore; and which was of a splendour in accordance with the taste of the age, but greatly beyond what was allowed by the sumptuary⑤ regulations of the colony.

---

① grisly: 可怕的
② threshold: 门口;起始点
③ dungeon: 土牢
④ haughty: 高傲的
⑤ sumptuary: 禁止奢侈的

The young woman was tall, with a figure of perfect elegance on a large scale. She had dark and abundant hair, so glossy that it threw off the sunshine with a gleam, and a face which, besides being beautiful from regularity of feature and richness of complexion, had the impressiveness belonging to a marked brow and deep black eyes. She was ladylike, too, after the manner of the feminine gentility of those days; characterised by a certain state and dignity, rather than by the delicate, evanescent, and indescribable grace, which is now recognised as its indication. And never had Hester Prynne appeared more ladylike, in the antique interpretation of the term, than as she issued from the prison. Those who had before known her, and had expected to behold her dimmed and obscured by a disastrous cloud, were astonished, and even startled, to perceive how her beauty shone out, and made a halo of the misfortune and ignominy① in which she was enveloped. It may be true, that, to a sensitive observer, there was something exquisitely painful in it. Her attire, which, indeed, she had wrought for the occasion, in prison, and had modelled much after her own fancy, seemed to express the attitude of her spirit, the desperate recklessness of her mood, by its wild and picturesque peculiarity. But the point which drew all eyes, and, as it were, transfigured the wearer-so that both men and women, who had been familiarly acquainted with Hester Prynne, were now impressed as if they beheld her for the first time—was that SCARLET LETTER, so fantastically embroidered and illuminated upon her bosom. It had the effect of a spell, taking her out of the ordinary relations with humanity, and enclosing② her in a sphere by herself.

Questions for discussion

1. What does the chapter mainly talk about?
2. What kind of woman do you think Hester Prynne is?
3. Have you found any impressive points in this chapter? What is the symbolic meaning of the scarlet letter A?

文学术语(Definition of Terms)

1. **Puritanism**: In the 16th and 17th centuries, a movement for reform in the Church of England that had a profound influence on the social, political, ethical, and theological ideas of England and America.
2. **Romanticism** can be seen as a rejection of the precepts of order, calmness, harmony, balance, idealization, and rationality that typified Classicism in general and late 18th-century Neoclassicism in particular.

---

① ignominy：耻辱
② enclose：围入，圈起

Section B Cultural Notes

Before You Read

1. Try to search on the Internet or in the library about Puritanism.
2. How would you explain the relationship between Puritanism and American culture?

Start to Read

Puritanism

Puritanism refers to the movement arising within the Church of England in the latter part of the 16th century that sought to purify, or reform, that church and establish a middle course between Roman Catholicism and the ideas of the Protestant reformers. It had a continuous life within the church until the Stuart Restoration (1660). Puritanism reached North America with the English settlers who founded Plymouth Colony in 1620. It remained the dominant religious force in New England throughout the 17th and 18th centuries.

The term Puritanism is also used in a broader sense to refer to attitudes and values considered characteristic of the Puritans. Thus, the Separatists in the 16th century, the Quakers (see Friends, Society of) in the 17th century, and Nonconformists[①] after the Restoration may be called Puritans, although they were no longer part of the established church. The founders of New England, for whom immigration to America constituted withdrawal from the mother church, are also commonly called Puritans.

Finally, the word Puritanism has often been used as a term of abuse in a way that does scant justice to historical Puritanism—for instance, when a rigid moralism[②], the condemnation of innocent pleasure, or religious narrowness is stigmatized as puritanical.

Even within the Church of England, a precise definition of Puritanism is elusive. The leading Puritan clergyman during the reign of Elizabeth I was Thomas Cartwright, who denied he was one. Cartwright advocated a presbyterian[③] form of church government that gave control to committees of ministers and lay members. His purpose was to free the church from the control of bishops appointed by the monarchy, which was hostile to Puritanism. Puritanism, however, cannot be identified with Presbyterianism[④] because a major segment of the movement eventually adopted

---

① Nonconformist: 不信奉英国国教的
② moralism: 道德主义,说教
③ presbyterian: 长老会的
④ Presbyterianism: 长老会制

congregationalism, in which there is no church hierarchy and each individual congregation is self-governing. The essence of Puritanism is an intense commitment to a morality, a form of worship, and a civil society strictly conforming to God's commandments.

Puritan theology is a version of Calvinism. It asserts the basic sinfulness of humankind; but it also declares that by an eternal decree God has determined that some will be saved through the righteousness of Christ despite their sins. No one can be certain in this life what his or her eternal destiny will be. Nevertheless, the experience of conversion, in which the soul is touched by the Holy Spirit, so that the inward bias of the heart is turned from sinfulness to holiness, is at least some indication that one is of the elect.

The experience of conversion was therefore central to Puritan spirituality. Much of Puritan preaching was concerned with it. This concern was evident in questions such as how conversion comes about—whether in a blinding flash as with Saint Paul on the road to Damascus, or following well-defined stages of preparation; how one can distinguish actual conversion from the counterfeit①; and why not everyone will be converted. Puritan spiritual life stressed self-discipline and introspection, through which one sought to determine whether particular spiritual strivings were genuine marks of sainthood. Although full assurance might never be attained, the conviction of having been chosen by God fortified the Puritans to contend with what they regarded as wantonness in society and faithfulness in the church, and to endure the hardships involved in trying to create a Christian commonwealth in America.

Puritanism was not static and unchanging. At first it simply stood for further reform of worship, but soon it began to attack episcopacy—church government by bishops, as in the Church of England—as unscriptural. At times the difference between the Puritans and the Anglicans (members of the Church of England) seems to have been as much a matter of differing cultural values as one of differing theological opinions. For example, their Sabbatarianism② came into conflict with a defense of sports and games on Sunday by King James I. Puritanism became a political as well as a religious movement during the English Revolution (1640-1660, also called the Puritan Revolution), when Parliament rebelled against the despotism of Stuart King Charles I. This rebellion gave the Puritans a chance to demand the abolition of bishops in the Church of England. Both in England during the Commonwealth (government established by Parliament, from 1649-1660) and in 17th-century New England, Puritanism meant the direction and control of civil authority.

---

① counterfeit: 伪造品
② Sabbatarianism: 严守星期日为安息日；严守安息日主义

After You Read

I. Questions for discussion
1. Why did Puritanism arise in the latter part of the 16th century?
2. What is the dominant religious force in New England throughout the 17th and 18th centuries?
3. Who can be called Puritans?
4. What is the essence of Puritanism?
5. How do you understand that "Puritanism was not static and unchanging"?

II. True or false
1. Puritanism sustained within the church until the Stuart Restoration. (   )
2. Puritanism only refers to the movement arising within the Church of England in the latter part of the 16th century. (   )
3. Only founders of New England are called Puritans. (   )
4. The word Puritanism has often been used as a term of abuse in a way different from historical Puritanism. (   )
5. Within the Church of England, there is a precise definition of Puritanism. (   )
6. According to Puritan theology, no one can be certain in this life what his or her eternal destiny will be. (   )
7. Through self-discipline and introspection, people sought to figure out whether particular spiritual strivings were real marks of sainthood. (   )
8. Puritanism indicated the direction and control of civil authority. (   )

For Fun

I. Movies to see
The Scarlet Letter (1995): *The Scarlet Letter* is a film based on Nathaniel Hawthorne's novel of the same name. It was directed by Roland Joffé. The story was set in Boston in 17th century.

II. Websites to visit
1. http://www.egs.edu/library/nathaniel-hawthorne/biography/
2. http://americanliterature.com/author/nathaniel-hawthorne/bio-books-stories
3. http://www.pbs.org/wnet/americannovel/timeline/hawthorne.html
4. http://sfs.scnu.edu.cn/hhzhang/webcourse2/kcln/13/5.htm

III. Writing
Can you write a brief summary of the novel *The Scarlet Letter*? Retell the story in about 300 words.

Chapter 5

Edgar Allan Poe (1809-1849)
埃德加·爱伦·坡

Section A Literary Focus

作者简介(About the Author)

【生平】 埃德加·爱伦·坡是美国小说家、诗人、批评家。坡以神秘故事和恐怖小说闻名于世,被尊为推理小说的开山鼻祖,也被誉为科幻小说的始祖。他是第一个尝试完全依赖写作谋生的知名美国作家。《莫格街谋杀案》(*The Murders in the Rue Morgue*)、《罗杰疑案》(*The Murder of Roger Ackroyd*)和《失窃的信》(*The Purloined Letter*)被奉为侦探小说的典范。《莫格街谋杀案》写密室凶杀,凶手居然是猩猩;《罗杰疑案》借新闻报道,纯粹用推理形式破案;《失窃的信》是对人类心理进行解剖与逻辑演示的范本。在这三篇小说中坡塑造的业余侦探杜宾的形象,可以说是柯南·道尔笔下福尔摩斯的前辈。

【主要作品】 作品有《怪诞故事集》(*Tales of the Grotesque and Arabesque*,1940)、《黑猫》(*The Black Cat*,1943)、《莫格街谋杀案》(*The Murders in the Rue Morgue*,1941)等。文学理论有《创作哲学》(*The Philosophy of Composition*,1946)、《诗歌原理》(*The Poetic Principle*,1948)等。诗歌代表作有《乌鸦》(*The Raven*,1945)、《安娜贝尔·李》(*Annabel Lee*,1949)等。

作品选读(Selected Writings)

The Cask of Amontillado

《一桶白葡萄酒》,是一部由爱伦·坡1846年所著的短篇小说,当时发布在女性杂志《戈迪妇女杂志》上。这则故事被设置在一座无名的意大利城市和一个未被具体说明的年份(也许是在18世纪)。小说以第一人称讲述了"我"对一个朋友实施的致命的复仇,因为对方羞辱了他。这篇小说和《黑猫》、《泄密的心》一样,从谋杀者的角度讲述恐怖故事。

The thousand injuries of Fortunato I had borne as I best could, but when he ventured upon insult, I vowed revenge. You, who so well know the nature of my soul, will not suppose, however, that I gave utterance to a threat. At length I would be avenged; this was a point definitely settled—but the very definitiveness with which it was resolved, precluded① the idea of risk. I must not only punish, but punish with impunity②. A wrong is unredressed when retribution③ overtakes its redresser. It is equally unredressed when the avenger fails to make himself felt as such to him who has done the wrong.

It must be understood that neither by word nor deed had I given Fortunato cause to doubt my good will. I continued, as was my wont④, to smile in his face, and he did not perceive that my smile now was at the thought of his immolation⑤.

He had a weak point—this Fortunato—although in other regards he was a man to be respected and even feared. He prided himself on his connoisseurship in wine. Few Italians have the true virtuoso spirit. For the most part their enthusiasm is adopted to suit the time and opportunity—to practise imposture upon the British and Austrian millionaires. In painting and gemmary, Fortunato, like his countrymen, was a quack—but in the matter of old wines he was sincere. In this respect I did not differ from him materially: I was skillful in the Italian vintages myself, and bought largely whenever I could.

It was about dusk, one evening during the supreme madness of the carnival season, that I encountered my friend. He accosted me with excessive warmth, for he had been drinking much. The man wore motley⑥. He had on a tight-fitting parti-striped dress, and his head was surmounted by the conical cap and bells. I was so pleased to see him that I thought I should never have done wringing his hand.

I said to him—"My dear Fortunato, you are luckily met. How remarkably well you are looking today! But I have received a pipe of what passes for Amontillado, and I have my doubts."

"How?" said he. "Amontillado? A pipe? Impossible! And in the middle of the carnival!"

"I have my doubts," I replied; "and I was silly enough to pay the full Amontillado price without consulting you in the matter. You were not to be found, and I was fearful of losing a bargain."

"Amontillado!"

"I have my doubts."

---

① preclude: 排除
② with impunity: 不受惩罚地
③ retribution: 报应,惩罚
④ wont: 习惯,惯常活动
⑤ immolation: 祭物
⑥ motley: 杂色衣服

"Amontillado!"

"And I must satisfy them."

"Amontillado!"

"As you are engaged, I am on my way to Luchesi. If any one has a critical turn, it is he. He will tell me—"

"Luchesi cannot tell Amontillado from Sherry."

"And yet some fools will have it that his taste is a match for your own."

"Come, let us go."

"Whither?"

"To your vaults①."

"My friend, no; I will not impose upon your good nature. I perceive you have an engagement. Luchesi—"

"I have no engagement;—come."

"My friend, no. It is not the engagement, but the severe cold with which I perceive you are afflicted. The vaults are insufferably damp. They are encrusted with nitre."

"Let us go, nevertheless. The cold is merely nothing. Amontillado! You have been imposed upon. And as for Luchesi, he cannot distinguish Sherry from Amontillado."

Thus speaking, Fortunato possessed himself of my arm. Putting on a mask of black silk, and drawing a roquelaire closely about my person, I suffered him to hurry me to my palazzo.

There were no attendants at home; they had absconded② to make merry in honour of the time. I had told them that I should not return until the morning, and had given them explicit orders not to stir from the house. These orders were sufficient, I well knew, to insure their immediate disappearance, one and all, as soon as my back was turned.

I took from their sconces two flambeaux, and giving one to Fortunato, bowed him through several suites of rooms to the archway that led into the vaults. I passed down a long and winding staircase, requesting him to be cautious as he followed. We came at length to the foot of the descent, and stood together on the damp ground of the catacombs of the Montresors.

The gait③ of my friend was unsteady, and the bells upon his cap jingled as he strode.

"The pipe," said he.

"It is farther on," said I, "but observe the white web-work which gleams from these cavern walls."

He turned towards me, and looked into my eyes with two filmy orbs that distilled

---

① vaults: 地窖

② abscond: 潜逃,逃匿

③ gait: 脚步

the rheum of intoxication.

"Nitre?" he asked, at length.

"Nitre," I replied. "How long have you had that cough?"

"Ugh! ugh! ugh! —ugh! ugh! ugh! —ugh! ugh! ugh! —ugh! ugh! ugh! —ugh! ugh! ugh!"

My poor friend found it impossible to reply for many minutes.

"It is nothing," he said, at last.

"Come," I said, with decision, "we will go back; your health is precious. You are rich, respected, admired, beloved; you are happy, as once I was. You are a man to be missed. For me it is no matter. We will go back; you will be ill, and I cannot be responsible. Besides, there is Luchesi—"

"Enough," he said; "the cough is a mere nothing; it will not kill me. I shall not die of a cough."

"True—true," I replied; "and, indeed, I had no intention of alarming you unnecessarily—but you should use all proper caution. A draught of this Medoc will defend us from the damps."

Here I knocked off the neck of a bottle which I drew from a long row of its fellows that lay upon the mould.

"Drink," I said, presenting him the wine.

He raised it to his lips with a leer. He paused and nodded to me familiarly, while his bells jingled.

"I drink," he said, "to the buried that repose around us."

"And I to your long life."

He again took my arm, and we proceeded.

"These vaults," he said, "are extensive."

"The Montresors," I replied, "were a great and numerous family."

"I forget your arms."

"A huge human foot d'or, in a field azure; the foot crushes a serpent rampant whose fangs[①] are imbedded in the heel."

"And the motto?"

"Nemo me impune lacessit."

"Good!" he said.

The wine sparkled in his eyes and the bells jingled. My own fancy grew warm with the Medoc. We had passed through walls of piled bones, with casks and puncheons intermingling, into the inmost recesses of catacombs. I paused again, and this time I made bold to seize Fortunato by an arm above the elbow.

"The nitre!" I said; "see, it increases. It hangs like moss upon the vaults. We are below the river's bed. The drops of moisture trickle among the bones. Come, we will go

---

① fangs: 尖牙

back ere it is too late. Your cough—"

"It is nothing," he said; "let us go on. But first, another draught of the Medoc."

I broke and reached him a flagon of De Grave. He emptied it at a breath. His eyes flashed with a fierce light. He laughed and threw the bottle upwards with a gesticulation① I did not understand.

I looked at him in surprise. He repeated the movement—a grotesque one.

"You do not comprehend?" he said.

"Not I," I replied.

"Then you are not of the brotherhood."

"How?"

"You are not of the masons."

"Yes, yes," I said; "yes, yes."

"You? Impossible! A mason?"

"A mason," I replied.

"A sign," he said, "a sign."

"It is this," I answered, producing a trowel from beneath the folds of my roquelaire.

"You jest," he exclaimed, recoiling a few paces. "But let us proceed to the Amontillado."

"Be it so," I said, replacing the tool beneath the cloak and again offering him my arm. He leaned upon it heavily.

We continued our route in search of the Amontillado. We passed through a range of low arches, descended, passed on, and descending again, arrived at a deep crypt, in which the foulness of the air caused our flambeaux rather to glow than flame.

At the most remote end of the crypt there appeared another less spacious. Its walls had been lined with human remains, piled to the vault overhead, in the fashion of the great catacombs of Paris. Three sides of this interior crypt were still ornamented in this manner. From the fourth side the bones had been thrown down, and lay promiscuously② upon the earth, forming at one point a mound of some size. Within the wall thus exposed by the displacing of the bones, we perceived a still interior recess, in depth about four feet, in width three, in height six or seven. It seemed to have been constructed for no especial use within itself, but formed merely the interval between two of the colossal supports of the roof of the catacombs, and was backed by one of their circumscribing walls of solid granite.

It was in vain that Fortunato, uplifting his dull torch, endeavoured to pry into the depth of the recess. Its termination the feeble light did not enable us to see.

"Proceed," I said; "herein is the Amontillado. As for Luchesi—"

---

① gesticulation：手势

② promiscuously：混杂地，杂乱地

"He is an ignoramus," interrupted my friend, as he stepped unsteadily forward, while I followed immediately at his heels. In an instant he had reached the extremity of the niche, and finding his progress arrested by the rock, stood stupidly bewildered. A moment more and I had fettered him to the granite. In its surface were two iron staples, distant from each other about two feet, horizontally. From one of these depended a short chain, from the other a padlock. Throwing the links about his waist, it was but the work of a few seconds to secure it. He was too much astounded to resist. Withdrawing the key I stepped back from the recess.

"Pass your hand," I said, "over the wall; you cannot help feeling the nitre. Indeed, it is very damp. Once more let me implore you to return. No? Then I must positively leave you. But I must first render you all the little attentions in my power."

"The Amontillado!" ejaculated my friend, not yet recovered from his astonishment.

"True," I replied; "the Amontillado."

As I said these words I busied myself among the pile of bones of which I have before spoken. Throwing them aside, I soon un-covered a quantity of building stone and mortar. With these materials and with the aid of my trowel, I began vigorously to wall up the entrance of the niche.

I had scarcely laid the first tier of the masonry when I discovered that the intoxication of Fortunato had in a great measure worn off. The earliest indication I had of this was a low moaning cry from the depth of the recess. It was not the cry of a drunken man. There was then a long and obstinate silence. I laid the second tier, and the third, and the fourth; and then I heard the furious vibrations of the chain. The noise lasted for several minutes, during which, that I might hearken to it with the more satisfaction, I ceased my labours and sat down upon the bones. When at last the clanking subsided, I resumed the trowel, and finished without interruption the fifth, the sixth, and the seventh tier. The wall was now nearly upon a level with my breast. I again paused, and holding the flambeaux over the mason-work, threw a few feeble rays upon the figure within.

A succession of loud and shrill① screams, bursting suddenly from the throat of the chained form, seemed to thrust me violently back. For a brief moment I hesitated—I trembled. Unsheathing② my rapier, I began to grope with it about the recess; but the thought of an instant reassured me. I placed my hand upon the solid fabric of the catacombs, and felt satisfied. I reapproached the wall; I replied to the yells of him who clamoured. I re-echoed—I aided—I surpassed them in volume and in strength. I did this, and the clamourer grew still.

It was now midnight, and my task was drawing to a close. I had completed the eighth, the ninth, and the tenth tier. I had finished a portion of the last and the

---

① shrill: 尖锐的,刺耳的

② unsheathe: 拔出

eleventh; there remained but a single stone to be fitted and plastered in. I struggled with its weight; I placed it partially in its destined position. But now there came from out the niche a low laugh that erected the hairs upon my head. It was succeeded by a sad voice, which I had difficulty in recognizing as that of the noble Fortunato. The voice said—

"Ha! ha! ha! —he! he! he! —a very good joke indeed—an excellent jest. We shall have many a rich laugh about it at the palazzo—he! he! he! —over our wine—he! he! he!"

"The Amontillado!" I said.

"He! he! he! —he! he! he! —yes, the Amontillado. But is it not getting late? Will not they be awaiting us at the palazzo, the Lady Fortunato and the rest? Let us be gone."

"Yes," I said, "let us be gone."

"For the love of God, Montresor!"

"Yes," I said, "for the love of God!"

But to these words I hearkened in vain for a reply. I grew impatient. I called aloud—

"Fortunato!"

No answer. I called again—

"Fortunato—"

No answer still. I thrust a torch through the remaining aperture and let it fall within. There came forth in reply only a jingling of the bells. My heart grew sick on account of the dampness of the catacombs. I hastened to make an end of my labour. I forced the last stone into its position; I plastered it up. Against the new masonry I re-erected the old rampart of bones. For the half of a century no mortal has disturbed them. In pace requiescat!

Questions for discussion

1. What kind of atmosphere can you figure out in this story? What are the supporting details?
2. What role does Amontillado play in terms of structure and the plot development?
3. This novel involves much conversation. Why do you think the author writes in this way? Do you have any ideas in constructing a story?

Annabel Lee

《安娜贝尔·李》是美国抒情诗中的上乘佳作。这是诗人坡1849年死后才发表的最后一篇诗作,代表其唯美主义风格的顶峰。许多评论家认为这是诗人为悼念亡妻而作,旨在把爱情融入理想化的永恒境界。全诗浓笔渲染了大海边亦真亦幻的浪漫氛围,既有纯洁的爱情,也有哀婉的悲剧。大海的波涛传递着悲切的旋律,而大海的永恒寓意着爱情的永恒。全诗情景交融,音乐和画面和谐,鲜明的视觉形象和忧郁抒情节奏既生动形象地呈现了一个爱情传奇,又委婉感人地抒发了诗人缠绵悲伤的心情。

It was many and many a year ago,
In a kingdom by the sea,
That a maiden there lived whom you may know
By the name of ANNABEL LEE;
And this maiden she lived with no other thought
Than to love and be loved by me.

I was a child and she was a child,
In this kingdom by the sea;
But we loved with a love that was more than love
I and my Annabel Lee;
With a love that the winged seraphs of heaven
Coveted her and me.

And this was the reason that, long ago,
In this kingdom by the sea,
A wind blew out of a cloud, chilling,
My beautiful Annabel Lee;
So that her highborn① kinsman came
And bore her away from me,
To shut her up in a sepulchre②
In this kindom by the sea.

The angels, not half so happy in the heaven,
Went evnying her and me
Yes! That was the reason (as all men know, In this kingdom by the sea)
That the wind came out of the cloud by night,
Chilling and killing my Annabel Lee.

But our love it was stronger by far than the love
Of those who were older than we
Of many far wiser than we
And neither the angels in heaven above,
Nor the demons down under the sea,
Can ever dissever my soul from the soul
Of the beautiful Annabel Lee.

---

① highborn: 高贵的,出身名贵的
② sepulchre: 坟墓

For the moon never beams without bringing me dreams
   Of the beautiful Annalbel Lee;
And the stars never rise but I see the bright eyes
   Of the beautiful Annabel Lee;
And so, all the night-tide, I lie down by the side
Of my darling, my darling, my life and my bride,
   In the sepulchre there by the sea,
   In her tomb by the side of the sea.

Questions for discussion
1. What kind of emotion does the author express for Annabel Lee?
2. What are the details that make the poem so impressive?
3. If you are going to write about a person you love deeply, in what aspect will you unfold your feeling?

To Helen

爱伦·坡写过两首《致海伦》。前一首发表于 1831 年,诗中的海伦是坡少年时暗恋过的简·斯坦纳德(Mrs. Jane Stith Stanard)。斯坦纳德夫人是坡的同学罗伯特·斯坦纳德的母亲,她端庄美丽,成了少年坡心中美的偶像。1824 年 4 月,31 岁的斯坦纳德夫人病故,坡为此非常伤心,其后很长一段时间神思恍惚。后一首《致海伦》发表于 1848 年,诗中的海伦指女诗人萨拉·海伦·惠特曼(Sarah Helen Whitman),坡曾于当年向她求过婚。

以下为第一首《致海伦》,从诗中提到的地理、历史背景来看,坡对斯坦纳德夫人的爱慕和对古希腊史诗《伊利亚特》中的绝世美人海伦的景仰合二为一。在最后一节里,对不可企及的美人的倾倒又升华为对艺术——甚至是对真、善、美的无穷无尽的追求。因为在西方人心中,古代的希腊和罗马已成为一种理想的境界,那里的一切似乎都是至美至善的。

TO HELEN

Helen, thy beauty is to me
Like those Nicéan barks of yore,
That gently, o'er a perfumed sea,
The weary, wayworn wanderer bore
To his own native shore.

On desperate seas long wont to roam,
Thy hyacinth hair, thy classic face,
Thy Naiad airs have brought me home
To the beauty of fair Greece,
And the grandeur of old Rome.

Lo! in yon little window-niche

How statue-like I see thee stand!
The folded scroll within thy hand!
Ah, Psyche, from the regions which
Are Holy-land!

文学术语(Definition of Literary Terms)

1. **Suspense** refers to the quality of a story, novel, or drama that makes readers uncertain or tense about the plot or outcome of events.
2. **Single effect**: A story is constructed to achieve "a certain unique or single effect". Every character, incident, and detail in a story should contribute to this effect.
3. **Imagery** is a way of using words or phrases that create pictures, or images in readers' mind.
4. **Metaphor** is a figure of speech in which a word or phrase that ordinarily designates one thing is used to designate another, thus making an implicit comparison.

Section B Cultural Notes

Before You Read

1. Try to search the internet or in the library about more information about Edgar Allan Poe. What are the main literary achievements of Edgar Allan Poe?
2. What different impressions do you have for Helen in the two different poems?
3. Can you find some images in the poem "To Helen"?

Start to Read

On "Helen"

"Helen" takes as its subject the woman who has been the literary and mythic symbol of sexual beauty and illicit love in western culture. Much has been written about her, but H. D.'s poem does something new: it implicitly attacks the traditional imagery of Helen and implies that such perspectives have silenced Helen's own voice.

Like Edgar Allan Poe's poem about Helen, this poem draws a portrait with careful references to Helen's eyes, face, hands, feet, and knees. But in contrast to Poe's poem, H. D.'s Helen does not stand alone, unveiled before the adoring eyes of the male poet. Instead, she is accompanied by a hate-filled gaze that never leaves the beauty of her body. H. D.'s poem operates on an opposition established between Helen and "all Greece," and the speaker stands outside this opposition to record the interaction between the two. Time, space, and situation are left uncertain with a sparse setting that presents an image rather than a realistic event. The action verbs outline the image: Helen "stands ... smiles" faintly, and grows more "wan and white" while "all Greece" regards first her face and then "sees ... the beauty of feet/and slenderest① knees."

  The process the speaker watches is the growing hatred of Helen and the overwhelming effect it has upon her. The emotion directed in judgment against Helen is intense—we are aware of this not only because the verbs "hates" and "reviles" stand out so starkly, but also because the impersonality② of "all Greece" generalizes the condemnation. In Poe's poem, he alone worships Helen. In W. B. Yeats's "No Second Troy," the poet's feelings for Helen are more ambivalent③, but Yeats still records a private experience between himself and his mythic mask for Maude Gonne. In her poem, however, H. D. generalizes those who regard Helen until they take on the dimensions of a collective culture. "Greece" is a country, not a person, not even a people. H. D.'s choice of "Greece" in place of the more logical "Greeks" suggests that the entire weight of a cultural tradition "reviles④" Helen. The structural repetition of "all" at the beginning of the first two stanzas reinforces the image of a whole culture set in powerful opposition to one woman. And the lack of a realistic setting in this portrait of "all Greece" regarding Helen underlines the real subject, of the poem: woman's place in male-dominated tradition.

  Helen's response to the hate-filled gaze of "all Greece" is not a static one. In fact, the stanzas of the poem subtly suggest the transformation of a living woman into a marble statue, a progression from life to death controlled by the force of hate. In the first stanza, Helen seems immobilized—her eyes are "still" and she simply "stands." The emphasis on the whiteness of her face and hands adds to this image of impassivity. But, read in the light of the last two stanzas, Helen in the first stanza still has the glow of life. The poet sees the rich "lustre as of olives/where she stands." This lustre begins to disappear in the second stanza. White hands and white face are conventional attributes of female beauty. But in the second stanza, white skin "grows wan and white" in the face of increasing hatred—that is, pale, bloodless, and seemingly lifeless. As if to appease "all Greece," her "wan face... smiles." According to some scholars, women have traditionally relied on a perpetual smile to render themselves more acceptable in an androcentric culture. Helen too smiles in a desperate attempt to counteract the condemnation that is growing "deeper still" for her part in the Trojan war.

  In the third stanza, "white" signals the final result of Greece's unmoving hatred, becoming the color of death: "white ash amid funereal cypresses⑤." The word

---

① slender: 苗条的
② impersonality: 非个人性
③ ambivalent: 矛盾情绪的
④ revile: 谩骂,诽谤
⑤ cypress: 柏树

"unmoved" to describe a lack of compassion is something of a pun (un-moving) that echoes in reverse the increasing immobility of Helen. Her smiles win no mercy, and the only way she can become loved is through her death ... The growing whiteness of her skin signals her death as a living woman and her birth as a statue, a symbol of beauty in the eyes of "all Greece."

In Poe's poem, Helen's appearance as a statue is an affirmation. But in H. D.'s poem, the speaker understands the connection between the traditional worship of woman as symbol and the death of the living woman. H. D.'s poem about Helen is a revision of the Medusa myth and an implicit attack on the processes of masculine mythmaking with female symbols. According to Greek myth, a man's direct sight of the fearful Medusa with her hair of snakes would turn him to stone. In his famous interpretation of this myth, Freud argued that Medusa's head represented the castrated state of female genitals, and the myth embodied castration[①] anxiety. But in H. D.'s reversal of psychoanalysis and myth, the hatred of a collective male tradition turns woman to stone, literally a statue. An added complexity, however, is that hatred becomes love once Helen's paralysis is complete. Like Joan of Arc, Helen, immobilized and silenced, is an object of worship. Alive, she was an object of hatred, a threat to the dominant culture ruled by men. As statue or symbol, she is safely controlled by the tradition that defines her through its art. What seems to be an adoration of woman, H. D. says, is rooted in reality in a hatred for the living woman who has the capacity to speak for herself.

In "To Helen," the poet cannot free Helen from the patriarchal cage of traditional hate and adoration. She stands outside the process, helpless to prevent Helen's growing silence and paralysis. She can and does attack tradition, but she cannot give the mute statue a voice. Because of her mother's name, Helen was always a personal and mythic mother-symbol for H. D. But at this point in her life, her mother-symbol was too overwhelmed to help her daughter the poet. To serve as "the Muse, the Creator" as the Goddess does in H. D.'s later poems, the daughter had to give birth to her own mother.

After You Read

I. Questions for discussion

1. What are the differences between the descriptions of Poe's and H. D's about Helen? Please describe based on the text.
2. How did H. D. achieve a totally opposite effect to Poe's poem?
3. What is the emotion expressed by the author in the poem?

---

① castration: 阉割

II. True or false

1. H. D. implicitly attacks the traditional imagery of Helen and implies that such perspectives have silenced Helen's own voice. (   )
2. Helen was freed from the patriarchal cage of traditional hate and adoration in H. D.'s description. (   )
3. In Edgar's poem, Helen was stared and controlled by a hate-filled gaze. (   )

For Fun

I. Websites to visit

1. http://www.poestories.com/
2. http://www.poets.org/poetsorg/poet/edgar-allan-poe
3. http://www.online-literature.com/poe/
4. http://www.poetryfoundation.org/bio/edgar-allan-poe
5. http://www.english.illinois.edu/maps/poets/g_l/hd/helen.htm

II. Writing

Poetry is a good way to express love and feelings of human beings. Write a love poem to your future husband or wife.

Chapter 6

Henry David Thoreau（1817–1862）
亨利·戴维·梭罗

Section A Literary Focus

作者简介（About the Author）

【生平】 亨利·戴维·梭罗是19世纪美国作家、哲学家,超验主义代表人物,也是一位废奴主义及自然主义者,有无政府主义倾向,曾任职土地勘测员。梭罗毕业于哈佛大学,曾协助爱默生编辑评论季刊《日晷》(The Dial)。其思想深受爱默生影响,提倡回归本心,亲近自然。他的《论公民不服从》(Civil Disobedience)则讨论面对政府和强权的不义,为公民主动拒绝遵守若干法律提出辩护。

梭罗的全部书本、散文、日记和诗集共有20册,其中他阐述了研究环境史和生态学的方法,对自然书写的影响甚远,也为现代环境保护主义奠定了基础。他的文体风格结合了对大自然的关怀、个人体验、象征手法和历史传说,善感敏锐,且富有诗意。

【主要作品】 《瓦尔登湖》(Walden,1854)、《论公民不服从》(Civil Disobedience,1849)、《没有规则的生活》(Life Without Principle,1863),游记《马萨诸塞自然史》(Natural History of Massachusetts)、《在康科德河与梅里麦克河上一周》(A Week on the Concord and Merrimac Rivers)、《缅因森林》(The Maine Woods)等。

作品选读（Selected Writings）

Walden

《瓦尔登湖》是梭罗独居瓦尔登湖畔的记录,描绘了他两年多时间里的所见、所闻和所思。这部著作区别于先前文学作品的第一个特征,是其对自然巨细靡遗的描摹和引申。大至四季交替造成的景色变化,小到两只蚂蚁的争斗,无不栩栩如生地再现于梭罗的生花妙笔之下。作者详细地描述两年多的湖畔独居生活,目的在于通过这次亲力亲为的实验向读者证明:其实不需要很多钱,也能够好好地活着,而且能够快快乐乐地活着。这本书内容丰厚,意义深远,语言生动,意境深邃。

The Pond

Sometimes, having had a surfeit① of human society and gossip, and worn out all my village friends, I rambled still farther westward than I habitually dwell, into yet more unfrequented parts of the town, "to fresh woods and pastures new," or, while the sun was setting, made my supper of huckleberries and blueberries on Fair Haven Hill, and laid up a store for several days. The fruits do not yield their true flavor to the purchaser of them, nor to him who raises them for the market. There is but one way to obtain it, yet few take that way. If you would know the flavor of huckleberries, ask the cowboy or the partridge②. It is a vulgar error to suppose that you have tasted huckleberries who never plucked them. A huckleberry never reaches Boston; they have not been known there since they grew on her three hills. The ambrosial③ and essential part of the fruit is lost with the bloom which is rubbed off in the market cart, and they become mere provender④. As long as Eternal Justice reigns, not one innocent huckleberry can be transported thither from the country's hills.

Occasionally, after my hoeing was done for the day, I joined some impatient companion who had been fishing on the pond since morning, as silent and motionless as a duck or a floating leaf, and, after practising various kinds of philosophy, had concluded commonly, by the time I arrived, that he belonged to the ancient sect of Coenobites⑤. There was one older man, an excellent fisher and skilled in all kinds of woodcraft, who was pleased to look upon my house as a building erected for the convenience of fishermen; and I was equally pleased when he sat in my doorway to arrange his lines. Once in a while we sat together on the pond, he at one end of the boat, and I at the other; but not many words passed between us, for he had grown deaf in his later years, but he occasionally hummed a psalm⑥, which harmonized well enough with my philosophy. Our intercourse was thus altogether one of unbroken harmony, far more pleasing to remember than if it had been carried on by speech. When, as was commonly the case, I had none to commune with, I used to raise the echoes by striking with a paddle on the side of my boat, filling the surrounding woods with circling and dilating sound, stirring them up as the keeper of a menagerie⑦ his wild beasts, until I elicited a growl from every wooded vale and hillside.

In warm evenings I frequently sat in the boat playing the flute, and saw the perch, which I seem to have charmed, hovering around me, and the moon travelling over the ribbed bottom, which was strewed with the wrecks of the forest. Formerly I had come

---

① surfeit: 过度
② partridge: 鹧鸪
③ ambrosial: 美味的
④ provender: 食品
⑤ coenobite: 修道院僧
⑥ psalm: 圣诗
⑦ menagerie: 动物园

to this pond adventurously, from time to time, in dark summer nights, with a companion, and, making a fire close to the water's edge, which we thought attracted the fishes, we caught pouts with a bunch of worms strung on a thread, and when we had done, far in the night, threw the burning brands high into the air like skyrockets, which, coming down into the pond, were quenched with a loud hissing, and we were suddenly groping in total darkness. Through this, whistling a tune, we took our way to the haunts of men again. But now I had made my home by the shore.

Sometimes, after staying in a village parlor till the family had all retired, I have returned to the woods, and, partly with a view to the next day's dinner, spent the hours of midnight fishing from a boat by moonlight, serenaded① by owls and foxes, and hearing, from time to time, the creaking note of some unknown bird close at hand. These experiences were very memorable and valuable to me—anchored in forty feet of water, and twenty or thirty rods from the shore, surrounded sometimes by thousands of small perch and shiners, dimpling the surface with their tails in the moonlight, and communicating by a long flaxen line with mysterious nocturnal fishes which had their dwelling forty feet below, or sometimes dragging sixty feet of line about the pond as I drifted in the gentle night breeze, now and then feeling a slight vibration along it, indicative of some life prowling about its extremity, of dull uncertain blundering purpose there, and slow to make up its mind. At length you slowly raise, pulling hand over hand, some horned pout squeaking and squirming to the upper air. It was very queer, especially in dark nights, when your thoughts had wandered to vast and cosmogonal themes in other spheres, to feel this faint jerk, which came to interrupt your dreams and link you to Nature again. It seemed as if I might next cast my line upward into the air, as well as downward into this element, which was scarcely more dense. Thus I caught two fishes as it were with one hook.

The scenery of Walden is on a humble scale, and, though very beautiful, does not approach to grandeur, nor can it much concern one who has not long frequented it or lived by its shore; yet this pond is so remarkable for its depth and purity as to merit a particular description. It is a clear and deep green well, half a mile long and a mile and three quarters in circumference②, and contains about sixty-one and a half acres; a perennial spring in the midst of pine and oak woods, without any visible inlet or outlet except by the clouds and evaporation. The surrounding hills rise abruptly from the water to the height of forty to eighty feet, though on the southeast and east they attain to about one hundred and one hundred and fifty feet respectively, within a quarter and a third of a mile. They are exclusively woodland. All our Concord waters have two colors at least; one when viewed at a distance, and another, more proper, close at hand. The first depends more on the light, and follows the sky. In clear weather, in summer, they

---

① serenade: 唱小夜曲

② circumference: 周长

appear blue at a little distance, especially if agitated, and at a great distance all appear alike. In stormy weather they are sometimes of a dark slate-color. The sea, however, is said to be blue one day and green another without any perceptible change in the atmosphere. I have seen our river, when, the landscape being covered with snow, both water and ice were almost as green as grass. Some consider blue "to be the color of pure water, whether liquid or solid." But, looking directly down into our waters from a boat, they are seen to be of very different colors. Walden is blue at one time and green at another, even from the same point of view. Lying between the earth and the heavens, it partakes① of the color of both. Viewed from a hilltop it reflects the color of the sky; but near at hand it is of a yellowish tint next the shore where you can see the sand, then a light green, which gradually deepens to a uniform dark green in the body of the pond. In some lights, viewed even from a hilltop, it is of a vivid green next the shore. Some have referred this to the reflection of the verdure; but it is equally green there against the railroad sandbank, and in the spring, before the leaves are expanded, and it may be simply the result of the prevailing blue mixed with the yellow of the sand. Such is the color of its iris. This is that portion, also, where in the spring, the ice being warmed by the heat of the sun reflected from the bottom, and also transmitted through the earth, melts first and forms a narrow canal about the still frozen middle. Like the rest of our waters, when much agitated, in clear weather, so that the surface of the waves may reflect the sky at the right angle, or because there is more light mixed with it, it appears at a little distance of a darker blue than the sky itself; and at such a time, being on its surface, and looking with divided vision, so as to see the reflection, I have discerned a matchless and indescribable light blue, such as watered or changeable silks and sword blades suggest, more cerulean than the sky itself, alternating with the original dark green on the opposite sides of the waves, which last appeared but muddy in comparison. It is a vitreous greenish blue, as I remember it, like those patches of the winter sky seen through cloud vistas in the west before sundown. Yet a single glass of its water held up to the light is as colorless as an equal quantity of air. It is well known that a large plate of glass will have a green tint, owing, as the makers say, to its "body," but a small piece of the same will be colorless. How large a body of Walden water would be required to reflect a green tint I have never proved. The water of our river is black or a very dark brown to one looking directly down on it, and, like that of most ponds, imparts to② the body of one bathing in it a yellowish tinge; but this water is of such crystalline purity that the body of the bather appears of an alabaster whiteness, still more unnatural, which, as the limbs are magnified and distorted withal, produces a monstrous effect, making fit studies for a Michael Angelo.

  The water is so transparent that the bottom can easily be discerned at the depth of

---

① partake: 分担

② impart to: 给予

twenty-five or thirty feet. Paddling over it, you may see, many feet beneath the surface, the schools of perch① and shiners②, perhaps only an inch long, yet the former easily distinguished by their transverse bars, and you think that they must be ascetic fish that find a subsistence there. Once, in the winter, many years ago, when I had been cutting holes through the ice in order to catch pickerel, as I stepped ashore I tossed my axe back on to the ice, but, as if some evil genius had directed it, it slid four or five rods③ directly into one of the holes, where the water was twenty-five feet deep. Out of curiosity, I lay down on the ice and looked through the hole, until I saw the axe a little on one side, standing on its head, with its helve erect and gently swaying to and fro with the pulse of the pond; and there it might have stood erect and swaying till in the course of time the handle rotted off, if I had not disturbed it. Making another hole directly over it with an ice chisel④ which I had, and cutting down the longest birch which I could find in the neighborhood with my knife, I made a slip-noose, which I attached to its end, and, letting it down carefully, passed it over the knob of the handle, and drew it by a line along the birch, and so pulled the axe out again.

Questions for discussion

1. What kind of impression does this chapter make on you?
2. What do you know about Thoreau's transcendentalism? Can you describe it in your own word with some examples?
3. If you have the chance to get close to nature, where do you want to go? Why?
4. What is the ideal relationship between the modern world and nature? What measure should be taken to achieve that goal?

文学术语 (Definition of Literary Terms)

1. **Motif** is a recurrent thematic element in an artistic or literary work.
2. **Narrator** is the one who narrates or tells a story.
3. **Pastoral poetry** holds a positive perspective towards nature and advocates simple country life.

---

① perch: 鲈鱼
② shiner: 银鱼
③ rod: 鱼竿
④ chisel: 凿子

Section B Cultural Notes

Before You Read

1. Try to search on the Internet or in the library about more information about Henry David Thoreau. What impression is the greatest Henry David Thoreau leave on you?
2. What does the title "Individualism" mean? What is your understanding of a person's individuality?
3. Have you ever bent your view or decision to either fit in a group or to please other people?

Start to Read

Individualism

In "Civil Disobedience," Thoreau expressed his belief in the power and, indeed, the obligation of the individual to determine right from wrong, independent of the dictates of society: "any man more right than his neighbors, constitutes a majority of one" (*Reform Papers*, 74). While many of his contemporaries espoused this view, few practiced it in their own lives as consistently as Thoreau. Thoreau exercised his right to dissent from the prevailing① views in many ways, large and small. He worked for pay intermittently; he cultivated relationships with several of the town's outcasts; he lived alone in the woods for two years; he never married; he signed off from the First Parish Church rather than be taxed automatically to support it every year.

Thoreau encouraged others to assert their individuality, each in his or her own way. When neighbors talked of emulating his lifestyle at the pond, he was dismayed rather than flattered.

> I would not have any one adopt *my* mode of living on any account; for, beside that before he has fairly learned it I may have found out another for myself, I desire that there may be as many different persons in the world as possible; but I would have each one be very careful to find out and pursue his own way, and not his father's or his mother's or his neighbor's instead. The youth may build or plant or sail, only let him not be hindered from doing that which he tells me he would like to do. It is by a mathematical point only that we are wise, as the sailor or the fugitive② slave keeps the polestar in his eye; but that is sufficient guidance for all our life. We may not arrive at our port

---

① prevailing: 普遍的,盛行的
② fugitive: 逃亡的,逃跑的

within a calculable period, but we would preserve the true course. (*Walden*, 71)

If a man does not keep pace with his companions, perhaps it is because he hears a different drummer. Let him step to the music which he hears, however measured or far away. (*Walden*, 326)

Thoreau also believed that independent, well-considered action arose naturally from a questing attitude of mind. He was first and foremost an explorer, of both the world around him and the world within him.

Be a Columbus to whole new continents and worlds within you, opening new channels, not of trade, but of thought. (Walden, 321)

Thoreau's celebration of solitude was a natural outgrowth of his commitment to the idea of individual action. His neighbors frequently saw him heading out for his regular afternoon walk which took him to every stream and meadow in Concord and the surrounding towns. Contemporaries attest that Thoreau was gregarious, and he left an extensive correspondence which demonstrates the depth and perseverance of his friendship. And although he had many visitors at Walden, much of the time he was alone, a condition he savored.

I never found the companion that was so companionable as solitude. (*Walden*, 135)

The man who goes alone can start today; but he who travels with another must wait till that other is ready (*Walden*, 72)

After You Read

I. Questions for discussion
1. What did Thoreau do to exercise his right to be different from the public?
2. What is your understanding of the sentence "any man more right than his neighbors, constitute a majority of one"?
3. Why was Thoreau displeased when people said that they wanted to follow his lifestyle?
4. What are the reasons that Thoreau cherished the notion of "solitude"? What do you think about the choice of being alone?

II. True or false
1. It is Thoreau's belief that people should follow the prevailing views of their days.
( )

2. Few people agreed with Thoreau's opinion that the individual should determine right or wrong independent of the influence of society. ( )
3. Thoreau endeavored to explore both the word around him and the world inside his mind. ( )
4. Thoreau usually stays at home and avoids contact with other people in order to be alone. ( )
5. The man who goes all by himself starts much earlier than those who go with a partner. ( )

For Fun

I. Websites to visit
1. http://www.quotationspage.com/quotes/Henry_David_Thoreau/
2. http://plato.stanford.edu/entries/thoreau/
3. http://global.britannica.com/EBchecked/topic/593225/Henry-David-Thoreau
4. http://www.thoreausociety.org/life-legacy
5. http://thoreau.library.ucsb.edu/thoreau_life.html
6. http://thoreau.library.ucsb.edu/thoreau_life.html

II. Writing

"The failures add dignity to human life." This is a quotation from Thoreau. What is your opinion on this? Use reasons and details to support your answer.

Chapter 7

Herman Melville (1819–1891)
赫尔曼·梅尔维尔

Section A Literary Focus

作者简介(About the Author)

【生平】 赫尔曼·梅尔维尔,19世纪美国小说家、散文家和诗人。做过农夫、职员、教师、水手、海军等。梅尔维尔著有很多小说及散文作品,晚年转而写诗。他的诗并没有获得高度评价,一些评论家认为他是美国首位现代主义(modernism)诗人,但是有些评论家则认为他的作品更富有后现代主义(postmodernism)的色彩。

【主要作品】 长篇小说:《白鲸》(Moby Dick, 1851)《皮埃尔》(Pierre, 1852)、《骗子的化装表演》(The Confidence-Man: His Masquerade, 1857)、《水手比利·巴德》(Billy Budd, Sailor)(1924);短篇小说:《代笔者巴特贝》(Bartleby, the Scrivener, 1853);诗作:《战事集》(Battle Pieces and Aspects of the War, 1866)、《克拉瑞尔》(Clarel, 1876)、《约翰·玛尔和其他水手》(John Marr and Other Sailors, 1888)和《梯摩里昂》(Timoleon, 1891)。

作品选读(Selected Writings)

Moby Dick

《白鲸》是赫尔曼·梅尔维尔于1851年发表的一篇海洋题材的小说,被认为是美国最伟大的小说之一。《白鲸》以充实的思想内容、史诗般的规模和沉郁瑰奇的文笔,成为杰出的作品,但在当时却没有得到重视。小说描写了亚哈船长为了追逐并杀死白鲸莫比·迪克,最终与白鲸同归于尽的故事。故事营造了一种置身海上航行、随时遭遇各种危险甚至是死亡的氛围。小说因描写了海上航行和纷繁的捕鲸生活,而被誉为"捕鲸业的百科全书"。

Chapter 41

I, Ishmael, was one of that crew; my shouts had gone up with the rest; my oath① had been welded with theirs; and stronger I shouted, and more did I hammer and clinch my oath, because of the dread in my soul. A wild, mystical, sympathetical feeling was in me; Ahab's quenchless② feud seemed mine. With greedy ears I learned the history of that murderous monster against whom I and all the others had taken our oaths of violence and revenge. For some time past, though at intervals only, the unaccompanied, secluded White Whale had haunted those uncivilized seas mostly frequented by the Sperm Whale fishermen. But not all of them knew of his existence; only a few of them, comparatively, had knowingly seen him; while the number who as yet had actually and knowingly given battle to him, was small indeed. For, owing to the large number of whale-cruisers; the disorderly way they were sprinkled over the entire watery circumference, many of them adventurously pushing their quest along solitary latitudes, so as seldom or never for a whole twelvemonth or more on a stretch, to encounter a single news-telling sail of any sort; the inordinate length of each separate voyage; the irregularity of the times of sailing from home; all these, with other circumstances, direct and indirect, long obstructed the spread through the whole world-wide whaling-fleet of the special individualizing tidings concerning Moby Dick. It was hardly to be doubted, that several vessels reported to have encountered, at such or such a time, or on such or such a meridian, a Sperm Whale of uncommon magnitude and malignity③, which whale, after doing great mischief to his assailants, has completely escaped them; to some minds it was not an unfair presumption, I say, that the whale in question must have been no other than Moby Dick. Yet as of late the Sperm Whale fishery had been marked by various and not unfrequent instances of great ferocity, cunning, and malice in the monster attacked; therefore it was, that those who by accident ignorantly gave battle to Moby Dick; such hunters, perhaps, for the most part, were content to ascribe the peculiar terror he bred, more, as it were, to the perils of the Sperm Whale fishery at large, than to the individual cause. In that way, mostly, the disastrous encounter between Ahab and the whale had hitherto been popularly regarded.

And as for those who, previously hearing of the White Whale, by chance caught sight of him; in the beginning of the thing they had every one of them, almost, as boldly and fearlessly lowered for him, as for any other whale of that species. But at length, such calamities did ensue④ in the sea assaults—not restricted to sprained wrists and ankles, broken limbs, or devouring amputations⑤—but fatal to the last degree of

---

① oath: 誓言
② quenchless: 难以压制的
③ malignity: 狠毒，凶猛
④ ensue: 接着发生
⑤ amputation: 截肢，肢体

fatality; those repeated disastrous repulses, all accumulating and piling their terrors upon Moby Dick; those things had gone far to shake the fortitude of many brave hunters, to whom the story of the White Whale had eventually come.

Nor did wild rumors of all sorts fail to exaggerate, and still the more horrify the true histories of these deadly encounters. For not only do fabulous rumors naturally grow out of the very body of all surprising terrible events, as the smitten tree gives birth to its fungi; but, in maritime life, far more than in that of terra firma①, wild rumors abound, wherever there is any adequate reality for them to cling to. And as the sea surpasses the land in this matter, so the whale fishery surpasses every other sort of maritime life, in the wonderfulness and fearfulness of the rumors which sometimes circulate there. For not only are whale men as a body unexempt from that ignorance and superstitiousness hereditary to all sailors; but of all sailors, they are by all odds the most directly brought into contact with whatever is appallingly astonishing in the sea; face to face they not only eye its greatest marvels, but, hand to jaw, give battle to them. Alone, in such remotest waters, that though you sailed a thousand miles, and passed a thousand shores, you would not come to any chiselled hearth-stone, or aught hospitable beneath that part of the sun; in such latitudes and longitudes, pursuing too such a calling as he does, the whale man is wrapped by influences all tending to make his fancy pregnant with many a mighty birth. No wonder, then, that ever gathering volume from the mere transit over the wildest watery spaces, the outblown rumors of the White Whale did in the end incorporate with themselves all manner of morbid hints, and half formed foetal suggestions of supernatural agencies, which eventually invested Moby Dick with new terrors unborrowed from anything that visibly appears. So that in many cases such a panic did he finally strike, that few who by those rumors, at least, had heard of the White Whale, few of those hunters were willing to encounter the perils of his jaw.

But there were still other and more vital practical influences at work. Nor even at the present day has the original prestige of the Sperm Whale, as fearfully distinguished from all other species of the leviathan, died out of the minds of the whale men as a body. There are those this day among them, who, though intelligent and courageous enough in offering battle to the Greenland or Right Whale, would perhaps—either from professional inexperience, or incompetency, or timidity, decline a contest with the Sperm Whale; at any rate, there are plenty of whale men, especially among those whaling nations not sailing under the American flag, who have never hostilely encountered the Sperm Whale, but whose sole knowledge of the leviathan② is restricted to the ignoble monster primitively pursued in the North; seated on their hatches, these men will hearken with a childish fireside interest and awe, to the wild, strange tales of Southern whaling. Nor is the preeminent tremendousness of the great Sperm Whale

---

① terra firma: 陆地
② leviathan: 海中怪兽

anywhere more feelingly comprehended, than on board of those prows which stem him.

And as if the now tested reality of his might had in former legendary times thrown its shadow before it; we find some book naturalists—Olassen and Povelson—declaring the Sperm Whale not only to be a consternation① to every other creature in the sea, but also to be so incredibly ferocious as continually to be a thirst for human blood. Nor even down to so late a time as Cuvier's, were these or almost similar impressions effaced. For in his Natural History, the Baron himself affirms that at sight of the Sperm Whale, all fish (sharks included) are "struck with the most lively terrors," and "often in the precipitancy of their flight dash themselves against the rocks with such violence as to cause instantaneous death." And however the general experiences in the fishery may amend such reports as these; yet in their full terribleness, even to the bloodthirsty item of Povelson, the superstitious belief in them is, in some vicissitudes of their vocation, revived in the minds of the hunters.

So that overawed② by the rumors and portents concerning him, not a few of the fishermen recalled, in reference to Moby Dick, the earlier days of the Sperm Whale fishery, when it was often times hard to induce long practised Right Whale men to embark in the perils of this new and daring warfare; such men protesting that although other leviathans might be hopefully pursued, yet to chase and point lances at such an apparition as the Sperm Whale was not for mortal man. That to attempt it, would be inevitably to be torn into a quick eternity. On this head, there are some remarkable documents that may be consulted.

Nevertheless, some there were, who even in the face of these things were ready to give chase to Moby Dick; and a still greater number who, chancing only to hear of him distantly and vaguely, without the specific details of any certain calamity, and without superstitious accompaniments were sufficiently hardy not to flee from the battle if offered.

One of the wild suggestions referred to, as at last coming to be linked with the White Whale in the minds of the superstitiously inclined, was the unearthly conceit that Moby Dick was ubiquitous; that he had actually been encountered in opposite latitudes at one and the same instant of time.

Nor, credulous as such minds must have been, was this conceit altogether without some faint show of superstitious probability. For as the secrets of the currents in the seas have never yet been divulged, even to the most erudite research; so the hidden ways of the Sperm Whale when beneath the surface remain, in great part, unaccountable to his pursuers; and from time to time have originated the most curious and contradictory speculations regarding them, especially concerning the mystic modes whereby, after sounding to a great depth, he transports himself with such vast swiftness to the most

---

① consternation: 恐怖
② overawed: 威慑,吓住

widely distant points.

It is a thing well known to both American and English whale-ships, and as well a thing placed upon authoritative record years ago by Scoresby, that some whales have been captured far north in the Pacific, in whose bodies have been found the barbs of harpoons darted in the Greenland seas. Nor is it to be gainsaid①, that in some of these instances it has been declared that the interval of time between the two assaults could not have exceeded very many days. Hence, by inference, it has been believed by some whale men, that the North West Passage, so long a problem to man, was never a problem to the whale. So that here, in the real living experience of living men, the prodigies related in old times of the inland Strello mountain in Portugal (near whose top there was said to be a lake in which the wrecks of ships floated up to the surface); and that still more wonderful story of the Arethusa fountain near Syracuse (whose waters were believed to have come from the Holy Land by an underground passage); these fabulous narrations are almost fully equalled by the realities of the whale men.

Forced into familiarity, then, with such prodigies as these; and knowing that after repeated, intrepid② assaults, the White Whale had escaped alive; it cannot be much matter of surprise that some whale men should go still further in their superstitions; declaring Moby Dick not only ubiquitous, but immortal (for immortality is but ubiquity in time); that though groves of spears should be planted in his flanks, he would still swim away unharmed; or if indeed he should ever be made to spout thick blood, such a sight would be but a ghastly deception; for again in ensanguined billows hundreds of leagues away, his unsullied jet would once more be seen.

But even stripped of these supernatural surmisings③, there was enough in the earthly make and incontestable character of the monster to strike the imagination with unwonted power. For, it was not so much his uncommon bulk that so much distinguished him from other sperm whales, but, as was elsewhere thrown out—a peculiar snow-white wrinkled forehead, and a high, pyramidical white hump. These were his prominent features; the tokens whereby, even in the limitless, uncharted seas, he revealed his identity, at a long distance, to those who knew him.

The rest of his body was so streaked, and spotted, and marbled with the same shrouded hue, that, in the end, he had gained his distinctive appellation④ of the White Whale; a name, indeed, literally justified by his vivid aspect, when seen gliding at high noon through a dark blue sea, leaving a milky-way wake of creamy foam, all spangled with golden gleamings.

Nor was it his unwonted magnitude, nor his remarkable hue, nor yet his deformed

---

① gainsay: 否认
② intrepid: 勇敢的,无畏的
③ surmise: 猜测
④ appellation: 名称

lower jaw, that so much invested the whale with natural terror, as that unexampled, intelligent malignity which, according to specific accounts, he had over and over again evinced in his assaults. More than all, his treacherous retreats struck more of dismay than perhaps aught else. For, when swimming before his exulting pursuers, with every apparent symptom of alarm, he had several times been known to turn around suddenly, and, bearing down upon them, either stave their boats to splinters, or drive them back in consternation to their ship.

Already several fatalities had attended his chase. But though similar disasters, however little bruited ashore, were by no means unusual in the fishery; yet, in most instances, such seemed the White Whale's infernal aforethought① of ferocity, that every dismembering or death that he caused, was not wholly regarded as having been inflicted by an unintelligent agent. Judge, then, to what pitches of inflamed, distracted fury the minds of his more desperate hunters were impelled, when amid the chips of chewed boats, and the sinking limbs of torn comrades, they swam out of the white curds of the whale's direful wrath into the serene, exasperating sunlight, that smiled on, as if at a birth or a bridal. His three boats stove around him, and oars and men both whirling in the eddies; one captain, seizing the line-knife from his broken prow, had dashed at the whale, as an Arkansas duellist at his foe, blindly seeking with a six inch blade to reach the fathom-deep life of the whale. That captain was Ahab. And then it was, that suddenly sweeping his sickle-shaped lower jaw beneath him, Moby Dick had reaped away Ahab's leg, as a mower a blade of grass in the field. No turbaned Turk, no hired Venetian or Malay, could have smote him with more seeming malice. Small reason was there to doubt, then, that ever since that almost fatal encounter, Ahab had cherished a wild vindictiveness② against the whale, all the more fell for that in his frantic morbidness he at last came to identify with him, not only all his bodily woes, but all his intellectual and spiritual exasperations. The White Whale swam before him as the monomaniac incarnation of all those malicious agencies which some deep men feel eating in them, till they are left living on with half a heart and half a lung. That intangible malignity which has been from the beginning; to whose dominion even the modern Christians ascribe one-half of the worlds; which the ancient Ophites of the east reverenced in their statue devil; Ahab did not fall down and worship it like them; but deliriously transferring its idea to the abhorred white whale, he pitted himself, all mutilated, against it. All that most maddens and torments; all that stirs up the lees of things; all truth with malice in it; all that cracks the sinews and cakes the brain; all the subtle demonisms of life and thought; all evil, to crazy Ahab, were visibly personified, and made practically assailable in Moby Dick. He piled upon the whale's white hump the sum of all the general rage and hate felt by his whole race from Adam down; and then,

---

① aforethought: 预谋的
② vindictiveness: 恶毒

as if his chest had been a mortar, he burst his hot heart's shell upon it.

It is not probable that this monomania① in him took its instant rise at the precise time of his bodily dismemberment. Then, in darting at the monster, knife in hand, he had but given loose to a sudden, passionate, corporal animosity; and when he received the stroke that tore him, he probably but felt the agonizing bodily laceration, but nothing more. Yet, when by this collision forced to turn towards home, and for long months of days and weeks, Ahab and anguish lay stretched together in one hammock, rounding in mid winter that dreary, howling Patagonian Cape; then it was, that his torn body and gashed soul bled into one another; and so interfusing, made him mad.

That it was only then, on the homeward voyage, after the encounter, that the final monomania seized him, seems all but certain from the fact that, at intervals during the passage, he was a raving lunatic; and, though unlimbed of a leg, yet such vital strength yet lurked in his Egyptian chest, and was moreover intensified by his delirium②, that his mates were forced to lace him fast, even there, as he sailed, raving in his hammock. In a strait-jacket, he swung to the mad rockings of the gales. And, when running into more sufferable latitudes, the ship, with mild stun' sails spread, floated across the tranquil tropics, and, to all appearances, the old man's delirium seemed left behind him with the Cape Horn swells, and he came forth from his dark den into the blessed light and air; even then, when he bore that firm, collected front, however pale, and issued his calm orders once again; and his mates thanked God the direful madness was now gone; even then, Ahab, in his hidden self, raved on. Human madness is oftentimes a cunning and most feline thing. When you think it fled, it may have but become transfigured into some still subtler form. Ahab's full lunacy subsided not, but deepeningly contracted; like the unabated③ Hudson, when that noble Northman flows narrowly, but unfathomably through the Highland gorge. But, as in his narrow-flowing monomania, not one jot of Ahab's broad madness had been left behind; so in that broad madness, not one jot of his great natural intellect had perished. That before living agent, now became the living instrument. If such a furious trope may stand, his special lunacy stormed his general sanity and carried it, and turned all its concentred cannon upon its own mad mark; so that far from having lost his strength, Ahab, to that one end, did now possess a thousand fold more potency than ever he had sanely brought to bear upon any one reasonable object.

This is much; yet Ahab's larger, darker, deeper part remains unhinted. But vain to popularize profundities, and all truth is profound. Winding far down from within the very heart of this spiked Hotel de Cluny where we here stand—however grand and wonderful, now quit it;—and take your way, ye nobler, sadder souls, to those vast

---

① monomania：偏执狂
② delirium：精神错乱
③ unabated：不减弱的，不衰减的

Roman halls of Thermes; where far beneath the fantastic towers of man's upper earth, his root of grandeur, his whole awful essence sits in bearded state; an antique buried beneath antiquities, and throned on torsoes! So with a broken throne, the great gods mock that captive king; so like a Caryatid, he patient sits, upholding on his frozen brow the piled entablatures of ages. Wind ye down there, ye prouder, sadder souls! Question that proud, sad king! A family likeness! Aye, he did beget ye, ye young exiled royalties; and from your grim sire only will the old State-secret come.

Now, in his heart, Ahab had some glimpse of this, namely; all my means are sane, my motive and my object mad. Yet without power to kill, or change, or shun the fact; he likewise knew that to mankind he did now long dissemble; in some sort, did still. But that thing of his dissembling was only subject to his perceptibility, not to his will determinate. Nevertheless, so well did he succeed in that dissembling①, that when with ivory leg he stepped ashore at last, no Nantucketer thought him otherwise than but naturally grieved, and that to the quick, with the terrible casualty which had overtaken him.

The report of his undeniable delirium at sea was likewise popularly ascribed to a kindred cause. And so too, all the added moodiness② which always afterwards, to the very day of sailing in the Pequod on the present voyage, sat brooding on his brow. Nor is it so very unlikely, that far from distrusting his fitness for another whaling voyage, on account of such dark symptoms, the calculating people of that prudent isle were inclined to harbor the conceit, that for those very reasons he was all the better qualified and set on edge, for a pursuit so full of rage and wildness as the bloody hunt of whales. Gnawed within and scorched without, with the infixed, unrelenting fangs of some incurable idea; such a one, could he be found, would seem the very man to dart his iron and lift his lance against the most appalling of all brutes. Or, if for any reason thought to be corporeally incapacitated for that, yet such a one would seem superlatively competent to cheer and howl on his underlings to the attack. But be all this as it may, certain it is, that with the mad secret of his unabated rage bolted up and keyed in him, Ahab had purposely sailed upon the present voyage with the one only and all-engrossing object of hunting the White Whale. Had anyone of his old acquaintances on shore but half dreamed of what was lurking in him then, how soon would their aghast and righteous souls have wrenched the ship from such a fiendish man! They were bent on profitable cruises, the profit to be counted down in dollars from the mint. He was intent on an audacious, immitigable③, and supernatural revenge. Here, then, was this grey-headed, ungodly old man, chasing with curses a Job's whale round the world, at the head of a

---

① dissemble: 掩饰
② moodiness: 喜怒无常,闷闷不乐
③ immitigable: 不能减轻的

crew, too, chiefly made up of mongrel renegades, and castaways, and cannibals①—morally enfeebled also, by the incompetence of mere unaided virtue or right mindedness in Starbuck, the invulnerable jollity② of indifference and recklessness in Stubb, and the pervading mediocrity in Flask. Such a crew, so officered, seemed specially picked and packed by some infernal fatality to help him to his monomaniac revenge. How it was that they so aboundingly responded to the old man's ire—by what evil magic their souls were possessed, that at times his hate seemed almost theirs; the White Whale as much their insufferable foe as his; how all this came to be—what the White Whale was to them, or how to their unconscious understandings, also, in some dim, unsuspected way, he might have seemed the gliding great demon of the seas of life, —all this to explain, would be to dive deeper than Ishmael can go. The subterranean③ miner that works in us all, how can one tell whither leads his shaft by the ever shifting, muffled sound of his pick? Who does not feel the irresistible arm drag? What skiff in tow of a seventy-four can stand still? For one, I gave myself up to the abandonment of the time and the place; but while yet all a-rush to encounter the whale, could see naught in that brute but the deadliest ill.

Questions for discussion

1. After reading the text, what do you learn about the sailor Ishmael?
2. What kind of information can you infer from the selected chapter? What's the function of the last paragraph?
3. What do you think are the symbolic meanings of Moby Dick and Captain Ahab?

文学术语(Definition of Literary Terms)

1. A **novel** is a long narrative, which describes fictional characters and events, usually in the form of a sequential story.
2. **Plot** is the plan of events or main story in a novel, narrative or drama.

Section B Cultural Notes

Before You Read

1. Try to search on the Internet or in the library about the term symbolism.
2. What is the definition of symbols?

---

① cannibal：食人族
② jollity：高兴
③ subterranean：地下的

Start to Read

Symbolism

Symbolism① originated in France, and was part of a 19th-century movement in which art became infused with mysticism. French Symbolism was both a continuation of the Romantic tradition and a reaction to the realistic approach of impressionism. It served as a catalyst② in the outgrowth of the darker sides of Romanticism and toward abstraction. The term Symbolism means the systematic use of symbols or pictorial conventions to express an allegorical meaning.

Symbolism is an important element of most religious arts and reading symbols which plays a main role in psychoanalysis. Thus, the Symbolist painters used these symbols from mythology and dream imagery for a visual language of the soul. Not so much a style of art, Symbolism was more an international ideological trend. Symbolists believed that art should apprehend more absolute truths which could only be accessed indirectly. Thus, they painted scenes from nature, human activities, and all other real world phenomena in a highly metaphorical and suggestive manner. They provided particular images or objects with esoteric③ attractions. There were several, rather dissimilar, groups of Symbolist painters and visual artists.

Symbolism in painting had a large geographical reach, reaching several Russian artists, as well as American. The closest to Symbolism was Aestheticism. The Pre-Raphaelites, also, were contemporaries of the earlier Symbolists, and have much in common with them. Symbolism had a significant influence on Expressionism and Surrealism, two movements which descend directly from Symbolism proper. The work of some Symbolist visual artists directly impacted the curvilinear forms of the contemporary Art Nouveau movements in Europe and Les Nabis.

After You Read

I. Questions for discussion

1. Where did symbolism originate?
2. What's the function of French symbolism?
3. How did Symbolist painters express a visual language of the soul?
4. What did Symbolists believe in terms of art?
5. What did Symbolists do to demonstrate their ideology?

---

① Symbolism: 象征主义
② catalyst: 催化剂
③ esoteric: 难领略的

II. True or false

1. When art became infused with mysticism, symbolism appeared. ( )
2. French symbolism is only a reaction to the realistic approach of impressionism. ( )
3. Symbolism is important not only in religious arts, but also in psychoanalysis. ( )
4. Symbolists believed that art should apprehend more absolute truths which could only be accessed directly. ( )
5. Symbolist painters and visual artists vary greatly geographically. ( )
6. Symbolism greatly influenced Expressionism and Surrealism, which descend directly from Symbolism. ( )

For Fun

I. Movies to see

Moby Dick (2010) is a movie based on the novel of the same name. It is directed by Trey Stokes.

II. Websites to visit

1. http://www.gradesaver.com/author/herman-melville/
2. http://www.pbs.org/wnet/americannovel/timeline/melville.html
3. http://www.online-literature.com/melville/
4. http://melvillesociety.org/
5. http://www.huntfor.com/arthistory/c19th/symbolism.htm

III. Writing

There are many similar stages during the development of different countries and the developing countries may learn something from the experiences of those developed ones. From your knowledge and what you have learnt in this unit, what do you think China can learn from the experiences of America?

Chapter 8

The Nineteenth Century American Poets
Walt Whitman (1819-1892)
沃尔特·惠特曼

Section A Literary Focus

作者简介(About the Author)

【生平】 沃尔特·惠特曼,美国现代诗歌之父,出生于纽约州长岛的穷苦家庭。他的一生颇为坎坷,11岁就辍学,先后曾在印刷所当过学徒、小学教师、地方报纸编辑。虽然没有受到过完整的学校正规教育,惠特曼从1839年起开始文学创作,写一些短诗,同时积极参加当地的政治活动,撰写文章表达自己的民主政治理念。他先后担任过几家报刊的编辑、主编,但终因政见不合于1840年离开新闻界。从1850年起,惠特曼一面从事体力劳动,一面展开了他的诗歌创作。1892年,惠特曼因病去世。

【主要作品】 诗集《草叶集》(*Leaves of Grass*,1855);诗集《桴鼓集》(*Drum Taps*,1865),诗集《桴鼓集·续集》(*Sequel to Drum Taps*,1865),散文《民主展望》(*Democratic Vistas*,1871)等。

作品选读(Selected Writings)

Leaves of Grass

19世纪美国作家惠特曼所创作的浪漫主义诗集《草叶集》奠定了美国诗歌的基础。1855年惠特曼出版了第一部诗集《草叶集》(*Leaves of Grass*)第一版。其中作为诗集名字的"草叶"以其顽强的生命力和勃勃生机象征着一切平凡的事物或平凡的普通人。诗集最初只有12首长诗,语言质朴,不拘泥传统诗歌中的格律和押韵,开创了独具一格的自由体诗(Free Verse)。这种风格的诗以民主的内容、革新的形式极大地影响了美国乃至世界诗坛。

惠特曼一生都在不断补充、修订、扩充诗集,直到第九版共收录300多首诗歌。这本诗集记录了诗人一生的思想和探索历程,也反映出时代和国家的面貌。诗集得名于集中这样一句诗:"这便是在有土有水的地方所长出来的青草。"草叶是最普通、最有生命力的东西,象征着当时正在蓬勃发展的美国。诗集中的诗歌像是长满美国大地的芳草,生气蓬勃并散发着诱人的芳香。诗集通过"自我"感受和"自我"形象,热情歌颂了资本主义上升时期的美国。《草叶集》的成功之处在于诗集里的每一片草叶都注入了鲜活的时代精神,正如诗人的心灵,时时随着时代的脉搏而跳动。在谈到这本诗集时,美国著名思想家、诗人拉尔夫·爱默生曾说道:"我在读它(《草叶集》)的时候,感到十分愉快,伟大的力量总是使我们感到愉快的。"

O Me! O Life!

O ME! O life! ... of the questions of these recurring[①];

Of the endless trains of the faithless—of cities fill'd with the foolish;

Of myself forever reproaching[②] myself,(for who more foolish than I, and who more faithless?)

Of eyes that vainly crave[③] the light—of the objects mean—of the struggle ever renew'd;

Of the poor results of all—of the plodding[④] and sordid[⑤] crowds I see around me;

Of the empty and useless years of the rest—with the rest me intertwined[⑥];

The question, O me! so sad, recurring—What good amid these, O me, O life?

Answer.

That you are here—that life exists, and identity;

That the powerful play goes on, and you will contribute a verse.

Questions for discussion
1. What is Whitman's view toward life?
2. What verse can you contribute in your life?

O Captain, My Captain[⑦]

O CAPTAIN! My Captain! Our fearful trip[⑧] is done;

The ship has weather'd every rack[⑨], the prize we sought is won;

---

① recurring:反复地出现
② reproach:责备
③ crave:渴望,热望
④ plodding:沉重的
⑤ sordid:肮脏的
⑥ intertwine:纠结,纠缠
⑦ 这首诗写于美国总统亚伯拉罕·林肯遇刺后不久,是惠特曼生前流传最广的诗歌之一。在诗中,惠特曼用一艘经历暴风雨后胜利返航的大船象征着废除奴隶制、平定南方分裂主义叛乱的美国;用船长和父亲来指代林肯总统。诗中采用对比和重复的手法,表达了对遇刺的林肯总统的怀念之情。
⑧ fearful trip:指经历南北战争的美国。
⑨ rack:痛苦

The port is near, the bells I hear, the people all exulting,①
  While follow eyes the steady keel②, the vessel③ grim and daring;
      But O heart! heart! heart!
        O the bleeding drops of red,
          Where on the deck my Captain lies,
            Fallen cold and dead.

O Captain! my Captain! rise up and hear the bells;
Rise up—for you the flag is flung④—for you the bugle⑤ trills⑥;
For you bouquets⑦ and ribbon'd wreaths⑧—for you the shores a-crowding;
For you they call, the swaying mass, their eager faces turning;
    Here Captain! dear father!
      This arm beneath your head;
        It is some dream that on the deck,
          You've fallen cold and dead.

My Captain does not answer, his lips are pale and still;
My father does not feel my arm, he has no pulse nor will;
The ship is anchor'd⑨ safe and sound⑩, its voyage closed and done;
From fearful trip, the victor ship, comes in with object won;
    Exult, O shores, and ring, O bell!
      But I, with mournful⑪ tread⑫,
        Walk the deck my Captain lies,
          Fallen cold and dead.

Questions for discussion

1. Can you find the sharp contrast between the speaker and the crowds on the shore?

---

① exult:狂欢

② While follow eyes the steady keel:人们的眼睛注视着平稳前进的大船。这里使用了倒装句,正常的语序是"While eyes follow the steady keel"。其中 eyes 和 keel 使用的是局部代替整体的提喻手法(synecdoche),用 eyes 代替岸上的人群,用 keel(船的龙骨)代替大船。

③ vessel:航船,货船

④ flung:fling 的过去分词,"抛,踢"的意思。

⑤ bugle:军号,号角

⑥ trill:发出颤音

⑦ bouquet:花束

⑧ wreath:花环,花冠

⑨ anchor:抛锚停泊

⑩ safe and sound:安然无恙,平安

⑪ mournful:悲哀的,凄切的

⑫ tread:脚步

What caused this contrast?
2. Who is this captain? Why is the first letter of "captain" capitalized?

文学术语(Definition of Literary Terms)

1. **Rhyme** is the type of echoing produced by the close placement of two or more words with similarly sounding final syllables. Rhyme is used in poetry (and occasionally in prose) to produce sounds that appeal to the ear and to unify and establish a poem's stanzaic form. End rhyme (i.e., rhyme used at the end of a line to echo the end of another line) is most common, but internal rhyme (occurring before the end of a line) is frequently used as an embellishment.
2. **Meter** in poetry is the recurrence of a rhythmic pattern, or the rhythm established by the regular or almost regular occurrence of similar units of sound pattern.
3. **Free verse** is a form of poetry which is free from meter patterns, rhyme, or any other musical patterns.

Section B Cultural Notes

Before You Read

1. Try to search on the internet or in the library about the cause of the American Civil War and the related information. Give a 3-minute classroom presentation.
2. Do you know Abraham Lincoln? Briefly summarize his life.

Start to Read

American Civil War

In the mid-19th century, while the United States was experiencing an era of tremendous growth, a fundamental economic difference existed between the country's northern and southern regions. While in the North, manufacturing and industry was well established, and agriculture was mostly limited to small-scale farms, the South's economy was based on a system of large-scale farming  that depended on the labor of black slaves to grow certain crops, especially cotton and tobacco. Growing abolitionist① sentiment in the North after the 1830s and northern opposition to slavery's extension into the new western territories led many southerners to fear that the existence of slavery in America—and thus the backbone of their economy—was in danger.

The American Civil War is also called the War Between the States, the War of Rebellion, or the War for Southern Independence. It broke out on April 12, 1861, when Confederate General opened fire on Fort Sumter, South Carolina, and lasted until May 26, 1865, when the last Confederate army surrendered②. The war took more than 600,000 lives, destroyed property valued at $5 billion, brought freedom to 4 million black slaves, and opened wounds that have not yet completely healed more than 125 years later.

The chief and immediate cause of the war was slavery. Southern states, including the 11 states that formed the confederacy③, depended on slavery to support their economy. Southerners used slave labor to produce crops, especially cotton. Although slavery was illegal in the Northern states, only a small proportion of Northerners actively opposed it. The main debate between the North and the South on the eve of the war was whether slavery should be permitted in the Western territories recently acquired during the Mexican War (1846-1848), including New Mexico, part of California, and Utah. Opponents of slavery were concerned about its expansion, in part because they did not want to compete against slave labor.

By 1860, the North and the South had developed into two different regions. Each tried to impose④ its point of view on the country as a whole. Although compromises⑤ had kept the Union together for many years, the situation was explosive in 1860. The election of Abraham Lincoln as president was viewed by the South as a threat to slavery and ignited⑥ the war.

During the first half of the 19th century, economic differences between the North and South also increased. By 1860, cotton was the chief crop of the South, and it represented 57 percent of all the U.S. exports. The profitability⑦ of cotton, known as King Cotton, completed the South's dependence on the plantation system and its essential component, slavery.

The North was by then firmly established an industrial society. Labor was needed, but not slave labor. Immigration was encouraged. Immigrants from Europe worked in factories, built the railroads of the North, and settled the West. Very few settled in the

---

① abolitionist: 废奴主义者
② surrender: 投降
③ confederacy: 联盟或同盟
④ impose: 强制实行,把……强加于
⑤ compromise: 妥协,折中
⑥ ignite: 点燃,引燃
⑦ profitability: 盈利性,收益率

South.

The South, resisting industrialization, manufactured little. Almost all manufactured goods had to be imported. Southerners, therefore, opposed high tariffs①, or taxes that were placed on imported goods and increased the price of manufactured articles. The manufacturing economy of the North, on the other hand, demanded high tariffs to protect its own products from cheap foreign competition.

The expanding Northwest Territory, which was made up of the present-day states of Ohio, Indiana, Illinois, Michigan, Wisconsin, and part of Minnesota, was far from the markets for its grain and cattle. It needed such internal improvement for survival, and so supported Northeast's demands for high tariffs. In return, the Northeast supported most federally financed improvement in the Northwest Territory.

As a result, the West allied② itself with the Northern, rather than the Southern, point of view although both the South and the West were agricultural, economic needs sharpened sectional differences, adding to the interregional hostility③.

After You Read

I. Questions for discussion

1. What was the immediate cause of the war?
2. When did the American Civil War break out?
3. What are the different attitudes towards slavery between the North and South?
4. How did the Southerners feel about the election of Abraham Lincoln? Why?
5. Why did the Southerners intend to keep slavery?
6. Why did the South take a different attitude towards tariffs from the North?

---

① tariff: 关税
② ally: 与……结盟
③ hostility: 敌对,对抗

II. True or false

1. The American Civil War is also called the War Between the States, the War of Rebellion, or the War for Southern Independence. ( )
2. By 1860, the North and the South had developed into one region. They always reached agreements on the country as a whole. ( )
3. The American Civil War broke out in 1860 and ended in 1865. ( )
4. By 1860, corn was the chief crop of the South, and it represented 57 percent of all the U. S. exports. ( )
5. The North was by then firmly established an industrial society. Labor was needed, but not slave labor. ( )
6. The expanding Northwest Territory, which was made up of the present-day states of Ohio, Indiana, Illinois, Michigan, Wisconsin, and part of Minnesota, was far from the markets for its grain and cattle. ( )
7. Westerners, therefore, opposed high tariffs, or taxes that were placed on imported goods and increased the price of manufactured articles. ( )
8. Growing abolitionist sentiment in the North after the 1830s and northern opposition to slavery's extension into the new western territories led many southerners to fear that the existence of slavery in America was in danger. ( )

For Fun

I. Movies to see

1. *Dead Poets Society* (1989)

　　It is a 1989 American drama film written by Tom Schulman, directed by Peter Weir and starring Robin Williams. Set at the conservative and aristocratic Welton Academy in the northeast United States in 1959, it tells the story of an English teacher who inspires his students through his teaching of poetry.

2. *Gone with the Wind* (1939)

　　The movie is adapted from a novel written by Margaret Mitchell, first published in 1936. The story is set in Clayton County, Georgia, and Atlanta during the American Civil War and Reconstruction era. It depicts the struggles of young Scarlett O'Hara, the spoiled daughter of a well-to-do plantation owner, who must use every means at her disposal to claw her way out of the poverty.

II. Websites to visit

1. http://www.loc.gov/exhibits/gad/
2. http://www.history.com/topics/american-civil-war

III. Writing

　　Poetry is a way of expressing passion. Do you have a role model? Imitate Walt

Whitman's "O Captain, My Captain" to compose a poem about a historical figure.

Emily Dickinson (1830–1886)
艾米莉·狄金森

Section A　Literary Focus

作者简介（About the Author）

【生平】　艾米莉·狄金森是美国 19 世纪杰出的抒情女诗人，也被公认为世界文学史上最为孤独的女诗人。她的诗不受传统形式的约束，不受当时社会思潮的左右。其独特的风格、敏锐的观察、深邃的思想及别具一格的创作技巧对后来不少西方现代派诗人产生过很大影响，是西方现代诗歌的一个重要渊源。狄金森一反浮夸的浪漫主义诗风，以不规则的韵律、奇特的对照和自由的联想，打开了通向美国现代诗的道路，被有的评论家称为"美国诗歌之母"，与惠特曼一道成为现当代美国诗歌的开拓者。

狄金森的诗通常短小精悍，简洁明快，擅用具体而独特的意象，感情真挚，寓意深刻，在平易自然中显出她对人生的思考。她的诗在形式上富于独创性，例如在诗句中使用许多短破折号，既可代替标点，又使正常的抑扬格音步节奏产生突兀的起伏跳动。她的诗大多押半韵（half rhyme），常省略句子成分，有时甚至连动词也省掉；句法多倒装，有学者指这是受拉丁文词序的影响。

在狄金森有生之年，她的作品未能获得青睐。然而周遭众人对她的不解与误会，却丝毫无法低损她丰富的创作天分。据统计，艾米莉为世人留下 1,800 多首诗，包括了定本的 1,775 首与新近发现的 25 首。

【主要作品】　《有另一片天空》(*There is Another Sky*)、《我们输了——因为我们赢了》(*We Lose—Because We Win*)、《我是无名小卒！你呢？》(*I'm Nobody! Who Are You?*)、《当它还存活》(*While It Is Alive*)等。

作品选读(Selected Writings)

I'm Nobody

I'm nobody! Who are you?
Are you nobody, too?
Then there's a pair of us—don't tell!
They'd banish① us, you know.

How dreary to be somebody!
How public, like a frog
To tell your name the livelong day
To an admiring bog②!

Questions for discussion
1. How do you understand "nobody" and "somebody" in this poem?
2. Why do you think the writer relate the public to a frog?
3. Do you want to be somebody? If yes, what will you do? If no, what is your goal in life?

I Heard a Fly Buzz—When I Died—

I heard a Fly buzz—when I died—
The stillness in the Room
Was like the stillness in the Air—
Between the Heaves of Storm—

The Eyes around—had wrung when them dry—
And breaths were gathering firm
For that last Onset—when the King
Be witnessed—in the Room—

I willed my keepsakes—Signed away
What portion of me be
Assignable③—and then it was
There interposed a Fly—

With Blue—uncertain stumbling Buzz—
Between the light—and me—
And the the windows failed—and then

---

① banish：放逐
② bog：泥塘
③ assignable：可分配的

I could not see to see—

Questions for discussion
1. What is the main idea of the poem?
2. How do you feel about the ending of the poem?
3. What do you think might be the possible setting of the poem?

Because I Could Not Stop for Death
Because I could not stop for Death—
He kindly stopped for me—
The Carriage held but just Ourselves—
And Immortality.

We slowly drove—He knew no haste—
And I had put away
My labor—and my leisure too,
For His Civility①.

We passed the School, where Children strove
At recess②—in the Ring③—
We passed the Fields of Gazing Grain—
We passed the Setting Sun—

Or rather—He④ passed Us—
The Dews drew quivering and chill—
For only Gossamer, my Gown—
My Tippet—only Tulle—

We paused before a House that seemed
A Swelling⑤ of the Ground—
The Roof was scarcely visible—
The Cornice⑥—in the Ground—

---

① civility: 礼貌
② recess: 课间休息
③ ring: 操场
④ He: 指落日
⑤ swelling: 隆起
⑥ cornice: 门檐

Since then—'tis① Centuries—and yet
Feels shorter than the Day
I first surmised the Horses' Heads
Were toward Eternity—

Questions for discussion
1. Why does the poet say "the horses's head toward eternity"?
2. How do you understand the images like "children," "gown," "horses' head" etc. in the poem?
3. How do you appreciate this poem?

文学术语(Definition of Literary Terms)

Rhythm: The arrangement of stressed and unstressed syllables into a pattern.

Section B Cultural Notes

Before You Read

Try to search on the Internet or in the library about the poet Emily Dickinson and the related information. Give a 3-minute classroom presentation.

Start to Read

Inside Emily Dickinson's Revealing Lost Papers

What will we learn about Dickinson as a poet from the new database? The first conclusion—far more visible in the manuscripts than in the print volumes—is how tenaciously she worked on perfecting her nearly two thousand poems. Innumerable instances of revision abound. Each one rethinks the matter or the manner of the poem, but more significantly, each one rethinks an intellectual question. Just as "The Bible is an Antique Volume"—a minor homiletics in itself—redefines what would be persuasive in the mediation of the Bible to the young, so "Shall I take thee" reflects on the premature attempt to force art, insisting on the essential relation between poetry and its initiating "Vision." Each of these poems end in satisfaction: biblical stories find their musical Orpheus, the struggling Poet's frustration is relieved.

Further study of Dickinson's path and procedures in her exact reconsiderations of her first thoughts would afford insight into several aspects of her art: it could pursue her

---

① 'tis: 即 it is

most frequent lines of self-correction—conjecture, denial, refutation, pathos; it could spell out the radiating possibilities of multiple poems constructed by a single word change (fourteen different poems retrospectively constructed by varying the successive adjectives for the persuasive "Teller" in the pulpit); it could illustrate the effect of changing nouns or gender pronouns from masculine to feminine; or it could examine the instances in which Dickinson refuses the sentimental in favor of the truthful. These are only a few illustrations of what the revisions might add to our sense of Dickinson's creative mind.

Her revisions allow us to admire her lexical fastidiousness as she weighs closely related words. In the strange riddle poem on the Soul (titled "The Spirit" by her first editors, spoiling thereby the reader's gradual solution of the riddle), should she say "imply" or "denote"? "Designate" or "intimate"? Should she prefer "function" to "customs"? Shall she say "unsurmised thing" or "Apocalyptic thing" or "Hyperbole"? These considerations are minutely related to the supernatural as Dickinson understands it or doubts it. I reproduce her riddle, showing the early choices to the right of the final version, in italics:

> 'Tis whiter than an Indian Pipe-
> 'Tis dimmer than a Lace—
> No stature has it, like a Fog
> When you approach the place—
> Not any voice imply it here-   *denote*
> Or intimate it there—   *designate*
> A spirit—how doth it accost—
> What function hath the Air?   *What customs*
> This limitless Hyperbole   *And this—this unsurmised thing—*
> Each one of us shall be—   *And this—Apocalyptic thing—*
> 'Tis Drama—if Hypothesis   *This*
> It be not Tragedy—

What shall we become after death? A Spirit? A Ghost? A Soul? Dickinson, facing the difficulty of describing something invisible, resorts at first to whimsical comparisons—with the slender white plant called the "Indian Pipe," with a piece of lace, with a fog. The early comparisons are queried (and replaced) only when the serious topic of voice arises: for a poet, the worst fear is the loss of voice. Dickinson first declares, by rejecting both "denote" and "designate," that these verbs are too material and positivistic; she finds them unsuited to the ethereality of this spirit and its putative voice. Better to use such verbs as "imply," which is secretive and tentative, or "intimate," which whispers and suggests.

When Dickinson imagines the posthumous dwelling of the spirit, she at first domesticates its air-home with an anthropological question: what "customs" has the Air? But she reproaches herself as she admits that customs are enacted materially in social environments; she therefore ascribes to the Air, the future habitation of the spirit, the abstract, unrevealing, even algebraic word "function." When she comes to describing what survives death, she begins vaguely: the spirit is "an unsurmised thing." True enough—one can hardly surmise a fog or a function. Her second thought returns to the Bible, her most frequent source; what will the spirit, formerly a temporal thing, become at the end of the world? An "Apocalyptic thing"? But this is to assume what remains to be proved, that there will *be* an Apocalypse. Leaping to a different level of language altogether—the imaginative linguistic level on which she herself lives—she says the spirit is a "Hyperbole," a conceptual exaggeration, something to which, on no evidence, we ascribe a "limitless" Eternity. Using the language of prophetic certainty (each one of us "shall" be—not "will" be—this entity), she invokes the Christian suspense of the soul's immortal destiny—"'Tis Drama"—before appending her subversive skeptical doubt, in which she returns to the rhetorical level of Hyperbole in advancing her grim Hypothesis in which our spirits, not immortal but mortal, are victims in an ineluctable tragedy.

After You Read

I. Questions for discussion

1. What are the differences between such words as "imply" and "denote," "intimate" and "designate"? Why do you think Dickson chose one word over the other in her riddle poem?
2. Do you think that revision plays an important role in poem writing? How the reconsideration of her initial thoughts contributes to Dickson's work?
3. What do you think is unique if the form of the poem contained in the text? What effects do the unconventional arrangement of lines produce for the readers?
4. If you are the editor of Emily Dickson's new anthology, what name will you give for this riddle poem or just no name at all?

For Fun

I. Websites to visit

1. http://www.poets.org/poetsorg/poet/emily-dickinson
2. http://www.online-literature.com/dickinson/
3. http://www.emilydickinsonmuseum.org/about_emily_dickinson
4. http://www.newrepublic.com/article/116788/emily-dickinsons-gorgeous-nothings-reviewed-helen-vendler

II. Writing

What is your explanation of success. Imitate Emily Dickinson's "I'm Nobody" to compose a poem to express your view about success.

Chapter 9

Mark Twain(1835–1910)
马克·吐温

Section A Literary Focus

作者简介(About the Author)

【生平】 马克·吐温(Mark Twain),美国著名作家,真实姓名是萨缪尔·兰亨·克莱门(Samuel Langhorne Clemens)。"马克·吐温"是他的笔名,原是密西西比河水手使用的表示在航道上所测水的深度的术语。马克·吐温12岁时,父亲去世,他只好停学,到工厂当小工。后来他又换了不少职业,曾做过密西西比河的领航员、矿工及新闻记者。渐渐地着手写一些有趣的小品,开始了自己的写作生涯。马克·吐温一生写了大量作品,题材涉及小说、剧本、散文、诗歌等各方面。从内容上说,他的作品批判了不合理现象或人性的丑恶之处,表达了这位当过排字工人和水手的作家强烈的正义感和对普通人民的关心;从风格上说,幽默和讽刺是他的写作特点。

马克·吐温是美国批判现实主义文学的奠基人,他经历了美国从初期资本主义到帝国主义的发展过程,其思想和创作也表现为从轻快调笑到辛辣讽刺再到悲观厌世的发展阶段,前期以辛辣的讽刺见长,到了后期语言更为激烈,被誉为"美国文学史上的林肯"。

【主要作品】《百万英镑》(*The Million Pound Note*,1893),《哈克贝利·费恩历险记》(*The Adventures of Huckleberry Finn*,1884),《汤姆·索亚历险记》(*The Adventures of Tom Sawyer*,1876)等。

作品选读(Selected Writings)

The Adventures of Tom Sawyer

《汤姆·索亚历险记》是马克·吐温1876年发表的代表作品,小说的故事发生在19世纪上半叶美国密西西比河畔的一个普通小镇上。主人公汤姆·索亚天真活泼,敢于探险,追求自由,不堪忍受束缚个性、枯燥乏味的生活,幻想干一番英雄事业。小说的时间设置在南北战争前,写的虽是圣彼得堡小镇,但该镇某种程度上可以说是当时美国社会的缩影。作品通过主人公的冒险经历，对美国虚伪庸俗的社会习俗、伪善的宗教仪式和刻板陈腐的学校教育进行了讽刺和批判，以欢快的笔调描写了少年儿童自由活泼的心灵。《汤姆·索亚历险记》以其浓厚的深具地方特色的幽默和对人物敏锐观察，一跃成为最伟大的儿童文学作品之一，也是一首美国"黄金时代"的田园牧歌。

The Adventures of Tom Sawyer (Excerpt)

A FEW minutes later Tom was in the shoal① water of the bar, wading toward the Illinois shore. Before the depth reached his middle he was halfway over; the current would permit no more wading, now, so he struck out confidently to swim the remaining hundred yards. He swam quartering② up-stream, but still was swept downward rather faster than he had expected. However, he reached the shore finally, and drifted along till he found a low place and drew himself out. He put his hand on his jacket pocket, found his piece of bark safe, and then struck through the woods, following the shore, with streaming garments. Shortly before ten o'clock he came out into an open place opposite the village, and saw the ferryboat lying in the shadow of the trees and the high bank. Everything was quiet under the blinking stars. He crept down the bank, watching with all his eyes, slipped into the water, swam three or four strokes and climbed into the skiff that did "yawl" duty at the boat's stern. He laid himself down under the thwarts and waited, panting. Presently the cracked bell tapped and a voice gave the order to "cast off." A minute or two later the skiff③'s head was standing high up, against the boat's swell, and the voyage was begun. Tom felt happy in his success, for he knew it was the boat's last trip for the night. At the end of a long twelve or fifteen minutes the wheels stopped, and Tom slipped overboard and swam ashore in the dusk, landing fifty yards down-stream, out of danger of possible stragglers.

He flew along unfrequented④ alleys, and shortly found himself at his aunt's back fence. He climbed over, approached the "ell," and looked in at the sitting-room window, for a light was burning there. There sat Aunt Polly, Sid, Mary, and Joe Harper's mother, grouped together, talking. They were by the bed, and the bed was between them and the door. Tom went to the door and began to softly lift the latch⑤; then he pressed gently and the door yielded a crack; he continued pushing cautiously, and quaking every time it creaked, till he judged he might squeeze through on his knees; so he put his head through and began, warily.

"What makes the candle blow so?" said Aunt Polly. Tom hurried up.

"Why, that door's open, I believe. Why, of course it is. No end of strange things

---

① shoal：浅滩
② quarter：（由于风或水流的影响）斜向行进
③ skiff：小帆船
④ unfrequented：人迹罕至的
⑤ latch：门闩

now. Go 'long and shut it, Sid."

Tom disappeared under the bed just in time. He lay and "breathed" himself for a time, and then crept to where he could almost touch his aunt's foot.

"But as I was saying," said Aunt Polly, "he warn't BAD, so to say—only mischievous. Only just giddy, and harum-scarum, you know. He warn't any more responsible than a colt. HE never meant any harm, and he was the best-hearted boy that ever was"—and she began to cry.

"It was just so with my Joe—always full of his devilment, and up to every kind of mischief, but he was just as unselfish and kind as he could be—and laws bless me, to think I went and whipped him for taking that cream, never once recollecting that I throwed it out myself because it was sour, and I never to see him again in this world, never, never, never, poor abused boy!" And Mrs. Harper sobbed as if her heart would break.

"I hope Tom's better off where he is," said Sid, "but if he'd been better in some ways—"

"SID!" Tom felt the glare of the old lady's eye, though he could not see it. "Not a word against my Tom, now that he's gone! God'll take care of HIM—never you trouble YOURself, sir! Oh, Mrs. Harper, I don't know how to give him up! I don't know how to give him up! He was such a comfort to me, although he tormented my old heart out of me, 'most."

"The Lord giveth and the Lord hath taken away—Blessed be the name of the Lord! But it's so hard—Oh, it's so hard! Only last Saturday my Joe busted① a firecracker right under my nose and I knocked him sprawling. Little did I know then, how soon—Oh, if it was to do over again I'd hug him and bless him for it."

"Yes, yes, yes, I know just how you feel, Mrs. Harper, I know just exactly how you feel. No longer ago than yesterday noon, my Tom took and filled the cat full of Pain-killer, and I did think the cretur would tear the house down. And God forgive me, I cracked Tom's head with my thimble, poor boy, poor dead boy. But he's out of all his troubles now. And the last words I ever heard him say was to reproach—"

But this memory was too much for the old lady, and she broke entirely down. Tom was snuffling, now, himself—and more in pity of himself than anybody else. He could hear Mary crying, and putting in a kindly word for him from time to time. He began to have a nobler opinion of himself than ever before. Still, he was sufficiently touched by his aunt's grief to long to rush out from under the bed and overwhelm her with joy—and the theatrical② gorgeousness of the thing appealed strongly to his nature, too, but he resisted and lay still. He went on listening, and gathered by odds and ends that it was conjectured at first that the boys had got drowned while taking a swim; then the small

---

① bust：使爆裂
② theatrica：戏剧性的

raft had been missed; next, certain boys said the missing lads had promised that the village should "hear some-thing" soon; the wise-heads had "put this and that together" and decided that the lads had gone off on that raft and would turn up at the next town below, presently; but toward noon the raft had been found, lodged against the Missouri shore some five or six miles below the village—and then hope perished; they must be drowned, else hunger would have driven them home by nightfall if not sooner. It was believed that the search for the bodies had been a fruitless effort merely because the drowning must have occurred in mid-channel, since the boys, being good swimmers, would otherwise have escaped to shore. This was Wednesday night. If the bodies continued missing until Sunday, all hope would be given over, and the funerals would be preached on that morning.

Tom shuddered.

Mrs. Harper gave a sobbing good-night and turned to go. Then with a mutual impulse the two bereaved women flung themselves into each other's arms and had a good, consoling cry, and then parted. Aunt Polly was tender far beyond her wont, in her good-night to Sid and Mary. Sid snuffled a bit and Mary went off crying with all her heart.

Aunt Polly knelt down and prayed for Tom so touchingly, so appealingly, and with such measureless love in her words and her old trembling voice, that he was weltering① in tears again, long before she was through. He had to keep still long after she went to bed, for she kept making broken-hearted ejaculations② from time to time, tossing unrestfully, and turning over. But at last she was still, only moaning a little in her sleep. Now the boy stole out, rose gradually by the bedside, shaded the candlelight with his hand, and stood regarding her. His heart was full of pity for her. He took out his sycamore scroll and placed it by the candle. But something occurred to him, and he lingered considering. His face lighted with a happy solution of his thought; he put the bark hastily in his pocket. Then he bent over and kissed the faded lips, and straightway made his stealthy③ exit, latching the door behind him.

Questions for discussion

1. What are the writing techniques that the author used in this part of the story?
2. Why did Tom leave a note to Aunt Polly? What kind of inner feeling did this action reveal?

---

① welter: 浸泡(welter in tears: 哭成了泪人)
② ejaculation: 惊叹声
③ stealthy: 偷偷摸摸的; 秘密的

文学术语(Definition of Terms)

1. **Local Color Fiction** refers to fiction that focuses on specific features—including characters, dialects, customs, history and landscape—of a particular region in America. Local colorism as a trend first made its presence felt in the late 1860s and early 1870s. It did not cease to be a dominant fashion until the turn of the 20th century. It formed an important part of the realistic movement. Mark Twain is a representative of this school.
2. **Frontier Literature**: A Literary school in America about the frontier and frontier life. 1890s is the time when all the free lands had generally been claimed, and from then on one aspect of American history was the steady westward movement of the frontier. Much of the writing of this frontier was sub-literary, confined to oral tradition, but it is a better way to understand frontier spirit in American culture.

Section B Cultural Notes

Before You Read

Try to search the Internet or in the library about the West Movement in American history and the related information. Give a 3-minute classroom presentation.

Start to Read

The Frontier of the American West

American Westward Movement, movement of people from the settled regions of the United States to lands farther west. Between the early 17th and late 19th centuries, Anglo-American peoples and their societies expanded from the Atlantic Coast to the Pacific Coast. This westward movement, across what was often called the American frontier, was of enormous significance. By expanding the nation's borders to include more than three million square miles, the United States became one of the most powerful nations of the 20th century. However, this expansion also resulted in great suffering, destruction, and cultural loss for the Native Americans of North America.

After the 13 colonies gained their independence from Great Britain and became the United States, they beganto settle the land to the west. The first area of settlement was the U.S. territory that spanned to the Mississippi River. The population of the United States in 1790 was 3,929,214.

Before Anglo-American westward expansion, North America had been shaped by many other forces and cultures. There were hundreds of Native American tribes who had been living on the continent for thousands of years before any Europeans arrived. Many of these tribes disappeared because of the assault① of European exploration and settlement.

England established its first Atlantic colonies in Virginia at Jamestown in 1607 and in Massachusetts. These first English frontiers illustrated two of the most common motivations for people moving westward. The first motivation was the hope of finding great wealth quickly through developing and trading the colonies' resources. Jamestown was settled for this reason. The earliest dreams of mining for gold and producing wine and silk came to nothing, but in time Virginians found prosperity in the rich soil, especially by raising and exporting tobacco. Over the next 400 years, the economic motive, in particular the desire for good and cheap farmland would be the most powerful attractions for people moving west.

The second common motivation was the hope of practicing their religion without government intervention. The Puritan settlers of Massachusetts wanted to build a community based on religious ideas that were opposed by the British government. The frontier was home to dozens of colonies looking for freedom, religious and otherwise.

Those first Atlantic colonies also illustrated the contradictory roles that government played in westward expansion. The Puritans settled in Massachusetts with the permission, and sometimes the protection, of the same government whose policies they were trying to escape. Governments, first England and then the United States, always encouraged movement westward in a variety of ways. These governments bought or seized land from others and gave it away or sold it cheaply to emigrants. The governments used their military to protect settlers and financed developments, such as transportation, that made settlement easier.

People heading west came to expect the government's aid and support. At the same time, settlers often resisted efforts by distant authorities to regulate how they used and lived on their new lands. From the first colonies to the final farming frontiers of the 20th century, this conflicting relationship between pioneers and government was a large part of the frontier story.

It took Americans a century and a half to expand as far west as the Appalachian Mountains, a few hundred miles from the Atlantic coast. It took another 50 years to push the frontier to the Mississippi River. By 1830 fewer than 100,000 pioneers had crossed the Mississippi.

Only a small number of explorers and traders had ventured far beyond the Mississippi River. These trailblazers drew a picture of the American West as a land of promise, a paradise of plenty, filled with fertile valleys and rich land. During the 1840s, tens of thousands of Americans began the process of settling the West beyond the Mississippi River. Thousands of families chalked GTT ("Gone to Texas") on their gates

---

① assualt: 攻击

or on their wagons, and joined the trek① westward. By 1850, pioneers had pushed the edge of settlement all the way to Texas, the Rocky Mountains, and the Pacific Ocean.

On January 24, 1848, less than 10 days before the signing of the peace treaty ending the Mexican War, James W. Marshall, a 36-year old carpenter and handyman, noticed several bright bits of yellow mineral near a sawmill that he was building. To test if the bits were "fool's gold," which shatters when struck by a hammer, Marshall "tried it between two rocks, and found that it could be beaten into a different shape but not broken." He told the men working with him: "Boys, by God, I believe I have found a gold mine."

On March 15, a San Francisco newspaper, *The Californian*, printed the first account of Marshall's discovery. Within two weeks, the paper had lost its staff and was forced to shut down its printing press. In its last edition it told its readers:

"The whole country, from San Francisco to Los Angeles ... resounds with the cry of Gold! Gold! Gold! While the field is left half-planted, the house half-built, and everything neglected but the manufacture of picks and shovels."

In 1849, 80,000 men arrived in California. Only half were Americans; the rest came from Britain, Australia, Germany, France, Latin America, and China. Sailors jumped ship; husbands left wives; apprentices② ran away from their masters; farmers and business people deserted their livelihoods. By July, 1850, sailors had abandoned 500 ships in San Francisco Bay. Within a year, California's population had swollen from 14,000 to 100,000. The population of San Francisco, which stood at 459 in the summer of 1847, reached 20,000 within a few months.

The Gold Rush transformed California from a sleepy society into one that was wild, unruly, ethnically-diverse, and violent. Philosopher Josiah Royce, whose family arrived in the midst of the gold rush, declared that the Californian was "morally and socially tried as no other American ever has been tried." In San Francisco alone there were more than 500 bars and 1,000 gambling dens. In the span of 18 months, the city burned to the ground six times.

The Gold Rush era in California lasted less than a decade. By 1860, the romantic era of California gold mining was over. Prospectors③ had found more than $350 million worth of gold.

The exploration and settlement of the Far West is one of the great epics of the 19th century history. But America's dramatic territorial expansion also created severe problems. In addition to providing the United States with its richest mines, greatest forests, and most fertile farm land, the Far West intensified the sectional conflict between the North and South and raised the ultimately divisive question of whether

---

① trek: 有组织的迁移；跋涉
② apprentice: 学徒工
③ prospectors: 探矿者

slavery would be permitted in the western territories.

After You Read

I. Questions for discussion

1. What was the significance of American Westward Movement?
2. What motivated people to expand the nation's borders westward?
3. What were the conflicting roles of the government in the westward expansion?
4. How did those explorers and traders view the American West?
5. Why was the Californian "morally and socially tried as no other American ever has been tried"?

II. True or false

1. Between the early 17th and late 19th centuries, Anglo-American peoples and their societies expanded from the Atlantic Coast to the Pacific Coast. ( )
2. England established its first Atlantic colonies in Virginia at Jamestown in 1607 and in California. ( )
3. One of the motivations to move westward was to find great wealth quickly through developing and trading the colonies' resources. ( )
4. It took Americans a century and a half to expand as far west as the Appalachian Mountains. ( )
5. In order to gain wealth, a large number of explorers and traders had ventured far beyond the Mississippi River. ( )
6. James W. Marshall was the first person to discover a gold mine in California. ( )
7. Most of the men arrived in California were Americans. ( )
8. The Gold Rush transformed California from a sleepy society into one that was wild, unruly, ethnically-diverse, and violent. ( )
9. The Gold Rush provided the United States with its richest mines, greatest forests, and most fertile farm land and made America one of the richest country. ( )
10. The gold rush was a period of feverish migration of workers into the area which witnessed a dramatic discovery of commercial quantities of gold. ( )

For Fun

I. Movies to see

The Adventures of Tom Sawyer (1938): It is a 1938 American literature adaption directed by Norman Taurog starring Tommy Kelly in the title role. The screenplay by John V. A. Weaver was based on the classic 1876 novel by Mark Twain. It is about a young boy growing up along the Mississippi River. The story is set in the fictional town of St. Petersburg, inspired by Hannibal, Missouri, where Twain lived.

II. Websites to visit

1. http://www.24en.com/novel/classics/the-adventures-of-tom-sawyer.html
2. http://www.qc99.com/e/yingwenyuedu/xiaoshu/10855.html

III. Writing

The balanced development of different areas is extremely significant to every country in the world, especially to those with vast territory. On the basis of the above written materials, can you offer some methods that may be useful in evenly developing the frontier areas and center parts of a country?

Chapter 10

Jack London (1876–1916)
杰克·伦敦

Section A Literary Focus

作者简介(About the Author)

【生平】 杰克·伦敦,原名为约翰·格利菲斯·伦敦(John Griffith London),美国著名的现实主义作家,生于旧金山。24 岁开始写作,去世时年仅 40 岁。从 1900 年起,他连续出版了多部小说,讲述美国下层人民的生活故事。他一生著述颇丰,16 年中留下了 19 部长篇小说、150 多篇短篇小说以及大量文学报告集,还写了 3 个剧本以及相当多的随笔和论文。最著名的有《马丁·伊登》、《野性的呼唤》、《白牙》、《热爱生命》等小说。这些作品共同为读者展示了一个陌生又异常广阔的世界:荒凉空旷又蕴藏宝藏的阿拉斯加、波涛汹涌、岛屿星罗棋布的太平洋、横贯大陆的铁路线,形形色色的鲜活人物,人与自然的严酷搏斗,人与人之间错综复杂的社会关系。他是世界文学史上最早的商业作家之一,因此被誉为商业作家的先锋。

【主要作品】 《马丁·伊登》(*Martin Eden*, 1909)、《野性的呼唤》(*The Call of the Wild*, 1903)、《白牙》(*White Fang*, 1906)、《热爱生命》(*Love of life*, 1907)、《海狼》(*The Sea Wolf*, 1904)、《铁蹄》(*The Iron Heel*, 1908)等。

作品选读(Selected Writings)

杰克·伦敦的作品《生命的法则》描写了部落首领老科斯库什生命的最后时刻。由于饥荒,他被部落家人遗弃在冬日的雪原上,孤独地等候死神的降临。自然主义观点在小说表现得非常清晰,认为人类从出生到死亡,在外部力量和内部遗传力量的综合作用下,完成种族传递的使命。人同自然及生存过程的一切不利因素作斗争,过着艰辛的生活,进行着徒劳的挣扎。但是在徒劳的挣扎、注定的死亡和无可奈何之中又倾注了些许生命的希冀。体现了达尔文物竞天择、弱肉强食、自然选择的进化论思想。

The Law of Life

Old Koskoosh listened greedily. Though his sight had long since faded, his hearing was still acute, and the slightest sound penetrated to the glimmering intelligence which yet abode behind the withered forehead, but which no longer gazed forth upon the things of the world. Ah! that was Sit-cum-to-ha, shrilly anathematizing the dogs as she cuffed① and beat them into the harnesses. Sit-cum-to-ha was his daughter's daughter, but she was too busy to waste a thought upon her broken grandfather, sitting alone there in the snow, forlorn and helpless. Camp must be broken. The long trail waited while the short day refused to linger. Life called her, and the duties of life, not death. And he was very close to death now.

The thought made the old man panicky for the moment, and he stretched forth a palsied② hand which wandered tremblingly over the small heap of dry wood beside him. Reassured that it was indeed there, his hand returned to the shelter of his mangy furs, and he again fell to listening. The sulky crackling of half-frozen hides told him that the chief's moose-skin lodge had been struck, and even then was being rammed and jammed into portable compass. The chief was his son, stalwart and strong, head man of the tribesmen, and a mighty hunter. As the women toiled with the camp luggage, his voice rose, chiding them for their slowness. Old Koskoosh strained his ears. It was the last time he would hear that voice. There went Geehow's lodge! And Tusken's! Seven, eight, nine; only the shaman's could be still standing. There! They were at work upon it now. He could hear the shaman③ grunt as he piled it on the sled. A child whimpered, and a woman soothed it with soft, crooning gutturals. Little Koo-tee, the old man thought, a fretful child, and not overstrong. It would die soon, perhaps, and they would burn a hole through the frozen tundra and pile rocks above to keep the wolverines away. Well, what did it matter? A few years at best, and as many an empty belly as a full one. And in the end, Death waited, ever-hungry and hungriest of them all.

What was that? Oh, the men lashing the sleds and drawing tight the thongs. He listened, who would listen no more. The whip-lashes snarled and bit among the dogs. Hear them whine! How they hated the work and the trail! They were off! Sled after sled churned④ slowly away into the silence. They were gone. They had passed out of his life, and he faced the last bitter hour alone. No. The snow crunched beneath a moccasin; a man stood beside him; upon his head a hand rested gently. His son was good to do this thing. He remembered other old men whose sons had not waited after the tribe. But his son had. He wandered away into the past, till the young man's voice brought him back.

---

① cuff: 掌击，拍打
② palsied: 麻痹的
③ shaman: 萨满教巫医
④ churn: 靠车轮、螺旋桨等旋转式构件前进

"Is it well with you?" he asked.

And the old man answered, "It is well."

"There be wood beside you," the younger man continued, "and the fire burns bright. The morning is gray, and the cold has broken. It will snow presently. Even now is it snowing."

"Ay, even now is it snowing."

"The tribesmen hurry. Their bales are heavy, and their bellies flat with lack of feasting. The trail is long and they travel fast. Go now. It is well?"

"It is well. I am as a last year's leaf, clinging lightly to the stem. The first breath that blows, and I fall. My voice is become like an old woman's. My eyes no longer show me the way of my feet, and my feet are heavy, and I am tired. It is well."

He bowed his head in content till the last noise of the complaining snow had died away, and he knew his son was beyond recall. Then his hand crept out in haste to the wood. It alone stood between him and the eternity that yawned in upon him. At last the measure of his life was a handful of fagots[①]. One by one they would go to feed the fire, and just so, step by step, death would creep upon him. When the last stick had surrendered up its heat, the frost would begin to gather strength. First his feet would yield, then his hands; and the numbness would travel, slowly, from the extremities to the body. His head would fall forward upon his knees, and he would rest. It was easy. All men must die.

He did not complain. It was the way of life, and it was just. He had been born close to the earth, close to the earth had he lived, and the law thereof was not new to him. It was the law of all flesh. Nature was not kindly to the flesh. She had no concern for that concrete thing called the individual. Her interest lay in the species, the race. This was the deepest abstraction old Koskoosh's barbaric mind was capable of, but he grasped it firmly. He saw it exemplified in all life. The rise of the sap, the bursting greenness of the willow bud, the fall of the yellow leaf—in this alone was told the whole history. But one task did Nature set the individual. Did he not perform it, he died. Did he perform it, it was all the same, he died. Nature did not care; there were plenty who were obedient, and it was only the obedience in this matter, not the obedient, which lived and lived always. The tribe of Koskoosh was very old. The old men he had known when a boy, had known old men before them. Therefore it was true that the tribe lived, that it stood for the obedience of all its members, way down into the forgotten past, whose very resting-places were unremembered. They did not count; they were episodes. They had passed away like clouds from a summer sky. He also was an episode, and would pass away. Nature did not care. To life she set one task, gave one law. To perpetuate was the task of life, its law was death. A maiden was a good creature to look upon, full-breasted and strong, with spring to her step and light in her eyes. But her task was yet

---

① fagot：柴

before her. The light in her eyes brightened, her step quickened, she was now bold with the young men, now timid, and she gave them of her own unrest. And ever she grew fairer and yet fairer to look upon, till some hunter, able no longer to withhold himself, took her to his lodge to cook and toil for him and to become the mother of his children. And with the coming of her offspring her looks left her. Her limbs dragged and shuffled, her eyes dimmed and bleared, and only the little children found joy against the withered cheek of the old squaw① by the fire. Her task was done. But a little while, on the first pinch of famine or the first long trail, and she would be left, even as he had been left, in the snow, with a little pile of wood. Such was the law. He placed a stick carefully upon the fire and resumed his meditations. It was the same everywhere, with all things. The mosquitoes vanished with the first frost. The little tree-squirrel crawled away to die. When age settled upon the rabbit it became slow and heavy, and could no longer outfoot its enemies. Even the big bald-face grew clumsy and blind and quarrelsome, in the end to be dragged down by a handful of yelping huskies. He remembered how he had abandoned his own father on an upper reach of the Klondike one winter, the winter before the missionary came with his talk-books and his box of medicines. Many a time had Koskoosh smacked his lips over the recollection of that box, though now his mouth refused to moisten. The "painkiller" had been especially good. But the missionary was a bother after all, for he brought no meat into the camp, and he ate heartily, and the hunters grumbled. But he chilled his lungs on the divide by the Mayo, and the dogs afterwards nosed the stones away and fought over his bones.

  Koskoosh placed another stick on the fire and harked back deeper into the past. There was the time of the Great Famine, when the old men crouched empty-bellied to the fire, and let fall from their lips dim traditions of the ancient day when the Yukon ran wide open for three winters, and then lay frozen for three summers. He had lost his mother in that famine. In the summer the salmon run had failed, and the tribe looked forward to the winter and the coming of the caribou②. Then the winter came, but with it there were no caribou. Never had the like been known, not even in the lives of the old men. But the caribou did not come, and it was the seventh year, and the rabbits had not replenished③, and the dogs were naught but bundles of bones. And through the long darkness the children wailed and died, and the women, and the old men; and not one in ten of the tribe lived to meet the sun when it came back in the spring. That was a famine!

  But he had seen times of plenty, too, when the meat spoiled on their hands, and the dogs were fat and worthless with overeating—times when they let the game go unkilled, and the women were fertile, and the lodges were cluttered with sprawling men-children

---

① squaw：印第安女子
② caribou：北美驯鹿
③ replenish：装满，补充

and women-children. Then it was the men became high-stomached, and revived ancient quarrels, and crossed the divides to the south to kill the Pellys, and to the west that they might sit by the dead fires of the Tananas. He remembered, when a boy, during a time of plenty, when he saw a moose pulled down by the wolves. Zing-ha lay with him in the snow and watched—Zing-ha, who later became the craftiest of hunters, and who, in the end, fell through an air-hole on the Yukon. They found him, a month afterward, just as he had crawled halfway out and frozen stiff to the ice.

But the moose. Zing-ha and he had gone out that day to play at hunting after the manner of their fathers. On the bed of the creek they struck the fresh track of a moose, and with it the tracks of many wolves. "An old one," Zing-ha, who was quicker at reading the sign, said—"an old one who cannot keep up with the herd. The wolves have cut him out from his brothers, and they will never leave him." And it was so. It was their way. By day and by night, never resting, snarling on his heels, snapping at his nose, they would stay by him to the end. How Zing-ha and he felt the blood-lust quicken! The finish would be a sight to see!

Eager-footed, they took the trail, and even he, Koskoosh, slow of sight and an unversed tracker, could have followed it blind, it was so wide. Hot were they on the heels of the chase, reading the grim tragedy, fresh-written, at every step. Now they came to where the moose had made a stand. Thrice the length of a grown man's body, in every direction, had the snow been stamped about and uptossed①. In the midst were the deep impressions of the splay-hoofed game, and all about, everywhere, were the lighter footmarks of the wolves. Some, while their brothers harried the kill, had lain to one side and rested. The full-stretched impress of their bodies in the snow was as perfect as though made the moment before. One wolf had been caught in a wild lunge of the maddened victim and trampled to death. A few bones, well picked, bore witness.

Again, they ceased the uplift of their snowshoes at a second stand. Here the great animal had fought desperately. Twice had he been dragged down, as the snow attested, and twice had he shaken his assailants clear and gained footing once more. He had done his task long since, but none the less was life dear to him. Zing-ha said it was a strange thing, a moose once down to get free again; but this one certainly had. The shaman would see signs and wonders in this when they told him.

And yet again, they come to where the moose had made to mount the bank and gain the timber. But his foes had laid on from behind, till he reared and fell back upon them, crushing two deep into the snow. It was plain the kill was at hand, for their brothers had left them untouched. Two more stands were hurried past, brief in time-length and very close together. The trail was red now, and the clean stride of the great beast had grown short and slovenly. Then they heard the first sounds of the battle—not the full-throated chorus of the chase, but the short, snappy bark which spoke of close quarters and teeth

---

① uptoss: 踩烂

to flesh. Crawling up the wind, Zing-ha bellied it through the snow, and with him crept he, Koskoosh, who was to be chief of the tribesmen in the years to come. Together they shoved aside the under branches of a young spruce① and peered forth. It was the end they saw.

The picture, like all of youth's impressions, was still strong with him, and his dim eyes watched the end played out as vividly as in that far-off time. Koskoosh marveled at this, for in the days which followed, when he was a leader of men and a head of councilors, he had done great deeds and made his name a curse in the mouths of the Pellys, to say naught of the strange white man he had killed, knife to knife, in open fight.

For long he pondered on the days of his youth, till the fire died down and the frost bit deeper. He replenished it with two sticks this time, and gauged his grip on life by what remained. If Sit-cum-to-ha had only remembered her grandfather, and gathered a larger armful, his hours would have been longer. It would have been easy. But she was ever a careless child, and honored not her ancestors from the time the Beaver, son of the son of Zing-ha, first cast eyes upon her. Well, what mattered it? Had he not done likewise in his own quick youth? For a while he listened to the silence. Perhaps the heart of his son might soften, and he would come back with the dogs to take his old father on with the tribe to where the caribou ran thick and the fat hung heavy upon them.

He strained his ears, his restless brain for the moment stilled. Not a stir, nothing. He alone took breath in the midst of the great silence. It was very lonely. Hark! What was that? A chill passed over his body. The familiar, long-drawn howl broke the void, and it was close at hand. Then on his darkened eyes was projected the vision of the moose—the old bull moose—the torn flanks and bloody sides, the riddled mane, and the great branching horns, down low and tossing to the last. He saw the flashing forms of gray, the gleaming eyes, the lolling② tongues, the slavered fangs. And he saw the inexorable circle close in till it became a dark point in the midst of the stamped snow.

A cold muzzle thrust against his cheek, and at its touch his soul leaped back to the present. His hand shot into the fire and dragged out a burning faggot. Overcome for the nonce by his hereditary fear of man, the brute retreated, raising a prolonged call to his brothers; and greedily they answered, till a ring of crouching, jaw-slobbered gray was stretched round about. The old man listened to the drawing in of this circle. He waved his brand wildly, and sniffs turned to snarls; but the panting brutes refused to scatter. Now one wormed his chest forward, dragging his haunches after, now a second, now a third; but never a one drew back. Why should he cling to life? he asked, and dropped the blazing stick into the snow. It sizzled③ and went out. The circle grunted uneasily,

---

① spruce: 云杉
② lolling: (舌头)垂在外面的
③ sizzle: 发咝咝声

but held its own. Again he saw the last stand of the old bull moose, and Koskoosh dropped his head wearily upon his knees. What did it matter after all? Was it not the law of life?

Questions for discussion
1. What is the law of life according to the story? Is it only confined to the Indians?
2. What is Old Koskoosh's idea about nature?
3. Is the author a social Darwinist?

文学术语(Definition of Terms)

1. **Realism** in the arts is the attempt to represent subject matter truthfully, without artificiality and avoiding artistic conventions, implausible, exotic and supernatural elements. Realism has been prevalent in the arts at many periods, and is in large part a matter of technique and training, and the avoidance of stylization.
2. **Naturalism** is a term used in writing, which demonstrates a deep interest in nature. It should properly be reserved to designate a literary movement in the late 19th and early 20th centuries in France, America, and England. In its simplest sense naturalism is the application of the principles of scientific Determinism to fiction and drama. It draws its name from its basic assumption that everything that is real exists in nature, nature being conceived as the world of objects, actions, and forces which yield the secrets of their causation and their being to objective scientific inquiry. The naturalists' fundamental view of human beings is that of animals in the natural world, responding to environmental forces an internal stresses and drives, over one of which they have control and none of which they fully understand.

Section B Cultural Notes

Before You Read

1. Try to search the internet or in the library about California Gold Rush and the related information. Give a 3-minute classroom presentation.
2. Do you know other gold rushes around the world?

Start to Read

California Gold Rush

The colorful history of the Gold Rush is being kept alive in a handful of towns in the Western U.S. State of California. VOA's Mike O'Sullivan has more from the town of

Jackson, a multicultural community in the heart of California's gold country.

Not far from here, gold was discovered at Sutter's Mill in 1848, and towns sprung up along the gold belt, called the Mother Lode, in the foothills of the Sierra Nevada mountains. One of the liveliest towns was Jackson.

Local historian Larry Cenotto says the lure of gold attracted people from many countries.

"There were a lot of French that were here in the early days," said Larry Cenotto. "Of course, an awful of Italians, a lot of Jewish merchants. I mean, Main Street in Jackson in the 1850s was at least half Jewish merchants. So *you had* an incredible society."

A walk through the city reveals its mixed heritage①, with 19th century cemeteries for the city's German Jews, Irish Catholics, and British Protestant residents. A Serbian Orthodox church dates to the 1890s. Longtime resident Gino Ricci says his Italian family was part of a polyglot② culture.

"You had a lot of Chinese, everything," said Gino Ricci. "We had all kinds of nationalities in here and they all got along. It was really a melting pot, but it was a good melting pot."

Ricci, now 84, is the town's only remaining barber. His father opened a barber shop here in 1913, and Ricci joined the business in 1941. He has seen the town flourish with mining, and later with timber. Through it all, there was gambling and there were houses of prostitution, illegal but tolerated until the 1950s.

"And we had the houses and we had gambling and we had no problems," he said. "Everything was just as smooth as silk."

Today, says Ricci dismissively, this is just a tourist town without its old excitement. But merchant Barbara Wierschem, who sells candy and ice cream, says it is a great place for visiting families.

"They like the oldness of the town, you know, the buildings, and people are all warm and friendly in the businesses," said Barbara Wierschem. "They like going to the gold mines, and also there are a lot of caverns③ up here that they go visit."

Larry Cenotto is a newcomer to Jackson, relatively speaking. He arrived in 1964 as a newspaper reporter, attracted by the town's friendliness. He says that living here, he got to know people as people, not just as part of the landscape, which he says is often the case in bigger cities.

"In small towns, you quickly learn that these are people, and you're going to see them again tomorrow, and the next day and the next day, and so you need to get along and understand them and then begin to value them," he said.

---

① heritage: 遗产
② polyglot: 多语言的
③ cavern: 挖空

For Jackson's 4,000 residents, life today is quiet, but visitors passing through California's Mother Lode country can hear tales of more boisterous times when the world descended on Jackson in search of gold.

After You Read

I. Questions for discussion

1. What is the cause of the California Gold Rush?
2. How many people rushed to California to find gold?
3. What are these people called by others and why?
4. What are the effects of the California Gold Rush?
5. What influence did the gold rush have on San Francisco?
6. What happened to Native Americans during the California Gold Rush?

II. True or false

1. The beginning of the gold rush is the discovery of gold in the foothills of the Sierra Nevada Mountains.　　(　)
2. In the 1850s, most part of the popularity in Jackson was still Americans.　　(　)
3. In Jackson at that time, a visitor could easily find Germany, British, Serbian, Chinese and Japanese cultures.　　(　)
4. Although there existed prostitutes and gamblers, the life in the town still went smoothly.　　(　)
5. Jackson has become a tourist town.　　(　)
6. Jackson's residents are not satisfied with their life now.　　(　)

For Fun

I. Websites to visit

1. http://www.jacklondons.net/
2. http://www.donnerpartydiary.com/

II. Writing

The relationship between nature and human beings has always been a topic that is discussed by people in various fields of studies. After reading Jack London's works, what is your attitude toward the relationship between nature and human beings? Write down your ideas.

Chapter 11

F・Scott Fitzgerald (1896–1940)
弗朗西斯・斯科特・菲茨杰拉德

Section A　Literary Focus

作者简介(About the Author)

【生平】 弗朗西斯・斯科特・菲茨杰拉德(Francis Scott Fitzgerald)是20世纪美国最杰出作家之一。1896年9月24日生于明尼苏达州圣保罗市,菲茨杰拉德的父亲是家具商。读完高中后考入普林斯顿大学。后因身体欠佳,中途辍学。1917年入伍,终日忙于军训,未曾出国打仗。退伍后坚持业余写作。

1920年出版了长篇小说《人间天堂》,一夜成名后与吉尔达结婚。婚后携妻寄居巴黎,结识了安德逊、海明威等多位美国作家。1925年《了不起的盖茨比》问世,奠定了他在现代美国文学史上的地位,成了20年代"爵士时代"的发言人和"迷惘的一代"的代表作家之一。菲兹杰拉德成名后继续勤奋笔耕,但婚后妻子讲究排场,后来又精神失常,挥霍无度,给他带来极大痛苦。他经济上入不敷出,一度去好莱坞写剧本挣钱维持生计。1936年不幸染上肺病,妻子又一病不起,使他几乎无法创作,精神濒于崩溃,终日酗酒。1940年12月21日并发心脏病,死于洛杉矶,年仅44岁。

【主要作品】《了不起的盖茨比》(*The Great Gatsby*,1925),《夜色温柔》(*Tender is the Night*,1934),《末代大亨的情缘》(*The Last Tycoon*,1941)

作品选读(Selected Writings)

The Great Gatsby

《了不起的盖茨比》是20世纪美国著名作家菲茨杰拉德的代表作。书中描述了出身贫寒的盖茨比如何历尽艰辛不择手段地攫取财富,从一个穷光蛋变成人们心中的"了不起"的富豪,又如何苦苦追求初恋时由于贫穷而失去的情人的故事。作品再现了20世纪20年代,也被称作"爵士乐时代"的美国社会,揭示了"美国梦"的诱惑和破灭。书中文字短小精悍,结构错落有致并以典型的场面和简洁、抒情的语言为读者提供了一部饱含韵味、极富美感的"最为动人的美国悲剧"。

After two years I remember the rest of that day, and that night and the next day, only as an endless drill of police and photographers and newspaper men in and out of Gatsby's front door. A rope stretched across the main gate and a policeman by it kept out the curious, but little boys soon discovered that they could enter through my yard, and there were always a few of them clustered open-mouthed about the pool. Someone with a positive manner, perhaps a detective, used the expression "madman" as he bent over Wilson's body that afternoon, and the adventitious① authority of his voice set the key for the newspaper reports next morning.

Most of those reports were a nightmare—grotesque②, circumstantial, eager, and untrue. When Michaelis's testimony at the inquest brought to light Wilson's suspicions of his wife I thought the whole tale would shortly be served up in racy pasquinade—but Catherine, who might have said anything, didn't say a word. She showed a surprising amount of character about it too—looked at the coroner with determined eyes under that corrected brow of hers, and swore that her sister had never seen Gatsby, that her sister was completely happy with her husband that her sister had been into no mischief whatever. She convinced herself of it, and cried into her handkerchief, as if the very suggestion was more than she could endure. S. Wilson was reduced to a man "deranged by grief" in order that the case might remain in its simplest form. And it rested there.

But all this part of it seemed remote and unessential. I found myself on Gatsby's side, and alone. From the moment I telephoned news of the catastrophe③ to West Egg village, every surmise about him, and every practical question, was referred to me. At first I was surprised and confused; then, as he lay in his house and didn't move or breathe or speak, hour upon hour, it grew upon me that I was responsible, because no one else was interested—interested, I mean, with that intense personal interest to which everyone has some vague right at the end.

I called up Daisy half an hour after we found him, called her instinctively and without hesitation. But she and Tom had gone away early that afternoon, and taken baggage with them.

"Left no address?"

"No."

"Say when they'd be back?"

"No."

"Any idea where they are? How I could reach them?"

---

① adventitious：偶然发生的
② grotesque：怪诞的
③ catastrophe：灾难

"I don't know. Can't say."

I wanted to get somebody for him. I wanted to go into the room where he lay and reassure him: "I'll get somebody for you, Gatsby. Don't worry. Just trust me and I'll get somebody for you—"

Meyer Wolfsheim's name wasn't in the phone book. The butler gave me his office address on Broadway, and I called Information, but by the time I had the number it was long after five, and no one answered the phone.

"Will you ring again?"

"I've rung them three times."

"It's very important."

"Sorry. I'm afraid no one's there."

I went back to the drawing-room and thought for an instant that they were chance visitors, all these official people who suddenly filled it. But, as they drew back the sheet and looked at Gatsby with unmoved eyes, his protest continued in my brain:

"Look here, old sport, you've got to get somebody for me. You've got to try hard. I can't go through this alone."

Someone started to ask me questions, but I broke away and going up-stairs looked hastily through the unlocked parts of his desk—he'd never told me definitely that his parents were dead. But there was nothing—only the picture of Dan Cody, a token of forgotten violence, staring down from the wall.

Next morning I sent the butler to New York with a letter to Wolfsheim, which asked for information and urged him to come out on the next train. That request seemed superfluous when I wrote it. I was sure he'd start when he saw the newspapers, just as I was sure there'd be a wire from Daisy before noon—but neither a wire nor Mr. Wolfsheim arrived; no one arrived except more police and photographers and newspaper men. When the butler① brought back Wolfsheim's answer I began to have a feeling of defiance, of scornful solidarity between Gatsby and me against them all.

Dear Mr. Carraway. This has been one of the most terrible shocks of my life to me I hardly can believe it that it is true at all. Such a mad act as that man did should make us all think. I cannot come down now as I am tied up in some very important business and cannot get mixed up in this thing now. If there is anything I can do a little later let me know in a letter by Edgar. I hardly know where I am when I hear about a thing like this and am completely knocked down and out.

Yours truly *Meyer Wolfshiem*

and then hasty addenda beneath:

Let me know about the funeral etc. Do not know his family at all.

When the phone rang that afternoon and Long Distance said Chicago was calling I thought this would be Daisy at last. But the connection came through as a man's voice,

---

① butler：男管家

very thin and far away.

"This is Slagle speaking..."

"Yes?" The name was unfamiliar.

"Hell of a note, isn't it? Get my wire?"

"There haven't been any wires."

"Young Parke's in trouble," he said rapidly. "They picked him up when he handed the bonds over the counter. They got a circular① from New York giving'em the numbers just five minutes before. What d'you know about that, hey? You never can tell in these hick towns—"

"Hello!" I interrupted breathlessly. "Look here—this isn't Mr. Gatsby. Mr. Gatsby's dead."

There was a long silence on the other end of the wire, followed by an exclamation... then a quick squawk as the connection was broken.

I think it was on the third day that a telegram signed Henry C. Gatz arrived from a town in Minnesota. It said only that the sender was leaving immediately and to postpone the funeral until he came.

It was Gatsby's father, a solemn old man, very helpless and dismayed, bundled up in a long cheap ulster② against the warm September day. His eyes leaked continuously with excitement, and when I took the bag and umbrella from his hands he began to pull so incessantly③ at his sparse gray beard that I had difficulty in getting off his coat. He was on the point of collapse, so I took him into the music room and made him sit down while I sent for something to eat. But he wouldn't eat, and the glass of milk spilled from his trembling hand.

"I saw it in the Chicago newspaper," he said. "It was all in the Chicago newspaper. I started right away."

"I didn't know how to reach you." His eyes, seeing nothing, moved ceaselessly about the room.

"It was a madman," he said. "He must have been mad."

"Wouldn't you like some coffee?" I urged him.

"I don't want anything. I'm all right now, Mr.—"

"Carraway."

"Well, I'm all right now. Where have they got Jimmy?" I took him into the drawing-room, where his son lay, and left him there. Some little boys had come up on the steps and were looking into the hall; when I told them who had arrived, they went reluctantly away.

After a little while Mr. Gatz opened the door and came out, his mouth ajar, his

---

① circular: 印刷信函
② ulster: 一种有带子的粗呢宽大衣
③ incessantly: 不停地

face flushed slightly, his eyes leaking isolated and unpunctual tears. He had reached an age where death no longer has the quality of ghastly① surprise, and when he looked around him now for the first time and saw the height and splendor of the hall and the great rooms opening out from it into other rooms, his grief began to be mixed with an awed pride. I helped him to a bedroom up-stairs; while he took off his coat and vest I told him that all arrangements had been deferred until he came.

"I didn't know what you'd want, Mr. Gatsby—"

"Gatz is my name."

"—Mr. Gatz. I thought you might want to take the body West."

He shook his head.

"Jimmy always liked it better down East. He rose up to his position in the East. Were you a friend of my boy's, Mr. —?"

"We were close friends."

"He had a big future before him, you know. He was only a young man, but he had a lot of brain power here."

He touched his head impressively, and I nodded.

"If he'd of lived, he'd of been a great man. A man like James J. Hill. He'd of helped build up the country."

"That's true," I said, uncomfortably.

He fumbled at the embroidered coverlet②, trying to take it from the bed, and lay down stiffly—was instantly asleep.

That night an obviously frightened person called up, and demanded to know who I was before he would give his name.

"This is Mr. Carraway," I said.

"Oh!" He sounded relieved. "This is Klipspringer." I was relieved too, for that seemed to promise another friend at Gatsby's grave. I didn't want it to be in the papers and draw a sightseeing crowd, so I'd been calling up a few people myself. They were hard to find.

"The funeral's to-morrow," I said. "Three o'clock, here at the house. I wish you'd tell anybody who'd be interested."

"Oh, I will," he broke out hastily. "Of course I'm not likely to see anybody, but if I do."

His tone made me suspicious.

"Of course you'll be there yourself."

"Well, I'll certainly try. What I called up about is—"

"Wait a minute," I interrupted. "How about saying you'll come?"

"Well, the fact is—the truth of the matter is that I'm staying with some people up

---

① ghastly: 可怕的
② coverlet: 床罩

here in Greenwich, and they rather expect me to be with them to-morrow. In fact, there's a sort of picnic or something. Of course I'll do my very best to get away."

I ejaculated an unrestrained "Huh!" and he must have heard me, for he went on nervously:

"What I called up about was a pair of shoes I left there. I wonder if it'd be too much trouble to have the butler send them on. You see, they're tennis shoes, and I'm sort of helpless without them. My address is care of B. F.—"

I didn't hear the rest of the name, because I hung up the receiver.

After that I felt a certain shame for Gatsby—one gentleman to whom I telephoned implied that he had got what he deserved. However, that was my fault, for he was one of those who used to sneer① most bitterly at Gatsby on the courage of Gatsby's liquor, and I should have known better than to call him.

The morning of the funeral I went up to New York to see Meyer Wolfsheim; I couldn't seem to reach him any other way. The door that I pushed open, on the advice of an elevator boy, was marked "The Swastika Holding Company," and at first there didn't seem to be any one inside. But when I'd shouted "hello" several times in vain, an argument broke out behind a partition, and presently a lovely Jewess appeared at an interior door and scrutinized② me with black hostile eyes.

"Nobody's in," she said. "Mr. Wolfsheim's gone to Chicago."

The first part of this was obviously untrue, for someone had begun to whistle "The Rosary," tunelessly, inside.

"Please say that Mr. Carraway wants to see him."

"I can't get him back from Chicago, can I?"

At this moment a voice, unmistakably Wolfsheim's, called "Stella!" from the other side of the door.

"Leave your name on the desk," she said quickly. "I'll give it to him when he gets back."

"But I know he's there."

She took a step toward me and began to slide her hands indignantly up and down her hips.

"You young men think you can force your way in here any time," she scolded. "We're getting sick and tired of it. When I say he's in Chicago, he's in Chicago."

I mentioned Gatsby.

"Oh—h!" She looked at me over again. "Will you just—What was your name?"

She vanished. In a moment Meyer Wolfsheim stood solemnly in the doorway, holding out both hands. He drew me into his office, remarking in a reverent③ voice that

---

① sneer：嘲笑

② scrutinize：审查

③ reverent：非常尊敬的

it was a sad time for all of us, and offered me a cigar.

"My memory goes back to when I first met him," he said. "A young major just out of the army and covered over with medals he got in the war. He was so hard up he had to keep on wearing his uniform because he couldn't buy some regular clothes. First time I saw him was when he come into Winebrenner's poolroom at Forty-third Street and asked for a job. He hadn't eat anything for a couple of days. 'come on have some lunch with me,' I said. He ate more than four dollars' worth of food in half an hour."

"Did you start him in business?" I inquired.

"Start him! I made him."

"Oh."

"I raised him up out of nothing, right out of the gutter. I saw right away he was a fine-appearing, gentlemanly young man, and when he told me he was at Oggsford I knew I could use him good. I got him to join up in the American Legion and he used to stand high there. Right off he did some work for a client of mine up to Albany. We were so thick like that in everything."—he held up two bulbous fingers—" always together."

I wondered if this partnership had included the World's Series transaction in 1919.

"Now he's dead," I said after a moment. "You were his closest friend, so I know you'll want to come to his funeral this afternoon."

"I'd like to come."

"Well, come then."

The hair in his nostrils quivered① slightly, and as he shook his head his eyes filled with tears.

"I can't do it—I can't get mixed up in it," he said.

"There's nothing to get mixed up in. It's all over now."

"When a man gets killed I never like to get mixed up in it in any way. I keep out. When I was a young man it was different—if a friend of mine died, no matter how, I stuck with them to the end. You may think that's sentimental, but I mean it—to the bitter end."

I saw that for some reason of his own he was determined not to come, so I stood up.

"Are you a college man?" he inquired suddenly.

For a moment I thought he was going to suggest a "gonnegtion," but he only nodded and shook my hand.

"Let us learn to show our friendship for a man when he is alive and not after he is dead," he suggested. "After that my own rule is to let everything alone."

When I left his office the sky had turned dark and I got back to West Egg in a drizzle. After changing my clothes I went next door and found Mr. Gatz walking up and down excitedly in the hall. His pride in his son and in his son's possessions was

---

① quivere: 颤抖

continually increasing and now he had something to show me.

"Jimmy sent me this picture." He took out his wallet with trembling fingers. "Look there."

It was a photograph of the house, cracked in the corners and dirty with many hands. He pointed out every detail to me eagerly. "Look there!" and then sought admiration from my eyes. He had shown it so often that I think it was more real to him now than the house itself.

"Jimmy sent it to me. I think it's a very pretty picture. It shows up well."

"Very well. Had you seen him lately?"

"He come out to see me two years ago and bought me the house I live in now. Of course we was broke up when he run off from home, but I see now there was a reason for it. He knew he had a big future in front of him. And ever since he made a success he was very generous with me." He seemed reluctant to put away the picture, held it for another minute, lingeringly①, before my eyes. Then he returned the wallet and pulled from his pocket a ragged old copy of a book called *Hopalong Cassidy*.

"Look here, this is a book he had when he was a boy. It just shows you."

He opened it at the back cover and turned it around for me to see. On the last fly-leaf was printed the word *Schedule*, and the date September 12, 1906, and underneath:

Rise from bed ························· 6.00 *a.m.*
Dumbbell exercise and wall-scaling ········· 6.15–6.30
Study electricity, etc ················· 7.15–8.15
Work ···························· 8.30–4.30 *p.m.*
Baseball and sports ··················· 4.30–5.00
Practice elocution, poise and how to attain it ······ 5.00–6.00
Study needed inventions ················ 7.00–9.00

General Resolves

No wasting time at Shafters or [a name, indecipherable]

No more smoking or chewing

Bath every other day

Read one improving book or magazine per week

Save $5.00 {crossed out} $3.00 per week

Be better to parents

"I come across this book by accident," said the old man. "It just shows you, don't it?"

"It just shows you."

"Jimmy was bound to get ahead. He always had some resolves like this or something. Do you notice what he's got about improving his mind? He was always great

---

① lingeringly: 延迟的

for that. He told me I ate like a hog once, and I beat him for it."

He was reluctant to close the book, reading each item aloud and then looking eagerly at me. I think he rather expected me to copy down the list for my own use.

A little before three the Lutheran minister arrived from Flushing, and I began to look involuntarily out the windows for other cars. So did Gatsby's father. And as the time passed and the servants came in and stood waiting in the hall, his eyes began to blink anxiously, and he spoke of the rain in a worried, uncertain way. The minister glanced several times at his watch, so I took him aside and asked him to wait for half an hour. But it wasn't any use. Nobody came.

About five o'clock our procession of three cars reached the cemetery and stopped in a thick drizzle beside the gate—first a motor hearse, horribly black and wet, then Mr. Gatz and the minister and I in the limousine, and a little later four or five servants and the postman from West Egg in Gatsby's station wagon, all wet to the skin. As we started through the gate into the cemetery I heard a car stop and then the sound of someone splashing after us over the soggy ground. I looked around. It was the man with owl-eyed glasses whom I had found marvelling① over Gatsby's books in the library one night three months before.

I'd never seen him since then. I don't know how he knew about the funeral, or even his name. The rain poured down his thick glasses, and he took them off and wiped them to see the protecting canvas unrolled from Gatsby's grave.

I tried to think about Gatsby then for a moment, but he was already too far away, and I could only remember, without resentment, that Daisy hadn't sent a message or a flower. Dimly I heard someone murmur, "Blessed are the dead that the rain falls on," and then the owl-eyed man said "Amen to that," in a brave voice.

We straggled down quickly through the rain to the cars. Owl-eyes spoke to me by the gate.

"I couldn't get to the house," he remarked.

"Neither could anybody else."

"Go on!" He started. "Why, my God! they used to go there by the hundreds." He took off his glasses and wiped them again, outside and in.

"The poor son-of-a-bitch," he said.

One of my most vivid memories is of coming back West from prep school and later from college at Christmas time. Those who went farther than Chicago would gather in the old dim Union Station at six o'clock of a December evening, with a few Chicago friends, already caught up into their own holiday gayeties②, to bid them a hasty good-by. I remember the fur coats of the girls returning from Miss This-or-that's and the chatter of frozen breath and the hands waving overhead as we caught sight of old

---

① marvel: 对……感到惊奇
② gayety: 欢乐的气氛

acquaintances, and the matchings of invitations: "Are you going to the Ordways'? the Herseys'? the Schultzes'?" and the long green tickets clasped tight in our gloved hands. And last the murky yellow cars of the Chicago, Milwaukee and St. Paul railroad looking cheerful as Christmas itself on the tracks beside the gate.

When we pulled out into the winter night and the real snow, our snow, began to stretch out beside us and twinkle against the windows, and the dim lights of small Wisconsin stations moved by, a sharp wild brace① came suddenly into the air. We drew in deep breaths of it as we walked back from dinner through the cold vestibules, unutterably aware of our identity with this country for one strange hour, before we melted indistinguishably into it again.

That's my Middle West—not the wheat or the prairies② or the lost Swede towns, but the thrilling returning trains of my youth, and the street lamps and sleigh bells in the frosty dark and the shadows of holly wreaths③ thrown by lighted windows on the snow. I am part of that, a little solemn with the feel of those long winters, a little complacent④ from growing up in the Carraway house in a city where dwellings are still called through decades by a family's name. I see now that this has been a story of the West, after all—Tom and Gatsby, Daisy and Jordan and I, were all Westerners, and perhaps we possessed some deficiency in common which made us subtly unadaptable to Eastern life.

Even when the East excited me most, even when I was most keenly aware of its superiority to the bored, sprawling, swollen towns beyond the Ohio, with their interminable inquisitions which spared only the children and the very old—even then it had always for me a quality of distortion. West Egg, especially, still figures in my more fantastic dreams. I see it as a night scene by El Greco: a hundred houses, at once conventional and grotesque, crouching under a sullen, overhanging sky and a lustreless⑤ moon. In the foreground four solemn men in dress suits are walking along the sidewalk with a stretcher on which lies a drunken woman in a white evening dress. Her hand, which dangles over the side, sparkles cold with jewels. Gravely the men turn in at a house—the wrong house. But no one knows the woman's name, and no one cares.

After Gatsby's death the East was haunted⑥ for me like that, distorted beyond my eyes' power of correction. So when the blue smoke of brittle leaves was in the air and the wind blew the wet laundry stiff on the line I decided to come back home.

There was one thing to be done before I left, an awkward, unpleasant thing that perhaps had better have been let alone. But I wanted to leave things in order and not just

---

① brace: 支架；夹子
② prairie: 大草原；牧场
③ wreath: 花圈
④ complacent: 自满的
⑤ lustreless: 暗淡的
⑥ haunted: 闹鬼的；忧心忡忡的

trust that obliging and indifferent sea to sweep my refuse away. I saw Jordan Baker and talked over and around what had happened to us together, and what had happened afterward to me, and she lay perfectly still, listening, in a big chair.

She was dressed to play golf, and I remember thinking she looked like a good illustration, her chin raised a little jauntily①, her hair the color of an autumn leaf, her face the same brown tint as the fingerless glove on her knee. When I had finished she told me without comment that she was engaged to another man. I doubted that, though there were several she could have married at a nod of her head, but I pretended to be surprised. For just a minute I wondered if I wasn't making a mistake, then I thought it all over again quickly and got up to say good-bye.

"Nevertheless you did throw me over," said Jordan suddenly. "You threw me over on the telephone. I don't give a damn about you now, but it was a new experience for me, and I felt a little dizzy for a while."

We shook hands.

"Oh, and do you remember,"—she added—"a conversation we had once about driving a car?"

"Why—not exactly."

"You said a bad driver was only safe until she met another bad driver? Well, I met another bad driver, didn't I? I mean it was careless of me to make such a wrong guess. I thought you were rather an honest, straightforward person. I thought it was your secret pride."

"I'm thirty," I said. "I'm five years too old to lie to myself and call it honor."

She didn't answer. Angry, and half in love with her, and tremendously sorry, I turned away.

One afternoon late in October I saw Tom Buchanan. He was walking ahead of me along Fifth Avenue in his alert, aggressive way, his hands out a little from his body as if to fight off interference, his head moving sharply here and there, adapting itself to his restless eyes. Just as I slowed up to avoid overtaking him he stopped and began frowning into the windows of a jewelry store. Suddenly he saw me and walked back, holding out his hand.

"What's the matter, Nick? Do you object to shaking hands with me?"

"Yes. You know what I think of you."

"You're crazy, Nick," he said quickly. "Crazy as hell. I don't know what's the matter with you."

"Tom," I inquired, "what did you say to Wilson that afternoon?" He stared at me without a word, and I knew I had guessed right about those missing hours. I started to turn away, but he took a step after me and grabbed my arm.

"I told him the truth," he said. "He came to the door while we were getting ready

---

① jauntily: 得意地

to leave, and when I sent down word that we weren't in he tried to force his way upstairs. He was crazy enough to kill me if I hadn't told him who owned the car. His hand was on a revolver in his pocket every minute he was in the house—" He broke off defiantly. "What if I did tell him? That fellow had it coming to him. He threw dust into your eyes just like he did in Daisy's, but he was a tough one. He ran over Myrtle like you'd run over a dog and never even stopped his car."

There was nothing I could say, except the one unutterable fact that it wasn't true.

"And if you think I didn't have my share of suffering—look here, when I went to give up that flat and saw that damn box of dog biscuits sitting there on the sideboard, I sat down and cried like a baby. By God it was awful—"

I couldn't forgive him or like him, but I saw that what he had done was, to him, entirely justified. It was all very careless and confused. They were careless people, Tom and Daisy—they smashed up things and creatures and then retreated back into their money or their vast carelessness, or whatever it was that kept them together, and let other people clean up the mess they had made ...

I shook hands with him; it seemed silly not to, for I felt suddenly as though I were talking to a child. Then he went into the jewelry store to buy a pearl necklace—or perhaps only a pair of cuff buttons—rid of my provincial squeamishness① forever.

Gatsby's house was still empty when I left—the grass on his lawn had grown as long as mine. One of the taxi drivers in the village never took a fare past the entrance gate without stopping for a minute and pointing inside; perhaps it was he who drove Daisy and Gatsby over to East Egg the night of the accident, and perhaps he had made a story about it all his own. I didn't want to hear it and I avoided him when I got off the train.

I spent my Saturday nights in New York because those gleaming, dazzling parties of his were with me so vividly that I could still hear the music and the laughter, faint and incessant②, from his garden, and the cars going up and down his drive. One night I did hear a material car there, and saw its lights stop at his front steps. But I didn't investigate. Probably it was some final guest who had been away at the ends of the earth and didn't know that the party was over.

On the last night, with my trunk packed and my car sold to the grocer, I went over and looked at that huge incoherent failure of a house once more. On the white steps an obscene word, scrawled by some boy with a piece of brick, stood out clearly in the moonlight, and I erased it, drawing my shoe raspingly③ along the stone. Then I wandered down to the beach and sprawled out on the sand.

Most of the big shore places were closed now and there were hardly any lights except the shadowy, moving glow of a ferryboat across the Sound. And as the moon rose

---

① squeamishness: 神经质;易受惊
② incessant: 持续不断的
③ raspingly: 刺耳地

higher the inessential houses began to melt away until gradually I became aware of the old island here that flowered once for Dutch sailors' eyes—a fresh, green breast of the new world. Its vanished trees, the trees that had made way for Gatsby's house, had once pandered in whispers to the last and greatest of all human dreams; for a transitory enchanted moment man must have held his breath in the presence of this continent, compelled into an aesthetic① contemplation② he neither understood nor desired, face to face for the last time in history with something commensurate to his capacity for wonder.

And as I sat there brooding on the old, unknown world, I thought of Gatsby's wonder when he first picked out the green light at the end of Daisy's dock. He had come a long way to this blue lawn, and his dream must have seemed so close that he could hardly fail to grasp it. He did not know that it was already behind him, somewhere back in that vast obscurity beyond the city, where the dark fields of the republic rolled on under the night.

Gatsby believed in the green light, the orgiastic③ future that year by year recedes before us. It eluded us then, but that's no matter—to-morrow we will run faster, stretch out our arms farther ... And one fine morning—

So we beat on, boats against the current, borne back ceaselessly into the past.

Questions for discussion

1. Do you think Gatsby deserves to be called "the great"? Why?
2. Does "the green light" Gatsby believed in exist in reality? Why or why not?
3. How do you think about Daisy and Tom?
4. Do you agree that Nick is an objective narrator?

文学术语(Definition of Terms)

1. **Lost Generation** is a term that refers to a group of American writers, most of whom were born around 1900. They fought in the First World War, and constituted a group reaching against the tendencies of the older writers in the 1920's. The term came from Gertrude Stein's remarks to Hemingway. Hemingway used it as a motto in his novel *The Sun Also Rises*, whose hero, the emasculated Jake Barnes, is often considered the archetypal man of the generation. Many of them spent much of their time in Paris, others lived and worked in New York, and some remained in the Middle West and the South. It was widely applied to such figures as F. Scott Fitzgerald, Ernest Hemingway, Hart Crane, Louis Bromfield, and Malcolm Cowley, as descriptive of the loss to them of traditional values as a result of the war and the

---

① aesthetic：美学的
② contemplation：沉思；凝视
③ orgiastic：极度兴奋的

nature of the modern city.

2. **The Jazz Age** describes the period from 1918 to 1929, the years between the end of World War I and the start of the Roaring Twenties; ending with the rise of the Great Depression, the traditional values of this age saw great decline while the American stock market soared. The age takes its name from F. Scott Fitzgerald and jazz music, which saw a tremendous surge in popularity among many segments of society. A great theme of the age was individualism and a greater emphasis on the pursuit of pleasure and enjoyment in the wake of the misery, destruction and perceived hypocrisy and waste of WWI and pre-war values.

Section B Cultural Notes

Before You Read

Search the Internet for some information about "The Lost Generation" and find out its features and representative writers.

Start to Read

The Lost Generation

Seeking the bohemian① lifestyle and rejecting the values of American materialism, a number of intellectuals, poets, artists and writers fled to France in the post World War I years. Paris was the center of it all.

American poet Gertrude Stein actually coined the expression "lost generation." Speaking to Ernest Hemingway, she said, "You are all a lost generation." The term stuck and the mystique surrounding these individuals continues to fascinate us.

Full of youthful idealism, these individuals sought the meaning of life, drank excessively, had love affairs and created some of the finest American literature to date.

There were many literary artists involved in the groups known as the Lost Generation. The three best known are F. Scott Fitzgerald, Ernest Hemingway and John Dos Passos. Others usually included among the list are: Sherwood Anderson, Kay Boyle, Hart Crane, Ford Maddox Ford and Zelda Fitzgerald.

Ernest Hemingway was the Lost Generation's leader in the adaptation of the naturalistic technique in the novel. Hemingway volunteered to fight with the Italians in World War I and his Midwestern American ignorance was shattered during the resounding② defeat of the Italians by the Central Powers at Caporetto. Newspapers of

---

① bohemian: 波西米亚的;放荡不羁的
② resounding: 巨大的;令人瞩目的

the time reported Hemingway, with dozens of pieces of shrapnel① in his legs, had heroically carried another man out. That episode even made the newsreels in America. These war time experiences laid the groundwork of his novel, *A Farewell to Arms* (1929). Another of his books, *The Sun Also Rises* (1926) was a naturalistic and shocking expression of post-war disillusionment②.

John Dos Passos had also seen the brutality of the war and questioned the meaning of contemporary life. His novel *Manhatten Transfer* reveals the extent of his pessimism as he indicated the hopeless futility③ of life in an American city.

F. Scott Fitzgerald is remembered as the portrayer of the spirit of the Jazz age. Though not strictly speaking an expatriate, he roamed Europe and visited North Africa, but returned to the US occasionally. Fitzgerald had at least two addresses in Paris between 1928 and 1930. He fulfilled the role of chronicler④ of the prohibition era.

His first novel, *This Side of Paradise* became a best-seller. But when first published, *The Great Gatsby* on the other hand, sold only 25,000 copies. The free spirited Fitzgerald, certain it would be a big hit, blew the publisher's advance money leasing a villa in Cannes. In the end, he owed his publishers, Scribners, money. Fitzgerald's Gatsby is the story of a somewhat refined and wealthy bootlegger whose morality is contrasted with the hypocritical attitude of most of his acquaintances. Many literary critics consider Gatsby his best work.

The impact of the war on the group of writers in the Lost Generation is aptly⑤ demonstrated by a passage from Fitzgerald's *Tender is the Night* (1933):

"This land here cost twenty lives a foot that summer ... See that little stream—we could walk to it in two minutes. It took the British a month to walk it—a whole empire walking very slowly, dying in front and pushing forward behind. And another empire walked very slowly backward a few inches a day, leaving the dead like a million bloody rugs. No Europeans will ever do that again in this generation."

The Lost Generation writers all gained prominence in 20th century literature. Their innovations challenged assumptions about writing and expression, and paved the way for subsequent generations of writers.

After You Read

I. Questions for discussion

1. What does the word "lost" refer to?

---

① shrapnel：飞溅的弹片
② disillusionment：幻想破灭
③ futility：无用；徒劳
④ chronicler：年代记录者
⑤ aptly：适当地

2. How is the quality of being "lost" shown in the representative writers' works?
3. Scott Fitzgerald is remembered as the portrayer of the spirit of the Jazz age. Have you ever read his novel *The Great Gatsby*? What's your comment on Gatsby and his life?
4. Who is regarded as the leader of The Lost Generation? What are the features of his writing?
5. What is John Dos Passos' attitude toward contemporary life? Why is that?

II. **True or false**

1. Ezra Pound coined the term "The Lost Generation" when he spoke to Ernest Hemingway in Europe. (　)
2. Gertrude Stein was the Lost Generation's leader in the adaptation of the naturalistic technique in the novel. (　)
3. John Dos Passos' novel *Manhatten Transfer* reveals the extent of his pessimism as he indicated the hopeless futility① of life in an American city. (　)
4. Fitzgerald's first novel, *The Great Gatsby* became a best-seller. (　)
5. Hemingway is remembered as the portrayer of the spirit of the Jazz age. (　)
6. The Lost Generation writers all gained prominence in 20th century literature. (　)

For Fun

I. **Movies to see**

　　The Great Gatsby (2013): It is a 2013 American epic romantic drama film based on F. Scott Fitzgerald's 1925 novel of the same name. The film was co-written and directed by Baz Luhrmann, and stars Leonardo DiCaprio as the eponymous Jay Gatsby, with Tobey Maguire, Carey Mulligan, Joel Edgerton, and Elizabeth Debicki in supporting roles. The film follows the life and times of millionaire Jay Gatsby and his neighbour Nick, who recounts his encounter with Gatsby at the height of the Roaring Twenties.

II. **Websites to visit**

1. http://movie.douban.com/subject/1485260/
2. http://www.360doc.com/content/12/1003/16/70559_239299623.shtml

III. **Writing**

　　Some people think that money is power and as long as you are rich, you can buy anything including true love. Others believe that love can conquer all and dollars can never win one's heart. What is your opinion after reading the story of Gatsby and Daisy?

---

① futility: 无用；徒劳

Chapter 12

William Faulkner(1897-1962)
威廉·福克纳

Section A Literary Focus

作者简介(About the Author)

【生平】 威廉·福克纳(William Faulkner 1897-1962),美国文学史上最具影响力的作家之一,意识流文学在美国的代表作家,1949年诺贝尔文学奖得主。一生共写了19部长篇小说与120多篇短篇小说,其中15部长篇与绝大多数短篇的故事都发生在约克纳帕塔法县,称为"约克纳帕塔法世系"小说。其主要脉络是这个县杰弗生镇及其郊区的属于不同社会阶层的若干个家族的几代人的故事,时间从1800年起直到第二次世界大战以后。世系中共600多个有名有姓的人物在各个长篇、短篇小说中穿插交替出现。最有代表性的作品是《喧哗与骚动》。福克纳的创作集现代主义、浪漫主义、现实主义于一身,大量使用了各种传统的和创新的手法,深刻而全面地探索了美国旧南方解体的根源,表现了处在历史性变革中的南方社会和南方人的精神危机。

【主要作品】《喧哗与骚动》(*Sound and Fury*,1929),《我弥留之际》(*As I Lay Dying*,1930),《去吧,摩西》(*Go Down,Moses*,1942)等。

作品选读(Selected Writings)

《献给爱米丽的玫瑰》(*A Rose for Emily*)是一篇美国现代南方哥特小说,自1931年发表以来一直是福克纳被收录入集最多的短篇小说。作品中阴森的大宅、心理扭曲的人物、谋杀、与死尸同眠都具有传统哥特小说的特点。作者借哥特式的阴郁和恐怖揭示了女主人公爱米丽的变态心理。她恋爱不成,不惜杀死自己的情人,并与之尸体同床共枕几十年,令人毛骨悚然。然而,福克纳并不满足于揭示爱米丽的变态心理,福克纳认为她是旧南方的牺牲品,其悲剧命运令人同情。福克纳塑造了一个敢于蔑视传统、勇于追求爱情的南方女子形象,批判了旧南方认为女子必须遵守门当户对的婚姻规范。

A Rose for Emily

I

When Miss Emily Grierson died, our whole town went to her funeral: the men through a sort of respectful affection for a fallen monument, the women mostly out of curiosity to see the inside of her house, which no one save an old man-servant—a combined gardener and cook—had seen in at least ten years.

It was a big, squarish frame house that had once been white, decorated with cupolas① and spires and scrolled balconies in the heavily lightsome style of the seventies, set on what had once been our most select street. But garages and cotton gins had encroached and obliterated② even the august names of that neighborhood; only Miss Emily's house was left, lifting its stubborn and coquettish decay above the cotton wagons and the gasoline pumps—an eyesore among eyesores. And now Miss Emily had gone to join the representatives of those august③ names where they lay in the cedar-bemused cemetery among the ranked and anonymous graves of Union and Confederate soldiers who fell at the battle of Jefferson.

Alive, Miss Emily had been a tradition, a duty, and a care; a sort of hereditary obligation upon the town, dating from that day in 1894 when Colonel Sartoris, the mayor—he who fathered the edict that no Negro woman should appear on the streets without an apron-remitted her taxes, the dispensation dating from the death of her father on into perpetuity. Not that Miss Emily would have accepted charity. Colonel Sartoris invented an involved tale to the effect that Miss Emily's father had loaned money to the town, which the town, as a matter of business, preferred this way of repaying. Only a man of Colonel Sartoris' generation and thought could have invented it, and only a woman could have believed it.

When the next generation, with its more modern ideas, became mayors and aldermen, this arrangement created some little dissatisfaction. On the first of the year they mailed her a tax notice. February came, and there was no reply. They wrote her a formal letter, asking her to call at the sheriff's office at her convenience. A week later the mayor wrote her himself, offering to call or to send his car for her, and received in reply a note on paper of an archaic④ shape, in a thin, flowing calligraphy in faded ink, to the effect that she no longer went out at all. The tax notice was also enclosed, without comment.

They called a special meeting of the Board of Aldermen. A deputation waited upon her, knocked at the door through which no visitor had passed since she ceased giving china-painting lessons eight or ten years earlier. They were admitted by the old Negro

---

① cupolas: 圆屋顶
② obliterate: 使消失,被忘却
③ august: 庄严的
④ archaic: 古老的,过时的

into a dim hall from which a stairway mounted into still more shadow. It smelled of dust and disuse—a close, dank smell. The Negro led them into the parlor. It was furnished in heavy, leather-covered furniture. When the Negro opened the blinds of one window, they could see that the leather was cracked; and when they sat down, a faint dust rose sluggishly about their thighs, spinning with slow motes in the single sun-ray. On a tarnished gilt easel before the fireplace stood a crayon portrait of Miss Emily's father.

They rose when she entered—a small, fat woman in black, with a thin gold chain descending to her waist and vanishing into her belt, leaning on an ebony cane with a tarnished① gold head. Her skeleton was small and spare; perhaps that was why what would have been merely plumpness in another was obesity in her. She looked bloated, like a body long submerged in motionless water, and of that pallid hue. Her eyes, lost in the fatty ridges of her face, looked like two small pieces of coal pressed into a lump of dough as they moved from one face to another while the visitors stated their errand.

She did not ask them to sit. She just stood in the door and listened quietly until the spokesman came to a stumbling② halt. Then they could hear the invisible watch ticking at the end of the gold chain.

Her voice was dry and cold. "I have no taxes in Jefferson. Colonel Sartoris explained it to me. Perhaps one of you can gain access to the city records and satisfy yourselves."

"But we have. We are the city authorities, Miss Emily. Didn't you get a notice from the sheriff, signed by him?"

"I received a paper, yes," Miss Emily said. "Perhaps he considers himself the sheriff ... I have no taxes in Jefferson."

"But there is nothing on the books to show that, you see we must go by the—"

"See Colonel Sartoris. I have no taxes in Jefferson."

"But, Miss Emily—"

"See Colonel Sartoris." (Colonel Sartoris had been dead almost ten years.) "I have no taxes in Jefferson. Tobe!" The Negro appeared. "Show these gentlemen out."

II

So she vanquished them, horse and foot, just as she had vanquished③ their fathers thirty years before about the smell.

That was two years after her father's death and a short time after her sweetheart— the one we believed would marry her—had deserted her. After her father's death she went out very little; after her sweetheart went away, people hardly saw her at all. A few of the ladies had the temerity to call, but were not received, and the only sign of life about the place was the Negro man—a young man then—going in and out with a market

---

① tarnish: 使生锈,失去光泽
② stumble: 蹒跚;绊倒
③ vanquish: 战胜;击败

basket.

"Just as if a man—any man—could keep a kitchen properly," the ladies said; so they were not surprised when the smell developed. It was another link between the gross, teeming world and the high and mighty Griersons.

A neighbor, a woman, complained to the mayor, Judge Stevens, eighty years old.

"But what will you have me do about it, madam?" he said.

"Why, send her word to stop it," the woman said. "Isn't there a law?"

"I'm sure that won't be necessary," Judge Stevens said. "It's probably just a snake or a rat that nigger of hers killed in the yard. I'll speak to him about it."

The next day he received two more complaints, one from a man who came in diffident deprecation①. "We really must do something about it, Judge. I'd be the last one in the world to bother Miss Emily, but we've got to do something." That night the Board of Aldermen met—three graybeards and one younger man, a member of the rising generation.

"It's simple enough," he said. "Send her word to have her place cleaned up. Give her a certain time to do it in, and if she don't ..."

"Dammit, sir," Judge Stevens said, "will you accuse a lady to her face of smelling bad?"

So the next night, after midnight, four men crossed Miss Emily's lawn and slunk about the house like burglars, sniffing② along the base of the brickwork and at the cellar openings while one of them performed a regular sowing motion with his hand out of a sack slung from his shoulder. They broke open the cellar door and sprinkled lime there, and in all the outbuildings. As they recrossed the lawn, a window that had been dark was lighted and Miss Emily sat in it, the light behind her, and her upright torso motionless as that of an idol. They crept quietly across the lawn and into the shadow of the locusts that lined the street. After a week or two the smell went away.

That was when people had begun to feel really sorry for her. People in our town, remembering how old lady Wyatt, her great-aunt, had gone completely crazy at last, believed that the Griersons held themselves a little too high for what they really were. None of the young men were quite good enough for Miss Emily and such. We had long thought of them as a tableau, Miss Emily a slender figure in white in the background, her father a spraddled③ silhouette in the foreground, his back to her and clutching④ a horsewhip, the two of them framed by the back-flung front door. So when she got to be thirty and was still single, we were not pleased exactly, but vindicated; even with insanity in the family she wouldn't have turned down all of her chances if they had really

---

① deprecation: 反对
② sniff: 闻,用力吸
③ spraddled: 叉开腿站立
④ clutch: 抓住,紧握

materialized.

When her father died, it got about that the house was all that was left to her; and in a way, people were glad. At last they could pity Miss Emily. Being left alone, and a pauper, she had become humanized. Now she too would know the old thrill and the old despair of a penny more or less.

The day after his death all the ladies prepared to call at the house and offer condolence and aid, as is our custom Miss Emily met them at the door, dressed as usual and with no trace of grief on her face. She told them that her father was not dead. She did that for three days, with the ministers calling on her, and the doctors, trying to persuade her to let them dispose of the body. Just as they were about to resort to law and force, she broke down, and they buried her father quickly.

We did not say she was crazy then. We believed she had to do that. We remembered all the young men her father had driven away, and we knew that with nothing left, she would have to cling to that which had robbed her, as people will.

III

She was sick for a long time. When we saw her again, her hair was cut short, making her look like a girl, with a vague resemblance to those angels in colored church windows—sort of tragic and serene.

The town had just let the contracts for paving the sidewalks, and in the summer after her father's death they began the work. The construction company came with riggers and mules and machinery, and a foreman named Homer Barron, a Yankee—a big, dark, ready man, with a big voice and eyes lighter than his face. The little boys would follow in groups to hear him cuss[①] the riggers, and the riggers singing in time to the rise and fall of picks. Pretty soon he knew everybody in town. Whenever you heard a lot of laughing anywhere about the square, Homer Barron would be in the center of the group. Presently we began to see him and Miss Emily on Sunday afternoons driving in the yellow-wheeled buggy and the matched team of bays from the livery stable.

At first we were glad that Miss Emily would have an interest, because the ladies all said, "Of course a Grierson would not think seriously of a Northerner, a day laborer." But there were still others, older people, who said that even grief could not cause a real lady to forget noblesse oblige—without calling it noblesse oblige. They just said, "Poor Emily. Her kinsfolk should come to her." She had some kin in Alabama; but years ago her father had fallen out with them over the estate of old lady Wyatt, the crazy woman, and there was no communication between the two families. They had not even been represented at the funeral.

And as soon as the old people said, "Poor Emily," the whispering began. "Do you suppose it's really so?" they said to one another. "Of course it is. What else could ... " This behind their hands; rustling of craned silk and satin behind jalousies closed upon the

---

① cuss: 咒骂

sun of Sunday afternoon as the thin, swift clop-clop-clop of the matched team passed: "Poor Emily."

She carried her head high enough—even when we believed that she was fallen. It was as if she demanded more than ever the recognition of her dignity as the last Grierson; as if it had wanted that touch of earthiness to reaffirm her imperviousness①. Like when she bought the rat poison, the arsenic. That was over a year after they had begun to say "Poor Emily," and while the two female cousins were visiting her.

"I want some poison," she said to the druggist②. She was over thirty then, still a slight woman, though thinner than usual, with cold, haughty black eyes in a face the flesh of which was strained across the temples and about the eyesockets as you imagine a lighthouse-keeper's face ought to look. "I want some poison," she said.

"Yes, Miss Emily. What kind? For rats and such? I'd recom—"

"I want the best you have. I don't care what kind."

The druggist named several. "They'll kill anything up to an elephant. But what you want is—"

"Arsenic," Miss Emily said. "Is that a good one?"

"Is...arsenic? Yes, ma'am. But what you want—"

"I want arsenic③."

The druggist looked down at her. She looked back at him, erect, her face like a strained flag. "Why, of course," the druggist said. "If that's what you want. But the law requires you to tell what you are going to use it for."

Miss Emily just stared at him, her head tilted back in order to look him eye for eye, until he looked away and went and got the arsenic and wrapped it up. The Negro delivery boy brought her the package; the druggist didn't come back. When she opened the package at home there was written on the box, under the skull and bones: "For rats."

IV

So the next day we all said, "She will kill herself;" and we said it would be the best thing. When she had first begun to be seen with Homer Barron, we had said, "She will marry him." Then we said, "She will persuade him yet," because Homer himself had remarked—he liked men, and it was known that he drank with the younger men in the Elks' Club—that he was not a marrying man. Later we said, "Poor Emily" behind the jalousies as they passed on Sunday afternoon in the glittering buggy, Miss Emily with her head high and Homer Barron with his hat cocked and a cigar in his teeth, reins and whip in a yellow glove.

Then some of the ladies began to say that it was a disgrace to the town and a bad

---

① imperviousness：密封性
② druggist：药剂师
③ arsenic：砷

example to the young people. The men did not want to interfere, but at last the ladies forced the Baptist minister—Miss Emily's people were Episcopal—to call upon her. He would never divulge① what happened during that interview, but he refused to go back again. The next Sunday they again drove about the streets, and the following day the minister's wife wrote to Miss Emily's relations in Alabama.

So she had blood-kin under her roof again and we sat back to watch developments. At first nothing happened. Then we were sure that they were to be married. We learned that Miss Emily had been to the jeweler's and ordered a man's toilet set in silver, with the letters H. B. on each piece. Two days later we learned that she had bought a complete outfit of men's clothing, including a nightshirt, and we said, "They are married." We were really glad. We were glad because the two female cousins were even more Grierson than Miss Emily had ever been.

So we were not surprised when Homer Barron—the streets had been finished some time since—was gone. We were a little disappointed that there was not a public blowing-off, but we believed that he had gone on to prepare for Miss Emily's coming, or to give her a chance to get rid of the cousins. (By that time it was a cabal, and we were all Miss Emily's allies to help circumvent the cousins.) Sure enough, after another week they departed. And, as we had expected all along, within three days Homer Barron was back in town. A neighbor saw the Negro man admit him at the kitchen door at dusk one evening.

And that was the last we saw of Homer Barron. And of Miss Emily for some time. The Negro man went in and out with the market basket, but the front door remained closed. Now and then we would see her at a window for a moment, as the men did that night when they sprinkled the lime, but for almost six months she did not appear on the streets. Then we knew that this was to be expected too; as if that quality of her father which had thwarted her woman's life so many times had been too virulent② and too furious to die.

When we next saw Miss Emily, she had grown fat and her hair was turning gray. During the next few years it grew grayer and grayer until it attained an even pepper-and-salt iron-gray, when it ceased turning. Up to the day of her death at seventy-four it was still that vigorous iron-gray, like the hair of an active man.

From that time on her front door remained closed, save for a period of six or seven years, when she was about forty, during which she gave lessons in china-painting. She fitted up a studio in one of the downstairs rooms, where the daughters and granddaughters of Colonel Sartoris' contemporaries were sent to her with the same regularity and in the same spirit that they were sent to church on Sundays with a twenty-five-cent piece for the collection plate. Meanwhile her taxes had been remitted.

---

① divulge: 泄露
② virulent: 致命的，剧毒的

Then the newer generation became the backbone and the spirit of the town, and the painting pupils grew up and fell away and did not send their children to her with boxes of color and tedious brushes and pictures cut from the ladies' magazines. The front door closed upon the last one and remained closed for good. When the town got free postal delivery, Miss Emily alone refused to let them fasten the metal numbers above her door and attach a mailbox to it. She would not listen to them.

Daily, monthly, yearly we watched the Negro grow grayer and more stooped, going in and out with the market basket. Each December we sent her a tax notice, which would be returned by the post office a week later, unclaimed. Now and then we would see her in one of the downstairs windows—she had evidently shut up the top floor of the house—like the carven torso of an idol in a niche, looking or not looking at us, we could never tell which. Thus she passed from generation to generation—dear, inescapable, impervious, tranquil, and perverse①.

And so she died. Fell ill in the house filled with dust and shadows, with only a doddering Negro man to wait on her. We did not even know she was sick; we had long since given up trying to get any information from the Negro.

He talked to no one, probably not even to her, for his voice had grown harsh and rusty, as if from disuse.

She died in one of the downstairs rooms, in a heavy walnut② bed with a curtain, her gray head propped on a pillow yellow and moldy with age and lack of sunlight.

V

The Negro met the first of the ladies at the front door and let them in, with their hushed, sibilant voices and their quick, curious glances, and then he disappeared. He walked right through the house and out the back and was not seen again.

The two female cousins came at once. They held the funeral on the second day, with the town coming to look at Miss Emily beneath a mass of bought flowers, with the crayon face of her father musing profoundly above the bier and the ladies sibilant③ and macabre④; and the very old men—some in their brushed Confederate uniforms—on the porch and the lawn, talking of Miss Emily as if she had been a contemporary of theirs, believing that they had danced with her and courted her perhaps, confusing time with its mathematical progression, as the old do, to whom all the past is not a diminishing road but, instead, a huge meadow which no winter ever quite touches, divided from them now by the narrow bottle-neck of the most recent decade of years.

Already we knew that there was one room in that region above stairs which no one had seen in forty years, and which would have to be forced. They waited until Miss

---

① perverse: 任性的;执拗的
② walnut: 核桃
③ sibilant: 发咝咝声的
④ macabre: 可怕的,恐怖的

Emily was decently in the ground before they opened it.

The violence of breaking down the door seemed to fill this room with pervading dust. A thin, acrid pall as of the tomb seemed to lie everywhere upon this room decked and furnished as for a bridal: upon the valance curtains of faded rose color, upon the rose-shaded lights, upon the dressing table, upon the delicate array of crystal and the man's toilet things backed with tarnished silver, silver so tarnished that the monogram was obscured. Among them lay a collar and tie, as if they had just been removed, which, lifted, left upon the surface a pale crescent in the dust. Upon a chair hung the suit, carefully folded; beneath it the two mute shoes and the discarded socks.

The man himself lay in the bed.

For a long while we just stood there, looking down at the profound and fleshless grin. The body had apparently once lain in the attitude of an embrace, but now the long sleep that outlasts love, that conquers even the grimace① of love, had cuckolded② him. What was left of him, rotted beneath what was left of the nightshirt, had become inextricable from the bed in which he lay; and upon him and upon the pillow beside him lay that even coating of the patient and biding dust.

Then we noticed that in the second pillow was the indentation of a head. One of us lifted something from it, and leaning forward, that faint and invisible dust dry and acrid in the nostrils, we saw a long strand of iron-gray hair.

Questions for discussion

1. Compare the character and background of Emily Grierson and Homer Barron. Why could not they get married according to Emily's father?
2. Who is the narrator of this story? Why does the narrator deliberately rearrange the chronology of the story's events? How does this technique reinforce the atmosphere?
3. What contrasts does the narrator draw between the changing reality and Emily's refusal to recognize the changes?
4. What do you think is Faulkner's attitude toward Emily Grierson? Why does the author give the story the title "A Rose for Emily"?

文学术语(Definition of Terms)

1. **Stream-of-consciousness novel** is an important part in Modernist Movement. The type of psychological novel taking the uninterrupted, uneven, and endless flow of the stream of consciousness of one or more of its characters as its subject matter. The stream-of-consciousness novel uses various techniques to represent this consciousness adequately. In general, most psychological novels report the flow of memory activated by

---

① grimace: 鬼脸,怪相
② cuckold: 使戴绿帽子

association. But the stream-of-consciousness novel tends to concentrate its attention chiefly on the pre-speech, non-verbalized level, where the image must express the unarticulated response and where the logic of grammar belongs to another world.

2. **The Southern Renaissance** was the reinvigoration of American Southern literature that began in the 1920s and 1930s with the appearance of writers such as William Faulkner, Katherine Anne Porter, Tennessee Williams, among others. The emergence of the Southern Renaissance as a literary and cultural movement has also been regarded as a consequence of the opening up of the predominantly rural South to outside influences due to the industrial expansion that took place in the region during and after the First World War. It focuses on the regional culture, rural life and racial conflicts in the Southern area.

Section B Cultural Notes

Before You Read

1. What do you know about the Civil Rights Movement in the history of the U.S.?
2. Try to find more information about America in the post-war period which interests you most. Get ready for a 5-minute presentation in class.
3. Choose a writer influenced much by the Civil Rights Movement and introduce him or her.

Start to Read

American Society in the 1950s

During the 1950s, many cultural commentators argued that a sense of uniformity pervaded American society. Though men and women had been forced into new employment patterns during World War II, once the war was over, traditional roles were reaffirmed. Men expected to be the breadwinners in each family; women, even when they worked, assumed their proper place was at home. In his influential book, *The Lonely Crowd*, sociologist David Riesman called this new society "other-directed," characterized by conformity, but also by stability. Television, still very limited in the choices it gave its viewers, contributed to the cultural trend by providing young and old with a shared experience reflecting accepted social patterns.

Yet beneath this seemingly peaceful surface, important segments of American society were filled with rebellion. A number of writers, collectively known as the "beat generation①," went out of their way to challenge the patterns of respectability and

---

① beat generation: 垮掉的一代

shock the rest of the culture.

The literary work of the beats displayed their sense of alienation① and quest for self-realization. Jack Kerouac typed his best-selling novel *On the Road* on a 75-meter roll of paper. Lacking traditional punctuation and paragraph structure, the book glorified the possibilities of the free life. Poet Allen Ginsberg gained similar notoriety for his poem "*Howl*," a critique of modern, mechanized civilization. When police charged that it was obscene and seized the published version, Ginsberg successfully challenged the ruling in court.

Musicians and artists rebelled as well. Tennessee singer Elvis Presley was the most successful of several white performers who popularized a sensual style of African-American music, which began to be called "rock and roll." At first, he outraged middle-class Americans with his ducktail haircut and undulating② hips. Similarly, it was in the 1950s that painters like Jackson Pollock discarded easels and laid out gigantic canvases on the floor, then applied paint, sand, and other materials in wild splashes of color. All of these artists and authors, whatever the medium, provided models for the wider and more deeply felt social revolution of the 1960s.

The Civil Rights Movement

African Americans became increasingly restive in the postwar years. During the war they had challenged discrimination in the military services and in the work force, and they had made limited gains. Millions of African Americans had left Southern farms for Northern cities, where they hoped to find better jobs. They found instead crowded conditions in urban slums. Now, African-American servicemen returned home, with many intent on rejecting second-class citizenship.

Jackie Robinson dramatized the racial question in 1947 when he broke baseball's color line and began playing in the major leagues. As a member of the Brooklyn Dodgers, he often faced trouble with opponents and teammates as well. But the outstanding first season led to his acceptance and eased the way for other African-American players, who now left the Negro leagues to which they had been confined.

Government officials, and many other Americans, discovered the connection between racial problems and Cold War politics. As the leader of the free world, the United States sought support in Africa and Asia. Discrimination at home impeded③ the effort to win friends in other parts of the world.

Harry Truman supported the early civil rights movement. He personally believed in political equality, though not in social equality, and recognized the growing importance of the African-American urban vote. When informed in 1946 of anti-black violence in the South, he appointed a committee on civil rights to investigate discrimination. Its

---

① alienation: 疏离,异化
② undulate: 使波动,使起伏
③ impede: 阻碍

report *To Secure These Rights*, issued the next year, documented African Americans' second-class status in American life and recommended numerous federal measures to secure the rights guaranteed to all citizens.

A number of the angriest, led by Governor Strom Thurmond of South Carolina, opposed the president in 1948. Truman thereupon issued an executive order barring① discrimination in federal employment, ordered equal treatment in the armed forces, and appointed a committee to work toward an end to military segregation, which was largely ended during the Korean War.

African Americans in the South in the 1950s still enjoyed few, if any, civil and political rights. In general, they could not vote. Those who tried to register faced the likelihood of beatings, loss of job, or loss of their land. Occasional lynchings② still occurred. Jim Crow laws enforced segregation of the races in streetcars, trains, hotels, restaurants, hospitals, recreational facilities, and employment.

After You Read

I. Questions for discussion

1. What was the women's social status in the 1950s? Did they win equal rights after WWII?
2. Why did Harry Truman support the early civil rights movement?
3. What were the situations of African Americans in the South in the 1950s?

II. True or false

1. Women have the same status on maintaining families as men after World War II. ( )
2. The representative literary work of the beats showed their sense of alienation and quest for self-realization. ( )
3. Elvis Presley popularized a sensual style of African-American music, which began to be called "rock and roll." ( )
4. Millions of African Americans had left Northern farms for Southern cities, where they hoped to find better jobs. ( )
5. Martin Luther King supported the early civil rights movement, and personally believed in political equality. ( )
6. After the 1950s, African Americans in the South enjoyed a lot of civil and political rights. ( )

---

① bar: 禁止,阻挡
② lynching: 私刑处死

For Fun

I. Works to Read

1. Riesman, David. *The Lonely Crowd*. This book was a 1950 sociological analysis by David Riesman, Nathan Glazer, and Reuel Denney. It is considered—along with "*White Collar: the American Middle Classes*" written by Riesman's friend and colleague C. Wright Mills—to be a landmark study of American character.
2. Kerouac, Jack. *On the Road*. It is largely an autobiographical work based on the spontaneous road trips of Kerouac and his friends across mid-century America. It is often considered a defining work of the postwar Beat Generation that was inspired by jazz, poetry, and drug experiences. While many of the names and details of Kerouac's experiences are changed for the novel, hundreds of references in *On the Road* have real-world counterparts.

II. Websites to visit

1. http://en.wikipedia.org/wiki/William_Faulkner
2. http://www.mcsr.olemiss.edu/~egjbp/faulkner/faulkner.html

III. Writing

Some people think that the tragedy of Emily is caused by the society while others believe that she should be responsible for her own fate. What is your opinion? Do you agree that Emily could have led a different life if she struggled hard?

Chapter 13

Ernest Miller Hemingway (1899-1961)
欧内斯特·米勒尔·海明威

Section A Literary Focus

作者简介(About the Author)

【生平】 欧内斯特·米勒尔·海明威,美国最具影响力的小说家之一。出生于美国伊利诺伊州芝加哥市郊区的奥克帕克,父亲是医生,母亲是音乐教师。父亲经常带他打猎和钓鱼,海明威因此一直亲近大自然,喜爱户外运动。高中毕业后成为报纸的见习记者。1917年以救护车司机身份参加第一次世界大战。晚年在爱达荷州凯彻姆的家中自杀身亡。海明威一生感情错综复杂,先后结过四次婚,是美国"迷惘的一代"(The Lost Generation)作家中的代表人物。

海明威一生中曾荣获不少奖项。1953年,他以《老人与海》一书获得普利策奖;1954年,《老人与海》又为海明威夺得诺贝尔文学奖。2001年,海明威的《太阳照样升起》与《永别了,武器》两部作品被美国现代图书馆列入"20世纪中的100部最佳英文小说"中。海明威的作品风格简洁,在美国文学史乃至世界文学史上都占有重要地位。

【主要作品】 《太阳照样升起》(The Sun Also Rises,1926),《永别了,武器》(A Farewell to Arms,1929),《老人与海》(The Old Man and the Sea,1951),《丧钟为谁而鸣》(For Whom the Bell Tolls,1940)

作品选读(Selected Writings)

A Day's Wait

海明威文风独特,用词俭省,但这种简洁不是简单,相反,简洁的背后意蕴无穷,耐人寻味。海明威曾用"冰山原则"来描述这种写作风格,"冰山的移动之所以雄伟壮观,因为它只有八分之一浮在水面上。"他的短篇小说是这一风格的典型体现。

海明威的创作有一般两大主题:一是死亡,一是勇气。读者在他的小说中能感受到死亡的气息,但死亡并不意味着怯懦,相反直面死亡更能显示一个人的勇气。《一天的等待》恰好印证了他的名言"人能够被毁灭,但是不能够被打败"(A Man can be destroyed but not defeated)。

A Day's Wait

He came into the room to shut the windows while we were still in bed and I saw he looked ill. He was shivering, his face was white, and he walked slowly as though it ached to move.

"What's the matter, Schatz?"

"I've got a headache."

"You better go back to bed."

"No. I'm all right."

"You go to bed. I'll be you when I'm dressed."

But when I came downstairs he was dressed, sitting by the fire, looking a very sick and miserable boy of nine years. When I put my hand on his forehead I knew he had a fever.

"You go up to bed," I said, "You're sick."

"I'm all right," he said.

When the doctor came he took the boy's temperature.

"What is it?" I asked him.

"One hundred and two."

Downstairs, the doctor left three different medicines in different colored capsules① with instruction for giving them. One was to bring down the fever, another a purgative②, the third to overcome an acid condition. The germs of influenza can only exist in an acid condition, he explained. He seemed to know all about influenza and said there was nothing to worry about if the fever did not go above one hundred and four degrees. This was a light epidemic of flu and there was no danger if you avoided pneumonia③.

Back in the room I wrote the boy's temperature down and made a note of the time to give the various capsules.

"Do you want me to read to you?"

"All right. If you want to," said the boy. His face was very white and there were dark areas under his eyes. He lay still in the bed and seemed very detached from what was going on.

I read aloud from Howard Pyle's Book of pirates; but I could see he was not following what I was reading.

"Just the same, so far," he said.

I sat at the foot of the bed and read to myself while I waited for it to be time to give another capsule. It would have been natural for him to go to sleep, but when I looked up

---

① capsule:胶囊

② purgative:泻药

③ pneumonia:肺炎

he was looking at the foot of the bed, looking very strangely.

"Why don't you try to sleep? I'll make you up for the medicine."

"I'd rather stay awake."

After a while he said to me,

"You don't have to stay in here with me, Papa, if it bothers you."

"It doesn't bother me."

"No, I mean you don't have to stay if it's going to bother you."

I thought perhaps he was a little lightheaded①, and after giving him the prescribed capsules at eleven o'clock I went out for a while. It was a bright, cold day, the ground covered with a sleet that had frozen so that it seemed as if all the bare trees, the bushes, the cut brush and all the grass and the bare ground had been varnished② with ice. I took the young Irish setter for a walk up the road and along a frozen creek, but it was difficult to stand or walk on the glassy surface and the red dog slipped and slithered and I fell twice, hard, once dropping my gun and having it slide away over the ice.

We flushed a covey of quail under a high clay bank with overhanging brush and I killed two as they went out of sight over the top of the blank. Some of the covey lit in trees, but most of them scattered into brush piles and it was necessary to jump on the ice-coated mounds of brush several times before they would flush. Coming out while you were poised unsteadily on the icy, springy brush they made difficult shooting and I killed two, missed five, and started back pleased to have found a covey close to the house and happy there were so many left to find on another day.

At the house they said the boy had refused to let anyone come into the room.

"You can't come in," he said. "You mustn't get what I have."

I went up to him and found him in exactly the position I had left him, white-faced, but with the tops of his cheeks flushed by the fever, staring still, as he had stared, at the foot of the bed.

I took his temperature.

"What is it?"

"Something like a hundred," I said. It was one hundred and two and four tenths.

"It was a hundred and two," he said.

"Who said so?"

"The doctor."

"Your temperature is all right," I said. "It's nothing to worry about."

"I don't worry," he said, "but I can't keep from thinking."

"Don't think," I said. "Just take it easy."

"I'm taking it easy," he said and looked straight ahead. He was evidently holding tight onto himself about something.

---

① lightheaded: 头晕

② varnish: 使表面光滑

"Take this with water."

"Do you think it will do any good?"

"Of course it will."

I sat down and opened the Pirate book and commenced to read, but I could see he was not following, so I stopped.

"About what time do you think I'm going to die?" he asked.

"What?"

"About how long will it be before I die?"

"You aren't going to die. What's the matter with you?"

"Oh, yes, I am, I heard him say a hundred and two."

"People don't die with a fever of one hundred and two. That's a silly way to talk."

"I know they do. At school in France the boys told me you can't live with forty-four degrees. I've got a hundred and two."

He had been waiting to die all day, ever since nine o'clock in the morning.

"You poor Schatz," I said. "Poor old Schatz, It's like miles and kilometers. You aren't going to die. That's different thermometer. On that thermometer thirty-seven is normal. On this kind it's ninety-eight."

"Are you sure?"

"Absolutely," I said, "It's like miles and kilometers. You know, like how many kilometers we make when we do seventy miles in the car?"

"Oh," he said.

But his gaze at the foot of the bed relaxed slowly. The hold over himself relaxed too, finally, and the next day it was very slack and he cried very easily at little things that were of no importance.

Questions for discussion

1. What does the word "wait" in the title suggest?
2. Why does the author mention the hunting scene in the story?
3. How do you think about the relationship between the father and the son?

文学术语(Definition of Terms)

1. **Iceberg Theory** (also known as the "theory of omission") is the writing style of American writer Ernest Hemingway. Hemingway believed the true meaning of a piece of writing should not be evident from the surface story; rather, the crux of the story lies below the surface and should be allowed to shine through. "The dignity of movement of an iceberg is due to only one-eighth of it being above water."
2. **Hemingway Code Hero** is a term to describe the protagonists as tough guys in Hemingway's works. Most of the time in Hemingway's fiction, the heroes are courageous, brave and determined to fight against the difficulties and hardships.

Section B Cultural Notes

Before You Read

1. What do you know about the role of the U.S. in World War I?
2. What negative and positive impacts did World War I exert on the U.S.?
3. Can you find an example to illustrate that WWI exerts impact on a writer?

The USA and World War I

A recent list of the hundred most important news stories of the 20th century ranked the onset of World War I as the 8th. This is a great error. Just about everything that happened in the remainder of the century was, in one way or another, a result of World War I, including the Bolshevik Revolution in Russia, World War II, the Holocaust, and the development of the atomic bomb①. The Great Depression, the Cold War, and the collapse of European colonialism② can also be traced, at least indirectly, to the First World War.

The Assassination of the Archduke

On June 28, 1914, a car carrying Archduke Franz Ferdinand made a wrong turn. As the car came to a halt and tried to turn around, a nervous teenager approached from a coffee house, pulled out a revolver③, and shot twice. Within an hour, the Archduke and his wife were dead.

The assassination provoked outrage in Austria-Hungary. The assassination of the archduke triggered a series of events that would lead to the outbreak of World War I five weeks later. When the conflict was over, 11 million people had been killed, four powerful European empires had been overthrown, and the seeds of World War II and the Cold War had been planted.

U.S. Neutrality in World War I

President Wilson was reluctant to enter World War I. When the War began, Wilson declared U.S. neutrality and demanded that the belligerents④ respect American rights as a neutral party.

The United States hoped to stay out of the way because war was viewed as wasteful, irrational, and immoral. There was no reason for the U.S. to intervene with European affairs. In addition, America would largely profit from trading with both the Allies and

---

① atomic bomb：原子弹
② colonialism：殖民主义
③ revolver：左轮手枪
④ belligerents：交战国

Central Powers. Siding with Britain would cause the U.S. to lose trade with Germany.

In 1914, he had warned that entry into the conflict would bring an end to Progressive reform. "Every reform we have won will be lost if we go into this war," he said. In 1916, President Wilson narrowly won reelection after campaigning on the slogan, "He kept us out of war."

U.S. Entry to World War I

Shortly after war erupted in Europe, President Wilson called on Americans to be "neutral in thought as well as deed." The United States, however, quickly began to lean toward Britain and France.

Convinced that wartime trade was necessary to fuel the growth of American trade, President Wilson refused to impose an embargo① on trade with the belligerents.

During the early years of the war, trade with the Allies tripled. This volume of trade quickly exhausted the Allies' cash reserves, forcing them to ask the United States for credit. In October 1915, President Wilson permitted loans to belligerents, a decision that greatly favored Britain and France. By 1917, American loans to the allies had soared to $2.25 billion.

In January 1917, Germany announced that it would resume unrestricted submarine warfare. This announcement gave rise to American entry into the conflict.

Then a fresh insult led Wilson to demand a declaration of war. In March 1917, newspapers published the Zimmerman Note, an intercepted telegram from the German Foreign Secretary Arthur Zimmerman to the German ambassador to Mexico. The telegram said that if Germany went to war with the United States, Germany promised to help Mexico recover the territory it had lost during the 1840s, including Texas, New Mexico, California, and Arizona. The Zimmerman telegram and German attacks on three U.S. ships in mid-March led Wilson to ask Congress for a declaration of war.

Treaty of Versailles

From the beginning of World War I, Wilson had hoped for a peace settlement promoting America's democratic ideals. President Wilson contributed greatly to an early end to the war by defining the war aims of the Allies, and by insisting that the struggle was being waged not against the German people but against their autocratic government. He wanted to end the war through a liberal peace agreement.

On January 8, 1918, Wilson made his famous "Fourteen Points" address, introducing the idea of a League of Nations—a League that would guarantee all nations "fundamental rights, equal sovereignty, freedom from aggression, freedom of the seas, and eventual of disarmament." The League of Nations, he announced, would "insure peace and justice throughout the world."

In January 1919, diplomats gathered at the château of Versailles near Paris to negotiate a peace treaty to end the Great War. By the time work began, it was clear that

---

① embargo: 禁止贸易令

the pre-war world map required drastic revision. The treaty formally placed the responsibility for the war on Germany and its allies and imposed on Germany the burden of the reparations① payments.

When the Treaty of Versailles was signed on June 28th, 1919, almost all the points that Wilson had proposed were rejected. Only the League of Nations was established, which was replaced in 1946 by the United Nations.

Consequences of the War

American involvement in World War I lasted from the summer of 1917 to the armistice that ended the war in November 1918—just over one year. For America the war was relatively brief, and the casualties, while large, could not be compared with those of the other major nations.

World War I killed more people (more than 9 million soldiers, sailors, and flyers and another 5 million civilians), involved more countries (28 nations), and cost more money ($186 billion in direct costs and another $151 billion in indirect costs), than any previous war in history. It was the first war to use airplanes, tanks, long-range artillery, submarines, and poison gas. It left at least 7 million men permanently disabled.

World War I probably had more far-reaching consequences than any other preceding war. Politically, it contributed to the Bolshevik rise to power in Russia in 1917 and the triumph of fascism② in Italy in 1922. It ignited colonial revolts in the Middle East and in Southeast Asia.

Economically, the war severely disrupted the European economies and allowed the United States to become the world's leading creditor and industrial power. The war also brought vast social consequences, including the mass murder of Armenians in Turkey and an influenza epidemic that killed over 25 million people worldwide.

Few events better reveal the uttermost unpredictability of the future. At the dawn of the 20th century, most Europeans anticipated a future of peace and prosperity. Europe had not fought a major war for 100 years. But a belief in human progress was shattered by World War I, a war few wanted or expected. At any point during the five weeks leading up to the outbreak of fighting, the conflict might have been averted. World War I was a product of miscalculation, misunderstanding, and miscommunication.

No one expected a war of such magnitude or duration as World War I. At first, the armies relied on outdated methods of communication, such as carrier pigeons③. The great powers mobilized more than a million horses. However, by the time the conflict was over, tanks, submarines, airplane-dropped bombs, machine guns, and poison gas had transformed the nature of modern warfare.

---

① reparations：赔款
② fascism：法西斯主义
③ carrier pigeons：信鸽

Chapter 13 Ernest Miller Hemingway (1899-1961)

After You Read

I. Questions for discussion
1. Why is it a great error to rank World War I the 8th in the news stories?
2. What did President Wilson's warning imply?
3. What events helped to involve the United States in the war?
4. What was the goal the League of Nations intended to achieve?
5. What was the political contribution of World War I?

II. True of false
1. In the writer's view, it was an error that the hundred most important news stories of the 20th century ranked the onset of World War I as the 8th.   (   )
2. World War I led to the Bolshevik Revolution in Russia, World War II, the Holocaust, and the development of the atomic bomb.   (   )
3. The assassination provoked outrage in Australia and Hungary.   (   )
4. In 1916, President Truman achieved an overwhelming majority in the reelection after campaigning on the slogan, "He kept us out of war."   (   )
5. "Treaty of Versailles" was signed on June 28th, 1919. Almost all the points proposed by Wilson had been accepted.   (   )
6. World War I was the first war to use airplanes, tanks, long-range artillery, submarines, nuclear weapon, and poisonous gas.   (   )

For Fun

I. Movies to see
Farewell to Arms (1932): It is a 1932 American romance drama film directed by Frank Borzage and starring Helen Hayes, Gary Cooper, and Adolphe Menjou. Based on the 1929 semi-autobiographical novel *A Farewell to Arms* by Ernest Hemingway, with a screenplay by Oliver H. P. Garrett and Benjamin Glazer, the film is about a romantic love affair between an American ambulance driver and an English nurse in Italy during World War I.

II. Websites to visit
http://en.wikipedia.org/wiki/Ernest_Hemingway

III. Writing
Nowadays, people live a life with higher quality than before but the distance among them is farther as well. More and more people have experienced the feeling of alienation. What is your opinion on the phenomenon?

Chapter 14

The Twentieth Century American Poets (I) Ezra Pound (1885–1972)
埃兹拉·庞德

Section A Literary Focus

作者简介(About the Author)

【生平】 埃兹拉·庞德,美国著名诗人,意象派诗歌的代表人物。1885 年 10 月 30 日出生于美国爱达荷州的海利镇。在去欧洲以前,他在宾夕法尼亚大学就学,攻读美国历史、古典文学、罗曼斯语言文学。两年后,他转至哈密尔顿大学(Hamilton College)学习,1906 年获硕士学位。1898 年庞德首次赴欧,以后于 1902 年,1906 年及 1908 年先后共四次去欧洲。1908 年定居伦敦,成为伦敦文坛上举足轻重的人物。他从中国古典诗歌、日本俳句中生发出"诗歌意象"的理论,为东西方诗歌的互相借鉴做出了卓越贡献。此外,庞德还是一名翻译家。但同时,庞德是一名极具争议性的人物,其中最轰动的便是1945 年填满美国各大报头版的庞德叛国案。他利用广播为敌对国家做宣传,阐述自己的观点,公开指责以罗斯柴尔德家族为首脑的银行家们为控制世界各国的银行而发动了第二次世界大战。1958 年经过阿奇博尔德·麦克利什(Archibald McLeish)、罗伯特·弗罗斯特(Robert Frost)、欧内斯特·海明威(Ernest Hemingway)的斡旋,庞德未经审判而被取消叛国罪,返回意大利。1972 年 11 月病逝于威尼斯。

【主要作品】 诗集《灯火熄灭之时》(*A Lume Spento*,1908)、中国古诗英译本《中国》(*Cathay*,1915),诗集《比萨诗章》(*The Pisan Cantos*,1948),《文学论文集》(*Literary Essays*,1954),《文选》(*Selected Prose* 1909–1965,1973)等。

作品选读(Selected Writings)

In a Station of the Metro

《在地铁站内》仅两行14个字,是一首单一意象诗(one-image poem)。它是庞德根据在巴黎协和广场地铁站的印象写成的。诗虽短,但诗人最后落笔定稿前经过相当一段时间的酝酿和推敲。

在地铁站庞德眼前闪过一张张美丽的脸。在归途中,这些脸在他眼前反复出现,直到最后他们逐渐变成了一片片彩色印花色底。这时他产生了一个念头,要做出一幅纯粹表现色彩的斑斑点点的非写实主义的画,但他不会作画,只能以诗代之。诗的两行互相依存。apparition是幻象、幽灵,使人们联想到来来往往的乘客的一张张脸。第二行的petal(花瓣)则传递了美的信息。这一信息由于有深色而又带湿气的树枝的反衬而变得突出鲜明了,同时也给人以模糊重叠之感,意境也就更丰满了。

In a Station of the Metro

The apparition① of these faces in the crowd;
Petals② on a wet, black bough③.

Questions for discussion

1. Which word is the one that overshadows all the rest in Line One? And why?
2. Can you put forward some of the figures of speech used in the poem?
3. What images do you have in your mind when you read the poem?
4. Can you dig out some deep meanings from these two lines?

A Pact

I make a pact with you, Walt Whitman—
I have detested④ you long enough.
I come to you as a grown child
Who has had a pig-headed⑤ father;
I am old enough now to make friends.
It was you that broke the new wood,
Now is a time for carving⑥.
We have one sap⑦ and one root—
Let there be commerce between us.

---

① apparition:幻影
② petal:花瓣
③ bough:树枝
④ detest:憎恶
⑤ pig-headed:固执的
⑥ carving:雕刻
⑦ sap:植物汁液

Questions for discussion
1. What is Ezra Pound's attitude towards Walt Whitman according to the poem?
2. What does Pound talk about in "A Pact"?
3. What does the poet mean in the last two lines?

文学术语(Definition of Literary Terms)

Imagism is a literary movement launched by British and American poets early in the 20th century in reaction against Victorian sentimentalism that advocated the use of free verse, common speech patterns, and clear concrete images.

Section B Cultural Notes

Before You Read

1. Try to search on the Internet or in the library about Multiculturalism and the related information. Give a 3-minute classroom presentation.
2. Do you agree that American culture is a melting pot? Or you prefer another version that it is a salad plate?
3. Do you know any Asian American writers?

Start to Read

Amy Tan

Amy Tan is a Chinese American writer whose works explore mother-daughter relationships. In 1993, Tan's adaptation of her first novel, *The Joy Luck Club*, became a commercially successful film. The book has been translated into 35 languages.

Amy Tan was born in Oakland, America to Chinese immigrants John Tan, an electrical engineer and Baptist minister, and Daisy, who was forced to leave her three daughters from a previous marriage behind in Shanghai. This incident provided the basis for Tan's first novel, 1989 *New York Times* bestseller *The Joy Luck Club*.

Amy is the middle child and only daughter among Daisy and John Tan's three children. In the late 1960s Amy's sixteen-year-old brother Peter died of a brain tumor. Within a year of Peter's death, Amy's father died of the same disease. After these family tragedies, Daisy moved Amy and her younger brother John Jr. to Switzerland, where Amy finished high school. During this period, Amy learned about her mother's former marriage to an abusive man in China, and of their four children, including three daughters and a son who died as a toddler. In 1987 Amy traveled with Daisy to China. There, Amy finally met her three half-sisters.

Tan received her bachelor's and master's degrees in English and Linguistics from San José State University, and later did doctoral linguistics studies at UC Santa Cruz and UC Berkeley.

She resides in Sausalito, California with her husband, Louis DeMattei, a lawyer whom she met on a blind date and married in 1974.

Tan is a member of the Rock Bottom Remainders, a rock band consisting of published writers, including Barbara Kingsolver, Matt Groening, Dave Barry, Kathi Kamen Goldmark, Sam Barry (Author), and Stephen King, among others.

After You Read

I. Questions for discussion
1. What is the main theme of Amy Tan's novels?
2. What do you think of the cultural conflicts in the world?

II. True or false
1. Tan's major exploration in her books is mother-daughter relationships. (　)
2. Tan's first novel, *The Joy Luck Club*, has been translated into 30 languages. (　)
3. Amy Tan's parents, together with her brother Peter, both died of brain tumor. (　)
4. Amy Tan and her husband first met when she was a little girl and her mother Daisy introduced her to Louis. (　)
5. Amy Tan is a Chinese American writer whose mother Daisy had a former marriage to an abusive man in China. (　)
6. Tan received her bachelor's and master's degrees from San José State University, and later did doctoral studies at an other university. (　)

For Fun

I. Movies to see
The Joy Luck Club (1993): *The Joy Luck Club* (喜福会) is a 1993 American film about the relationships between Chinese-American women and their Chinese mothers. Directed by Wayne Wang, the film is based on the eponymous 1989 novel by Amy Tan, who co-wrote the screenplay with Ronald Bass. Four older women, all Chinese immigrants living in San Francisco, meet regularly to play mahjong, eat, and tell stories. Each of these women has an adult Chinese-American daughter. The film reveals the hidden pasts of the older women and their daughters and how their lives are shaped by the clash of Chinese and American cultures as they strive to understand their family bonds and one another.

II. Websites to visit

1. http://en.wikipedia.org/wiki/Multiculturalism
2. http://plato.stanford.edu/entries/multiculturalism/

III. Writing

In recent years, studying abroad has flourished. Thousands of schloars and students have gone to foreign countries to study. Many people are sparing no efforts in applying for going abroad. Do you think it will do good to our country? Write a composition about 250 words to express your idea about it.

Robert Frost (1874-1963)
罗伯特·弗罗斯特

Section One Literary Focus

作者简介(About the Author)

【生平】 罗伯特·弗罗斯特是最受人喜爱的美国诗人之一。1874年3月26日,出生于旧金山。父亲做过校长与新闻记者,在他11岁时逝世。他随母亲迁回祖籍马萨诸塞州,并由其母抚养成人。其母的苏格兰人的虔诚的宗教信仰对弗罗斯特的个性和文学事业有很大影响,使他的作品既崇尚实际又富有神秘色彩。他从小就对诗歌有浓厚的兴趣,但年少时并没有一举成名。在成为诗人的道路上,他从事过各种工作。

在诗歌创作手法上,弗罗斯特不进行诗歌形式的试验与改革,而是反复声称满足于用"旧形式表达新内容"。他采用通俗上口的语言、人们熟知的韵律、日常生活中常见的比喻和象征手法,描写新英格兰地区宁静乡村的道德风尚。然而,他的诗歌并不仅仅记录为人忽略的自然界事物或乡野村民的举止行为。他对大自然的描写常常蕴涵深刻的、象征性的、甚至是形而上学的意义。晚年的他是人人称赞的非官方桂冠诗人。弗罗斯特常被称为"交替性的诗人",意指他处在传统诗歌和现代派诗歌交替的一个时期。1963年1月29日,弗罗斯特在波士顿去世。

【主要作品】 诗集《山间》(*Mountain Interval*, 1916),诗集《新罕布什尔》(*New

Hampshire, 1923),诗集《西去的溪流》(*West-Running Brook*, 1928),诗集《林间空地》(*In the Clearing*, 1962)等。

作品选读(Selected Writings)

The Road Not Taken

《未选之路》是美国诗人罗伯特·弗罗斯特的作品。这首诗表面上似乎是在写自然界的道路,但实质上暗示的却是人生之路。它告诉我们:人生的道路千万条,但一个人一生中往往只能选择其中一条。所以必须慎重;人生道路上不要随波逐流,而要经过自己的思考,作出自己的选择。

Two roads diverged① in a yellow wood,
And sorry I could not travel both
And be one traveler, long I stood
And looked down one as far as I could
To where it bent in the undergrowth②;
Then took the other, as just as fair③,
And having perhaps the better claim④,
Because it was grassy and wanted wear⑤;
Though as for that the passing there
Had worn them really about the same,
And both that morning equally lay
In leaves no step had trodden⑥ black.
Oh, I kept the first for another day!
Yet knowing how way leads on to way,
I doubted if I should ever come back.
I shall be telling this with a sigh⑦
Somewhere ages and ages hence⑧:
Two roads diverged in a wood, and I—
I took the one less traveled by,
And that has made all the difference.

---

① diverge:分叉
② undergrowth:草丛,灌木丛
③ as just as fair:又公正,又正确
④ claim:风景,景色
⑤ wanted wear:人迹罕至的
⑥ trodden:tread 过去分词,被踩踏
⑦ sigh:叹气
⑧ somewhere ages and ages hence:很多年后

Questions for discussion
1. Please compare and contrast the two roads in the poem. Why does the speaker choose the other road?
2. Have you ever experienced such a choice, and how do you feel now, a kind of nostalgic relief or regret?
3. Do you agree that it is choosing itself that makes "all the difference"?

Mending Wall

《修墙》是美国现代诗人罗伯特·弗洛斯特最有名的诗之一。这首诗描绘的是在新英格兰地区的许多农场，人们常用石头砌成墙作为篱笆使用，以及在春季来临时人们习惯性地修补石墙的事。在诗的开始，作者描写了石墙因冬天雨水浸润而冻结，从而出现裂缝甚至倒塌的状况；接着，作者向我们描绘了诗中叙事者与其邻居一起补墙的经过；在诗的最后一节，叙事者向其邻居提出了他的疑问：既然此墙没有起到丝毫的作用，完全没有存在的必要，干嘛还要修补它呢？但是他那无知而又不假思索的邻居却告诉叙事者说，是他父亲告诉他的，"有了好篱笆才能有好邻家"。显然，这个邻居从未去探究过：父亲这么说对吗？而我照父亲说的这么去做又对不对？真的有必要这么去做吗？

Something there is that doesn't love a wall,
That sends the frozen-ground-swell① under it
And spills② the upper boulders③ in the sun,
And makes gaps even two can pass abreast.
The work of hunters④ is another thing:
I have come after them and made repair
Where they have left not one stone on a stone,
But they would have the rabbit out of hiding,
To please the yelping⑤ dogs. The gaps I mean,
No one has seen them made or heard them made,
But at spring mending-time⑥ we find them there.
I let my neighbor know beyond the hill;
And on a day we meet to walk the line
And set the wall between us once again.
We keep the wall between us as we go.
To each the boulders that have fallen to each.

---

① frozen-ground-swell：冻地涨得隆起
② spill：散落
③ boulder：卵石，石头
④ hunter：人类
⑤ yelp：尖叫
⑥ at spring mending-time：春季修墙

And some are loaves① and some so nearly balls
We have to use a spell② to make them balance:
"Stay where you are until our backs are turned!"
We wear our fingers rough with handling them.
Oh, just another kind of outdoor game,
One on a side. It comes to little more:
There where it is we do not need the wall:
He is all pine and I am apple orchard.
My apple trees will never get across
And eat the cones under his pines, I tell him.
He only says, "Good fences make good neighbors."
Spring is the mischief in me, and I wonder
If I could put a notion in his head③:
Why do they make good neighbors? Isn't it
Where there are cows? But here there are no cows.
Before I built a wall I'd ask to know
What I was walling in or walling out,
And to whom I was like to give offense.
Something there is that doesn't love a wall,
That wants it down. I could say "Elves" to him,
But it's not elves exactly, and I'd rather
He said it for himself. I see him there,
Bringing a stone grasped firmly by the top
In each hand, like an old-stone savage armed④.
He moves in darkness as it seems to me,
Not of woods only and the shade of trees.
He will not go behind his father's saying,
And he likes having thought of it so well
He says again, "Good fences make good neighbors."

Questions for discussion

1. What does the "wall" symbolize?
2. What is your interpretation of "something" in the first line of the poem? And why?
3. Do you agree that "Good fences make good neighbors"? Why?
4. Have you had any experience about the necessity of keeping distance from your

---

① loaf: 长块
② spell: 魔法
③ put a notation in his head: 让邻居明白
④ an old-stone savage armed: 旧石器时代的武装野蛮人

neighbors?

文学术语(Definition of Literary Terms)

1. **Blank verse** is a type of poetry, distinguished by having a regular meter, but no rhyme. In English, the meter most commonly used with blank verse has been iambic pentameter.
2. **Symbol**: Any object, person, place, or action that has a meaning in itself and also stands for something larger than itself, such as a quality, attitude, or belief.
3. **Symbolism**: A literary movement in the late 19th century, characterized by the use of symbols to represent things.

Section B Cultural Notes

Before You Read

1. Try to search on the Internet or in the library about American contemporary poetry and the related information. Give a 3-minute classroom presentation.
2. Do you know Philip Levine? Briefly summarize his literary life.
3. Have you read any poems of other American poets? Please share your reading experience with your classmates.

Start to Read

Philip Levine

"A large, ironic Whitman of the industrial heartland" according to Edward Hirsch in the *New York Times Book Review*, Philip Levine is one of the elder statesmen of contemporary American poetry. The son of Russian-Jewish immigrants, Levine was born and raised in industrial Detroit. As a young boy in the midst of the Great Depression① of the 1930s, he was fascinated by the events of the Spanish Civil War. His heroes were not only those individuals who struggled against fascism but also ordinary folks who worked at hopeless jobs simply to stave off poverty. Noted for his interest in the grim reality of blue-collar work and workers, Levine resolved "to find a voice for the voiceless" while working in the auto plants of Detroit during the 1950s. "I saw that the people that I was working with ... were voiceless in a way," he explained in *Detroit Magazine*. "In terms of the literature of the United States they weren't being heard. Nobody was speaking for them. And as young people will, you know, I took this foolish

---

① the Great Depression: 大萧条时期

vow that I would speak for them and that's what my life would be. And sure enough I've gone and done it. Or I've tried anyway ..."

Because of its subject matter, critics have described Levine's work as dark, brooding, and grim. Time contributor Paul Gray called Levine's speakers "guerrillas, trapped in an endless battle long after the war is lost." This sense of defeat is particularly strong when the poet recalls scenes from his Detroit childhood, where unemployment and violence colored his life. But despite its painful material, Levine's verse can also display a certain joyfulness, suggested Marie Borroff. Writing in the Yale Review, she described the title poem of "They Feed They Lion" (1972) as "a litany celebrating, in rhythms and images of unflagging, piston-like force, the majestic strength of the oppressed, rising equally out of the substances of the poisoned industrial landscape and the intangibles of humiliation." Richard Hugo commented in the *American Poetry Review*: "Levine's poems are important because in them we hear and we care." Though Levine's poems are full of loss, regret and inadequacy[①], Hugo felt that they also embody the triumphant potential of language and song. Levine has kept alive in himself "the impulse to sing," Hugo concluded, adding that Levine "is destined to become one of the most celebrated poets of the time."

I. Questions for discussion
1. Why was he fascinated by the events of the Spanish Civil War?
2. Why have critics described Levine's work as dark, brooding, and grim?
3. What is Richard Hugo's comment about Levine's poems?

II. True or false
1. According to Edward Hirsch in the *New York Times Book Review*, Philip Levine is one of the elder statesmen of contemporary American poetry. ( )
2. Although he never experienced the Great Depression of the 1930s, Philip was fascinated by the events of the Spanish Civil War. ( )
3. Levine tended to articulate for the people who had no power of expressing their own ideas while working in the auto plants of Detroit during the 1950s. ( )
4. Because of its subject matter in his works, critics have described Levine's work as dark, brooding, and grim. ( )
5. During the childhood of Levine, his life was filled with unemployment and violence. ( )
6. Richard Hugo commented in the *American Poetry Review*: "Levine's poems are important because in them we hear and we care." ( )
7. Hugo concluded in his book that Levine was destined to become the most celebrated poet of the time. ( )

---

① inadequacy: 不足,缺陷

For Fun

I. Websites to visit

1. http://en.wikipedia.org/wiki/American_Poets_Laureate
2. http://en.wikipedia.org/wiki/United_States_Poet_Laureate
3. http://www.loc.gov/rr/program/bib/poetslaureate/
4. http://www.poetryfoundation.org/bio/philip-levine

II. Writing

  Nowadays animals are used for the testing of newly developed medicines. Some people think this is very cruel and unnecessary. However, others believe that it is justified in the interest of human beings. Discuss these two points of view and give your own opinion.

Chapter 15

The Twentieth Century American Drama Eugene Glastone O'Neill (1888–1953)
尤金·奥尼尔

Section A Literary Focus

作者简介(About the Author)

【生平】 尤金·奥尼尔,美国著名剧作家。奥尼尔出生于纽约一个演员家庭,父亲是爱尔兰人。1909年至1911年期间,奥尼尔曾至南美、非洲各地流浪,淘过金,当过水手、小职员、无业游民。1911年回国后在父亲的剧团里当临时演员。父亲不满意他的演出,他却不满意剧团的传统剧目。1914年到哈佛大学选读戏剧技巧方面的课程,并开始创作。1929年耶鲁大学授予他名誉文学博士学位。此后他居住在美国佐治亚州一个远离海岸的岛上专心写作。一生写作45个剧本,题材广泛,戏剧风格多样。由于他的努力,美国的戏剧事业得以在20世纪20年代发展起来,成为美国文化领域中堪与小说、绘画、音乐作品相提并论的艺术形式。奥尼尔一生坚持不懈地革新戏剧艺术。他把戏剧从19世纪的传统束缚中解放出来,使之在现实生活中扎根、成长。他首次把现实主义乃至自然主义的传统手法运用于美国戏剧的创作中,艺术风格以多种多样和精深圆熟而著称,因而被公认为美国最重要的戏剧作家。1936年获诺贝尔文学奖。

【主要作品】 《天边外》(*Beyond the Horizon*,1918),《安娜·克里斯蒂》(*Anna Christie*,1922),《毛猿》(*The Hairy Ape*,1922),《榆树下的欲望》(*Desire Under the Elms*,1924),《奇妙的插曲》(*Strange Interlude*,1927)和《进入黑夜的漫长旅程》(*Long Day's Journey into Night*,1941)。

作品选读(Selected Writings)

Desire Under the Elms

《榆树下的欲望》是尤金·奥尼尔的作品。1924年首演，主要描写农场主卡伯特为了农场所有权同儿子埃本和妻子爱碧之间发生的三角纠纷。前妻所生的儿子埃本对继承农场抱有希望，76岁高龄的父亲却娶了年轻美貌的爱碧做第三任妻子。爱碧嫁给行将就木的老头，就是为了这份遗产，但是她跟年迈的卡伯特生不出孩子，继承权眼看要落空，于是引诱埃本同她发生关系，并生下了儿子。在利用、引诱埃本的过程中，她对埃本产生了真正的爱情。而埃本一直认为爱碧对他并无感情，只是为了生个继承人夺取农场。爱碧百般表白也不能证明自己的真心，于是忍痛杀死了新生婴儿。她与埃本的隔阂消除了，但等待着他们的却是法律的制裁。

发生在这个家庭中的悲剧向人们揭示出，在金钱占统治地位的社会里，人的自然的情感与本性是如何被压抑与扭曲的，对财产的欲望使父子、母子、夫妻与兄弟之间尔虞我诈，虎视眈眈，一个个贪婪、狡诈、邪恶、虚伪。作者也写了人性中美好的一面，当爱情的火花迸发而出，冲破对金钱的占有欲时，他们会变得真诚、善良，为了得到一份真情而奋不顾身地追求。但是这种追求所表现出的疯狂依然造成了毁灭，这正是悲剧性所在。

Characters

EPHRAIM CABOT

SIMEON

PETER

EBEN

ABBIE PUTNAM

Young Girl, Two Farmers, The Fiddler①, A Sheriff②, and other folk from the neighboring farms

SCENE FOUR

About an hour later. Same as Scene Three. Show the kitchen and Cabot's bedroom. It is after dawn. The sky is brilliant with the sunrise. In the kitchen, Abbie sits at the table, her body limp and exhausted, her head bowed down over her arms, her face hidden. Upstairs, Cabot is still asleep but awakens with a start. He looks toward the window and gives a snort of surprise and irritation—throws back the covers and begins hurriedly pulling on his clothes. Without looking behind him, he begins talking to Abbie, whom he supposes beside him.

CABOT—Thunder 'n' lightnin', Abbie! I hain't slept this late in fifty year! Looks's if the sun was full riz a'most. Must've been the dancin 'an' likker. Must be gittin' old. I hope Eben's t' wuk. Ye might've tuk the trouble t' rouse me, Abbie. (He turns—sees no one there—surprised) Waal—whar air she? Gittin' vittles, I calc'late. (He tiptoes to the cradle and peers down—proudly) Mornin', sonny. Putty's a picter! Sleepin' sound. He don't beller all night like most o'em. (He goes quietly out the door in rear—a few moments later enters

---

① Fiddler：小提琴手
② Sheriff：警长

kitchen—sees Abbie—with satisfaction) So thar ye be. Ye got any vittles cooked?

ABBIE—(without moving) No.

CABOT—(coming to her, almost sympathetically) Ye feelin' sick?

ABBIE—No.

CABOT—(pats her on shoulder. She shudders.) Ye'd best lie down a spell. (half jocularly①) Yer son'll be needin' ye soon. He'd ought t' wake up with a gnashin' appetite, the sound way he's sleepin'.

ABBIE—(shudders②—then in a dead voice) He hain't never goin' t' wake up.

CABOT—(jokingly) Takes after me this mornin'. I hain't slept so late in ...

ABBIE—He's dead.

CABOT—(stares at her—bewilderedly) What ...

ABBIE—I killed him.

CABOT—(stepping back from her—aghast) Air ye drunk—'r crazy—'r ... !

ABBIE—(suddenly lifts her head and turns on him—wildly) I killed him, I tell ye! I smothered③ him. Go up an' see if ye don't b'lieve me! (Cabot stares at her a second, then bolts out the rear door, can be heard bounding up the stairs, and rushes into the bedroom and over to the cradle④. Abbie has sunk back lifelessly into her former position. Cabot puts his hand down on the body in the crib. An expression of fear and horror comes over his face.)

CABOT—(shrinking away—tremblingly) God A'mighty! God A'mighty. (He stumbles out the door—in a short while returns to the kitchen—comes to Abbie, the stunned expression still on his face—hoarsely⑤) Why did ye do it? Why? (As she doesn't answer, he grabs her violently by the shoulder and shakes her.) I ax ye why ye done it! Ye'd better tell me'r ... !

ABBIE—(gives him a furious push which sends him staggering back and springs to her feet—with wild rage and hatred) Don't ye dare tech me! What right hev ye t' question me'bout him? He wa'n't yewr son! Think I'd have a son by yew? I'd die fust! I hate the sight o' ye an' allus did! It's yew I should've murdered, if I'd had good sense! I hate ye! I love Eben. I did from the fust. An' he was Eben's son—mine an' Eben's—not your'n!

CABOT—(stands looking at her dazedly—a pause—finding his words with an effort—dully) That was it—what I felt—pokin' round the corners—while ye lied—holdin' yerself from me—sayin' ye'd a'ready conceived—(He lapses into

---

① jocularly: 风趣地
② shudder: 颤抖
③ smother: 使窒息而死
④ cradle: 摇篮
⑤ hoarsely: 沙哑地

crushed silence—then with a strange emotion) He's dead, sart'n. I felt his heart. Pore little critter①! (He blinks back one tear, wiping his sleeve across his nose.)

ABBIE—(hysterically) Don't ye! Don't ye! (She sobs unrestrainedly.)

CABOT—(with a concentrated effort that stiffens② his body into a rigid line and hardens his face into a stony mask—through his teeth to himself) I got t' be-like a stone—a rock o' jedgment! (A pause. He gets complete control over himself—harshly) If he was Eben's, I be glad he air gone! An' mebbe I suspicioned it all along. I felt they was somethin' onnateral—somewhars—the house got so lonesome—an' cold—drivin' me down t' the barn—t' the beasts o' the field.... Ay-eh. I must've suspicioned—somethin'. Ye didn't fool me—not altogether, leastways—I'm too old a bird—growin' ripe on the bough ... (He becomes aware he is wandering, straightens again, looks at Abbie with a cruel grin.) So ye'd liked t' hev murdered me'stead o' him, would ye? Waal, I'll live to a hundred! I'll live t' see ye hung! I'll deliver ye up t' the jedgment o' God an' the law! I'll git the Sheriff now. (starts for the door)

ABBIE—(dully) Ye needn't. Eben's gone fur him.

CABOT—(amazed) Eben—gone fur the Sheriff?

ABBIE—Ay-eh.

CABOT—T' inform agen ye?

ABBIE—Ay-eh.

CABOT—(considers this—a pause—then in a hard voice) Waal, I'm thankful fur him savin' me the trouble. I'll git t' wuk. (He goes to the door—then turns—in a voice full of strange emotion) He'd ought t' been my son, Abbie. Ye'd ought t' loved me. I'm a man. If ye'd loved me, I'd never told no Sheriff on ye no matter what ye did, if they was t' brile me alive!

ABBIE—(defensively) They's more to it nor yew know, makes him tell.

CABOT—(dryly) Fur yewr sake, I hope they be. (He goes out—comes around to the gate—stares up at the sky. His control relaxes. For a moment he is old and weary. He murmurs despairingly) God A'mighty, I be lonesomer'n ever! (He hears running footsteps from the left, immediately is himself again. Eben runs in, panting exhaustedly, wild-eyed and mad looking. He lurches③ through the gate. Cabot grabs him by the shoulder. Eben stares at him dumbly.) Did ye tell the Sheriff?

EBEN—(nodding stupidly) Ay-eh.

CABOT—(gives him a push away that sends him sprawling—laughing with withering

---

① critter: 动物
② stiffen: 使……变硬
③ lurch: 突然倾斜

contempt) Good fur ye! A prime chip o' yer Maw ye be! (He goes toward the barn, laughing harshly. Eben scrambles to his feet. Suddenly Cabot turns—grimly threatening) Git off this farm when the Sheriff takes her—or, by God, he'll have t' come back an' git me fur murder, too! (He stalks off. Eben does not appear to have heard him. He runs to the door and comes into the kitchen. Abbie looks up with a cry of anguished① joy. Eben stumbles over and throws himself on his knees beside her—sobbing brokenly)

EBEN—Fergive me!

ABBIE—(happily) Eben! (She kisses him and pulls his head over against her breast.)

EBEN—I love ye! Fergive me!

ABBIE—(ecstatically) I'd fergive ye all the sins in hell fur sayin' that! (She kisses his head, pressing it to her with a fierce passion of possession.)

EBEN—(brokenly) But I told the Sheriff. He's comin' fur ye!

ABBIE—I kin b'ar what happens t' me—now!

EBEN—I woke him up. I told him. He says, wait till I git dressed. I was waiting. I got to thinkin' o' yew. I got to thinkin' how I'd loved ye. It hurt like somethin' was bustin' in my chest an' head. I got t' cryin'. I knowed sudden I loved ye yet, an' allus would love ye!

ABBIE—(caressing his hair—tenderly) My boy, hain't ye?

EBEN—I begun t' run back. I cut across the fields an' through the woods. I thought ye might have time t' run away—with me—an' ... .

ABBIE—(shaking her head) I got t' take my punishment—t' pay fur my sin.

EBEN—Then I want t' share it with ye.

ABBIE—Ye didn't do nothin'.

EBEN—I put it in yer head. I wisht he was dead! I as much as urged ye t' do it!

ABBIE—No. It was me alone!

EBEN—I'm as guilty as yew be! He was the child o' our sin.

ABBIE—(lifting her head as if defying God) I don't repent that sin! I hain't askin' God t' fergive that!

EBEN—Nor me—but it led up t' the other—an' the murder ye did, ye did' count o' me—an' it's my murder, too, I'll tell the Sheriff—an' if ye deny it, I'll say we planned it t'gether—an' they'll all b'lieve me, fur they suspicion everythin' we've done, an' it'll seem likely an' true to' em. An' it is true—way down. I did help ye—somehow.

ABBIE—(laying her head on his—sobbing) No! I don't want yew t' suffer!

EBEN—I got t' pay fur my part o' the sin! An' I'd suffer wuss leavin' ye, goin' West, thinkin' o' ye day an' night, bein' out when yew was in—(lowering his voice) 'rbein' alive when yew was dead. (a pause) I want t' share with ye, Abbie—

---

① anguished: 极度痛苦的

prison'r death'r hell'r anythin'! (He looks into her eyes and forces a trembling smile.) If I'm sharin' with ye, I won't feel lonesome①, leastways.

ABBIE—(weakly) Eben! I won't let ye! I can't let ye!

EBEN—(kissing her—tenderly) Ye can't he'p yerself. I got ye beat fur once!

ABBIE—(forcing a smile—adoringly) I hain't beat—s'long's I got ye!

EBEN—(hears the sound of feet outside) Ssshh! Listen! They've come t' take us!

ABBIE—No, it's him. Don't give him no chance to fight ye, Eben. Don't say nothin'—no matter what he says. An' I won't, neither. (It is Cabot. He comes up from the barn in a great state of excitement and strides② into the house and then into the kitchen. Eben is kneeling beside Abbie, his arm around her, hers around him. They stare straight ahead.)

CABOT—(stares at them, his face hard. A long pause—vindictively③) Ye make a slick pair o' murderin' turtle doves! Ye'd ought t' be both hung on the same limb an' left thar t' swing in the breeze an' rot—a warnin' t' old fools like me t' b'ar their lonesomeness alone—an' fur young fools like ye t' hobble their lust. (A pause. The excitement returns to his face, his eyes snap, he looks a bit crazy.) I couldn't work today. I couldn't take no interest. T' hell with the farm. I'm leavin' it! I've turned the cows an' other stock loose. I've druv'em into the woods whar they kin be free! By freein'em, I'm freein' myself! I'm quittin' here today! I'll set fire t' house an' barn an' watch'em burn, an' I'll leave yer Maw t' haunt the ashes, an' I'll will the fields back t' God, so that nothin' human kin never touch'em! I'll be a-goin' to Californi-a—t' jine Simeon an' Peter—true sons o' mine if they be dumb fools—an' the Cabots'll find Solomon's Mines t'gether! (He suddenly cuts a mad caper.) Whoop! What was the song they sung? "Oh, Californi-a! That's the land fur me." (He sings this—then gets on his knees by the floorboard under which the money was hid.) An' I'll sail thar on one o' the finest clippers I kin find! I've got the money! Pity ye didn't know whar this was hidden so's ye could steal ... (He has pulled up the board. He stares—feels—stares again. A pause of dead silence. He slowly turns, slumping into a sitting position on the floor, his eyes like those of a dead fish, his face the sickly green of an attack of nausea④. He swallows painfully several times—forces a weak smile at last.) So—ye did steal it!

EBEN—(emotionlessly) I swapped it t' Sim an' Peter fur their share o' the farm—t' pay their passage t' Californi-a.

---

① lonesome：孤单的

② stride：阔步行走

③ vindictively：报复地

④ nausea：恶心

CABOT—(with one sardonic) Ha! (He begins to recover. Gets slowly to his feet—strangely) I calc'late God give it to'em—not yew! God's hard, not easy! Mebbe they's easy gold in the West, but it hain't God's gold. It hain't fur me. I kin hear His voice warnin' me agen t' be hard an' stay on my farm. I kin see his hand usin' Eben t' steal t' keep me from weakness. I kin feel I be in the palm o' His hand, His fingers guidin' me. (A pause—then he mutters① sadly) It's a-goin' t' be lonesomer now than ever it war afore—an' I'm gittin' old, Lord—ripe on the bough ... (then stiffening) Waal—what d'ye want? God's lonesome, hain't He? God's hard an' lonesome! (A pause. The sheriff with two men comes up the road from the left. They move cautiously to the door. The sheriff knocks on it with the butt of his pistol②.)

SHERIFF—Open in the name o' the law! (They start.)

CABOT—They've come fur ye. (He goes to the rear door.) Come in, Jim! (The three men enter. Cabot meets them in doorway.) Jest a minit, Jim. I got'em safe here. (The sheriff nods. He and his companions remain in the doorway.)

EBEN—(suddenly calls) I lied this mornin', Jim. I helped her do it. Ye kin take me, too.

ABBIE—(brokenly) No!

CABOT—Take'em both. (He comes forward—stares at Eben with a trace of grudging admiration.) Putty good—fur yew! Waal, I got t' round up the stock. Good-by.

EBEN—Good-by.

ABBIE—Good-by. (Cabot turns and strides past the men—comes out and around the corner of the house, his shoulders squared, his face stony, and stalks grimly toward the barn. In the meantime the sheriff and men have come into the room.)

SHERIFF—(embarrassedly) Waal—we'd best start.

ABBIE—Wait, (turns to Eben) I love ye, Eben.

EBEN—I love ye, Abbie. (They kiss. The three men grin and shuffle embarrassedly. Eben takes Abbie's hand. They go out the door in rear, the men following, and come from the house, walking hand in hand to the gate. Eben stops there and points to the sunrise sky.) Sun's a-rizin'. Purty, hain't it?

ABBIE—Ay-eh. (They both stand for a moment looking up raptly in attitudes strangely aloof③ and devout④.)

SHERIFF—(looking around at the farm enviously—to his companion) It's a jim-dandy farm, no denyin'. Wished I owned it!

(The Curtain Falls)

---

① mutter：嘟哝，轻声抱怨
② pistol：手枪
③ aloof：冷漠的
④ devout：虔诚的

Questions for discussion
1. What tragic elements are there in the play?
2. What do you think of the love between Eben and Abbie?
3. What is your opionion of the Father Cabot?

文学术语(Definition of Literary Terms)

The Expressionist plays often dramatize the struggle against bourgeois values and established authority, often personified in the figure of the Father. Its typical trait is to present the world solely from a subjective perspective, distorting it radically for emotional effect in order to evoke moods or ideas. Expressionist artists sought to express meaning or emotional experience rather than physical reality.

Section B Cultural Notes

Before You Read

1. Try to search on the Internet or in the library about the history of American drama and the related information. Give a 3-minuteclassroom presentation.
2. Briefly summarize Eugene O'Neill's life.
3. What role do eminent playwrights such as Shakespeare play in modern society?

Start to Read

The Absent Voice: American Drama and the Critic

In recent years attempts have been made to fill some of the more obvious absence in the literary canon. The battle for the future, as ever, begins with the past. First blacks and then women chose to define present reality in terms of a redefined tradition. The project was an implicit critique of a critical practice that had filtered out experiences not felt to be normative, that had denied a voice to those marginalized① by the social or economic system—hence the significance of the title of Tillie Olsen's book *Silences* and the potency of Richard Wright's image of laboratory dogs, their vocal chords② cut, silently baying to the moon, in *American Hunger*. Language is power, the shaping of language into art is power and the codification of that literature in the form of literary history is also a source of power.

It is, however, not merely the literary expression of the experiences of particular

---

① marginalize: 使边缘化
② vocal chord: 声带

sections of American society that have fallen below the threshold of critical attention. There is also another surprising absence, another silence, another example of critical reticence①. Whatever happened to American drama? Why is it that literary critics, cultural historians, literary theorists, those interested in the evolution of genre, in discourse and ideology, find so little to say about the theatre in general and the American theatre in particular? Can it really be that an entire genre has evaded the critic who was once drawn to the poem and then the novel and who, more recently, has chosen to concentrate on literary theory? There are, of course, honorable exceptions, but on the whole the silence has been remarkable.

Any account of American drama must begin by noting the casual disregard with which it has been treated by the critical establishment. There is no single history of its development, no truly comprehensive analysis of its achievement. In the standard histories of American literature it is accorded at best a marginal position. Why should this be? Is it perhaps the nature of drama which takes it outside the parameters of critical discourse, unless, like Shakespeare, its canonical② status as scholarly text has been established by time? After all, it is drama, and the theatre in which it takes place, not inherently ideological? Does the transformation of the word on the page into the mobility of performance not raise questions about discourse and text? Is the stage, the most public of the arts, not a place to see dramatized the tensions and concerns of a society? Is a concern with the reception of a work, with the way in which it is read, not of special significance to an art in which that reception may profoundly modify the work in question? May questions of authorship not have special bearing on an art which might be thought to be collaborative? Is the very nature and status of criticism not challenged by work which to a large degree incorporates a critical reading in the very processes of its transmission③? These might be thought to be rhetorical questions, but the history of literary criticism and cultural studies suggests otherwise.

It was Umberto Eco who reminded us that though the intervention of the actor complicates the act of reception, the process remains the same in that every "reading," "contemplation" or "enjoyment" of a work of art represents a tacit form of "performance": and every performance, a reading. That reader may, of course, be in the theatre. He or she may be on their own, confronted with the printed word. It could even be argued that the latter may, in a perverse way, be in a more privileged if exposed position in that the individual imagination I not coerced④ by the interpretative strategy of director and actor. As David Mamet has said, "the best production takes place in the mind of the beholder." But of course the theatre's attraction lies in its power to

---

① reticence: 沉默, 缄默
② canonical: 经典的
③ transmission: 传输, 传播
④ coerce: 强制, 胁迫

transcend the written word. That is the key. It is physical, three-dimensional, immediate, and perhaps that very fact has itself intimidated the critic. It should instead have challenged him. Too often, we are offered reductive versions, even by those who acknowledge drama as an aspect of literature. Thus, in his diatribe against the American playwright, Robert Brustein, as a young critic, had denounced Eugene O'Neill as a "charter member of a cult of inarticulacy①" who perversely suggested that the meaning of one of his plays might lie in its silences, and Tennessee Williams for emphasizing "the incontinent blaze of live theatre, a theatre meant for seeing and feeling," a plastic theatre which did not reward the literary critic. This view, expressed in *Harper*'s magazine in 1959, has been echoed sufficiently and widely since then to merit consideration.

After You Read

I. Discuss the following questions based on the text.
1. How do you understand that "language is power"?
2. What differences do you think are there among poems, novels and plays?
3. From your perspective, why does American drama be marginalized in history?
4. Why does the author say "every performance a reading"?
5. How do you understand David Mamet's remark that "the best production takes place in the mind of the beholder"?
6. What's the relationship between critics and plays? Please give an example and analyze it.
7. How do you understand the term "the absent voice" in the title?
8. Have you read any play? Please share your reading experience with your parterners.

II. True or false
1. Blacks and then women chose to define present reality in terms of the past. (   )
2. There is also another surprising absence, another silence, another example of critical reticence. (   )
3. There is a single history of its development, no truly comprehensive analysis of the achievement of American drama. (   )
4. The very nature and status of criticism is, to some extent, not challenged by work which to a large degree incorporates a critical reading in the very processes of its transmission. (   )
5. It was Tillie Olsen who reminded us that the intervention of the actor complicates the act of reception. (   )
6. Robert Brustein, as a young critic, had denounced Eugene O'Neill as a "charter

---

① inarticulacy: 口齿不清

member of a cult of inarticulacy" who perversely suggested that the meaning of one of his plays might lie in its silences.　　　　　　　　　　　　　　　　　　　　　　（　）

For Fun

I. Movies to see:

Desire Under the Elms (1958): It is a 1958 American film version of the 1924 play *Desire Under the Elms* written by Eugene O'Neill. The film was directed by Delbert Mann from a screenplay by O'Neill and Irwin Shaw. The cast included Sophia Loren as Abbie (known as Anna in the film), Anthony Perkins as Eben, Burl Ives as Ephraim, Frank Overton as Simeon and Pernell Roberts as Peter. The film was nominated for Best Black and White Cinematography (Daniel L. Fapp) at the Academy Awards and Laurel Awards in 1959.

II. Websites to visit

1. http://www.questia.com/library/music-and-performing-arts/theater/drama-and-dramatists/american-drama#/
2. http://www.imdb.com/name/nm0642156/
3. http://assets.cambridge.org/97805217/90895/excerpt/9780521790895_excerpt.pdf

III. Writing

The government should control the amount of violence in films and on television in order to decrease the violent crimes in society. To what extent do you agree or disagree? Write a composition about 250 words to express your ideas.

Tennessee Williams (1911–1983)
田纳西·威廉斯

Section A　Literary Focus

作者简介(About the Author)

【生平】　田纳西·威廉斯,美国著名剧作家,生于一个混乱不安的家庭,这样的环境也激发了他许多的写作灵感。他出生在密西西比州的哥伦布市,身为牧师的外祖父的家中。

1918年威廉斯全家搬到密苏里州的圣路易斯。威廉斯的剧本中的角色常直接代表了他的家庭成员。他与他的助理兼同性爱人法兰克·梅洛的关系从1947年开始，直到1963年梅洛过世为止。威廉斯是反同性恋社会气氛下的受害者。一些评论家说病态的堕落呈现在他的作品里，另一些则相信这是威廉斯在反抗自己是同性恋者的事实。在四十多年的创作生涯中，他为世人留下了六十几部剧作，八九部电影剧本，几部电视剧本，两部长篇小说，六七本短篇小说集，两本诗集，两本书信集，一本评论集和一部回忆录。甚至在其身后还陆续发现不少在构思  中的手稿和素材札记，有些佚作、遗作都已出版。在1945、1948、1955和1962年这四年中，威廉斯先后获得四次纽约剧评界奖；在1948和1955这两年中，又两度获得普利策奖；1996年获得美国文学研究院金质奖；1979年又获得纽约肯尼迪艺术中心艺术奖。1976年成为美国艺术学院院士。

【主要作品】《玻璃动物园》(*The Glass Menagerie*, 1944)，《欲望号街车》(*A Streetcar Named Desire*, 1947)，《热铁皮屋顶上的猫》(*Cat on a Hot Tin Roof*, 1955)等。

作品选读(Selected Writings)

A Streetcar Named Desire

本剧是田纳西·威廉斯的代表作之一。徐娘半老风味犹存的"南部美女"白兰琪因"不适当"的行为被解除家庭教师职务后，来到新奥尔良投靠妹妹。妹妹家在一栋肮脏的公寓内，其丈夫斯坦利是波兰移民的儿子，性格粗鲁莽撞，且酗酒嗜赌。因为从小娇生惯养，受过旧式的南方教育，白兰琪多少有些神经质，她认为斯坦利是个很没教养的人，而斯坦利也正因为她所表现出的娇弱敏感，认为她会带坏自己的妻子，甚至威胁到他作为家中主人的地位，对她时常加以言语侮辱以示憎恶。在这样的环境中，白兰琪的悲剧一点点展开。

白兰琪与斯坦利见面伊始就对对方毫无好感。斯坦利认为白兰琪不值得信任，侵吞了妻子本来应该得到的家产。白兰琪却认为斯坦利是个没受过教育的粗鲁小子。白兰琪和斯坦利的同事米奇相识。米奇好心而友善，很喜欢白兰琪。斯坦利发现了白兰琪的秘密，原来她并非那么纯洁，他把这个秘密告诉了沉醉在爱河中的米奇。米奇感觉自己受到了白兰琪的愚弄，抛弃了她。妹妹即将临盆，被送进了医院。从医院醉酒回家的斯坦利在酒精的刺激下，强奸了白兰琪。白兰琪发疯了，最后被送进了疯人院。

THE CHARACTERS

BLANCHE
STELLA
STANLEY
MITCH
EUNICE
STEVE

PABLO
A NEGRO WOMAN
A DOCTOR
A NURSE
A YOUNG COLLECTOR
A MEXICAN WOMAN

SCENE ONE

The exterior of a two-story corner building on a street in New Orleans which is named Elysian Fields and runs between the L & N tracks and the river. The section is poor but, unlike corrsponding sections in other American cities, it has a raffish① charm. The houses are mostly white frame, weathered grey, with rickety outside stairs and galleries and quaintly ornamented gables. This building contains two flats, upstairs and down. Faded white stairs ascend to the entrances of both.

It is first dark of an evening early in May. The sky that shows around the dim white building is a peculiarly tender blue, almost a turquoise②, which invests the scene with a kind of lyricism and gracefully attenuates③ the atmosphere of decay. You can almost feel the warm breath of the brown river beyond the river warehouses with their faint redolence of bananas and coffee. A corresponding air is evoked by the music of Negro entertainers at a ballroom around the corner. In this part of New Orleans you are practically always just around the corner, or a few doors down the street, from a tinny piano being played with the infatuated④ fluency of brown fingers. This "Blue Piano" expresses the spirit of the life which goes on here.

Two women, one white and one colored, are taking the air on the steps of the building. The white woman is Eunice, who occupies the upstairs flat; the colored woman a neighbor, for New Orleans is a cosmopolitan city where there is a relatively warm and easy intermingling of races in the old part of town.

Above the music of the "Blue Piano" the voices of people on the street can be heard overlapping.

Two men come around the corner, Stanley Kowalski and Mitch. They are about twenty-eight or thirty years old, roughly dressed in blue denim work clothes. Stanley carries his bowling jacket and a red-stained package from a butcher's. They stop at the foot of the steps.

STANLEY [bellowing]: Hey, there! Stella, Baby! [Stella comes out on the first floor landing, a gentle young woman, about twenty-five, and of a

---

① raffish: 放荡不羁的
② turquoise: 绿松石
③ attenuate: 减弱
④ infatuated: 痴迷的

background obviously quite different from her husband's.]

STELLA [mildly]: Don't holler at me like that. Hi, Mitch.

STANLEY: Catch!

STELLA: What?

STANLEY: Meat! [He heaves the package at her. She cries out in protest but manages to catch it; then she laughs breathlessly. Her husband and his companion have already started back around the corner.]

STELLA [calling after him]: Stanley! Where are you going?

STANLEY: Bowling!

STELLA: Can I come watch?

STANLEY: Come on. [He goes out.]

STELLA: Be over soon. [To the white woman] Hello, Eunice. How are you?

EUNICE: I'm all right. Tell Steve to get him a poor boy's sandwich' cause nothing's left here. [They all laugh; the colored woman does not stop. Stella goes out.]

COLORED WOMAN: What was that package he th'ew at'er?

[She rises from steps, laughing louder.]

EUNICE: You hush, now!

NEGRO WOMAN: Catch what! [She continues to laugh. Blanche comes around the corner, carrying a valise. She looks at a slip of paper, then at the building, then again at the slip and again at the building. Her expression is one of shocked disbelief. Her appearance is incongruous① to this setting. She is daintily dressed in a white suit with a fluffy bodice, necklace and earrings of pearl, white gloves and hat, looking as if she were arriving at a summer tea or cocktail party in the garden district. She is about five years older than Stella. Her delicate beauty must avoid a strong light. There is something about her uncertain manner, as well as her white clothes, that suggests a moth.]

EUNICE [finally]: What's the matter, honey? Are you lost?

BLANCHE [with faintly hysterical humor]: They told me to take a street-car named Desire, and then transfer to one called Cemeteries and ride six blocks and get off at-Elysian Fields!

EUNICE: That's where you are now.

BLANCHE: At Elysian Fields?

EUNICE: This here is Elysian Fields.

BLANCHE: They mustn't have-understood-what number I wanted ...

EUNICE: What number you lookin' for? [Blanche wearily refers to the slip of paper.]

BLANCHE: Six thirty-two.

---

① incongruous: 不协调的

EUNICE: You don't have to look no further.
BLANCHE [uncomprehendingly]: I'm looking for my sister, Stella DuBois. I mean Mrs. Stanley Kowalski.
EUNICE: That's the party. —You just did miss her, though.
BLANCHE: This—can this be—her home?
EUNICE: She's got the downstairs here and I got the up.
BLANCHE: Oh. She's—out?
EUNICE: You noticed that bowling alley around the corner?
BLANCHE: I'm—not sure I did.
EUNICE: Well, that's where she's at, watchin' her husband bowl. [There is a pause.] You want to leave your suitcase here an' go find her?
BLANCHE: No.
NEGRO WOMAN: I'll go tell her you come.
BLANCHE: Thanks.
NEGRO WOMAN: You welcome. [She goes out.]
EUNICE: She wasn't expecting you?
BLANCHE: No. No, not tonight.
EUNICE: Well, why don't you just go in and make yourself at home till they get back.
BLANCHE: How could I—do that?
EUNICE: We own this place so I can let you in. [She gets up and opens the downstairs door. A light goes on behind the blind, turning it light blue. Blanche slowly follows her into the downstairs flat. The surrounding areas dim out as the interior is lighted.] [Two rooms can be seen, not too clearly defined. The one first entered is primarily a kitchen but contains a folding bed to be used by Blanche. The room beyond this is a bedroom. Off this room is a narrow door to a bathroom.]
EUNICE [defensively, noticing Blanche's look]: It's sort of messed up right now but when it's clean it's real sweet.
BLANCHE: Is it?
EUNICE: Uh-huh, I think so. So you're Stella's sister?
BLANCHE: Yes. [Wanting to get rid of her] Thanks for letting me in.
EUNICE: Por nada, as the Mexicans say, por nada! Stella spoke of you.
BLANCHE: Yes?
EUNICE: I think she said you taught school.
BLANCHE: Yes.
EUNICE: And you're from Mississippi, huh?
BLANCHE: Yes.
EUNICE: She showed me a picture of your home—place, the plantation.
BLANCHE: Belle Reve?
EUNICE: A great big place with white columns.

BLANCHE: Yes ...

EUNICE: A place like that must be awful hard to keep up.

BLANCHE: If you will excuse me, I'm just about to drop.

EUNICE: Sure, honey. Why don't you set down?

BLANCHE: What I meant was I'd like to be left alone.

EUNICE [offended]: Aw. I'll make myself scarce, in that case.

BLANCHE: I didn't mean to be rude, but—

EUNICE: I'll drop by the bowling alley an' hustle her up. [She goes out the door.]

[Blanche sits in a chair very stiffly with her shoulders slightly hunched and her legs pressed close together and her hands tightly clutching her purse as if she were quite cold. After a while the blind look goes out of her eyes and she begins to look slowly around. A cat screeches. She catches her breath with a startled gesture. Suddenly she notices something in a half opened closet. She springs up and crosses to it, and removes a whiskey bottle. She pours a half tumbler① of whiskey and tosses it down. She carefully replaces the bottle and washes out the tumbler at the sink. Then she resumes her seat in front of the table.]

BLANCHE [faintly to herself]: I've got to keep hold of myself! [Stella comes quickly around the corner of the building and runs to the door of the downstairs flat.]

STELLA [calling out joyfully]: Blanche! [For a moment they stare at each other. Then Blanche springs up and runs to her with a wild cry.]

BLANCHE: Stella, oh, Stella, Stella! Stella for Star! [She begins to speak with feverish② vivacity③ as if she feared for either of them to stop and think. They catch each other in a spasmodic④ embrace.]

BLANCHE: Now, then... Let me look at you. But don't you look at me, Stella, no, no, no, not till later, not till I've bathed and rested! And turn that over-light off! Turn that off! I won't be looked at in this merciless glare! [Stella laughs and complies] Come back here now! Oh, my baby! Stella! Stella for Star! [She embraces her again] I thought you would never come back to this horrible place! What am I saying? I didn't mean to say that. I meant to be nice about it and say—Oh, what a convenient location and such-Ha-a-ha! Precious lamb! You haven't said a word to me.

STELLA: You haven't given me a chance to, honey! [She laughs, but her glance at Blanche is a little anxious.]

---

① tumbler：玻璃杯

② feverish：发烧的

③ vivacity：活泼

④ spasmodic：一阵阵的

BLANCHE: Well, now you talk. Open your pretty mouth and talk while I look around for some liquor. I know you must have some liquor on the place! Where could it be, I wonder? Oh, I spy, I spy! [She rushes to the closet and removes the bottle, she is shaking all over and panting for breath as she tries to laugh. The bottle nearly slips from her grasp.]

STELLA [noticing]: Blanche, you sit down and let me pour the drinks. I don't know what we've got to mix with. Maybe a coke's in the icebox. Look'n see, honey, while I'm—

BLANCHE: No coke, honey, not with my nerves tonight! Where where—where is—?

STELLA: Stanley? Bowling! He loves it. They're having a—found some soda I— tournament ...

BLANCHE: Just water, baby, to chase it! Now don't get worried, your sister hasn't turned into a drunkard, she's just all shaken up and hot and tired and dirty! You sit down, now, and explain this place to me. What are you doing in a place like this?

STELLA: Now, Blanche—

BLANCHE: Oh, I'm not going to be hypocritical, I'm going to be honestly critical about it! Never, never, never in my worst dreams could I picture— Only Poe! Only Mr. Edgar Allan Poe ! —could do it justice! Out there I suppose is the ghoul—haunted woodland of Weir! [She laughs.]

STELLA: No, honey, those are the L & N tracks.

BLANCHE: No, now seriously, putting joking aside. Why didn't you tell me, why didn't you write me, honey, why didn't you let me know?

STELLA [carefully, pouring herself a drink]: Tell you what, Blanche?

BLANCHE: Why, that you had to live in these conditions!

STELLA: Aren't you being a little intense about it? It's not that bad at all! New Orleans isn't like other cities.

BLANCHE: This has got nothing to do with New Orleans. You might as well say— forgive me, blessed baby! [She suddenly stops short] The subject is closed.

STELLA [a little drily]: Thanks. [During the pause, Blanche stares at her. She smiles at Blanche.]

BLANCHE [looking down at her glass, which shakes in her hand]: You're all I've got in the world, and you're not glad to see me!

STELLA [sincerely]: Why, Blanche, you know that's not true.

BLANCHE: No? —I'd forgotten how quiet you were.

STELLA: You never did give me a chance to say much, Blanche. So I just got in the habit of being quiet around you.

BLANCHE [vaguely]: A good habit to get into ... [then, abruptly] You haven't asked me how I happened to get away from the school before the spring term ended.

STELLA: Well, I thought you'd volunteer that information—if you wanted to tell me.

BLANCHE: You thought I'd been fired?

STELLA: No, I—thought you might have—resigned ...

BLANCHE: I was so exhausted by all I'd been through my—nerves broke. [Nervously tamping cigarette] I was on the verge of lunacy①, almost! So Mr. Graves—Mr. Graves is the high school superintendent—he suggested I take a leave of absence. I couldn't put all of those details into the wire ... [She drinks quickly] Oh, this buzzes right through me and feels so good!

STELLA: Won't you have another?

BLANCHE: No, one's my limit.

STELLA: Sure?

BLANCHE: You haven't said a word about my appearance.

STELLA: You look just fine.

BLANCHE: God love you for a liar! Daylight never exposed so total a ruin. But you-you've put on some weight, yes, you're just as plump as a little partridge②. And it's so becoming to you!

STELLA: Now, Blanche—

BLANCHE: Yes, it is, it is or I wouldn't say it. You just have to watch around the hips a little. Stand up.

STELLA: Not now.

BLANCHE: You hear me? I said stand up! [Stella complies reluctantly] You messy child, you, you've spilt something on that pretty white lace collar. About your hair—you ought to have it cut in a feather bob with your dainty features. Stella, you have a maid, don't you?

STELLA: No. With only two rooms it's—

BLANCHE: What? Two rooms, did you say?

STELLA: This one and—[She is embarrassed.]

BLANCHE: The other one? [She laughs sharply. There is an embarrassed silence.]

BLANCHE: I am going to take just one little tiny nip more, sort of to put the stopper on, so to speak ... Then put the bottle away so I won't be tempted. [She rises] I want you to look at my figure! [She turns around] You know I haven't put on one ounce in ten years, Stella? I weigh what I weighed the summer you left Belle Reve. The summer Dad died and you left us ...

STELLA [a little wearily]: It's just incredible, Blanche, how well you're looking.

BLANCHE: [They both laugh uncomfortably] But, Stella, there's only two rooms, I don't see where you're going to put me!

STELLA: We're going to put you in here.

---

① lunacy：精神错乱

② partridge：山鹑

BLANCHE: What kind of bed's this—one of those collapsible things? [She sits on it.]
STELLA: Does it feel all right?
BLANCHE [dubiously①]: Wonderful, honey. I don't like a bed that gives much. But there's no door between the two rooms, and Stanley—will it be decent?
STELLA: Stanley is Polish, you know.
BLANCHE: Oh, yes. They're something like Irish, aren't they?
STELLA: Well—
BLANCHE: Only not so—highbrow? [They both laugh again in the same way] I brought some nice clothes to meet all your lovely friends in.
STELLA: I'm afraid you won't think they are lovely.
BLANCHE: What are they like?
STELLA: They're Stanley's friends.
BLANCHE: Polacks?
STELLA: They're a mixed lot, Blanche.
BLANCHE: Heterogeneous—types?
STELLA: Oh, yes. Yes, types is right.
BLANCHE: Well—anyhow—I brought nice clothes and I'll wear them. I guess you're hoping I'll say I'll put up at a hotel, but I'm not going to put up at a hotel. I want to be near you, got to be with somebody, I can't be alone! Because—as you must have noticed—I'm-not very well ... " [Her voice drops and her look is frightened.]
STELLA: You seem a little bit nervous or overwrought or something.
BLANCHE: Will Stanley like me, or will I be just a visiting in-law, Stella? I couldn't stand that.
STELLA: You'll get along fine together, if you'll just try not to well compare him with men that we went out with at home.
BLANCHE: Is he so—different?
STELLA: Yes. A different species.
BLANCHE: In what way; what's he like?
STELLA: Oh, you can't describe someone you're in love with! Here's a picture of him! [She hands a photograph to Blanche.]
BLANCHE: An officer?
STELLA: A Master Sergeant② in the Engineers' Corps. Those are decorations!
BLANCHE: He had those on when you met him?
STELLA: I assure you I wasn't just blinded by all the brass.
BLANCHE: That's not what!
STELLA: But of course there were things to adjust myself to later on.

---

① dubiously: 犹疑地
② Sergeant: 中士

BLANCHE: Such as his civilian background. [Stella laughs uncertainly] How did he take it when you said I was coming?

STELLA: Oh, Stanley doesn't know yet.

BLANCHE [frightened]: You—haven't told him?

STELLA: He's on the road a good deal.

BLANCHE: Oh. Travels?

STELLA: Yes.

BLANCHE: Good. I mean—isn't it?

STELLA [half to herself]: I can hardly stand it when he is away for a night ...

BLANCHE: Why, Stella!

STELLA: When he's away for a week I nearly go wild!

BLANCHE: Gracious!

STELLA: And when he comes back I cry on his lap like a baby ... [She smiles to herself.]

BLANCHE: I guess that is what is meant by being in love ... [Stella looks up with a radiant smile.] Stella—

STELLA: What?

BLANCHE [in an uneasy rush]: I haven't asked you the things you probably thought I was going to ask. And so I'll expect you to be understanding about what I have to tell you.

STELLA: What, Blanche? [Her face turns anxious.]

BLANCHE: Well, Stella—you're going to reproach me, I know that you're bound to reproach me—but before you do—take into consideration—you left. I stayed and struggled. You came to New Orleans and looked out for yourself! I stayed at Belle Reve and tried to hold it together! I'm not meaning this in any reproachful① way, but all the burden descended on my shoulders.

STELLA: The best I could do was make my own living, Blanche. [Blanche begins to shake again with intensity.]

BLANCHE: I know, I know. But you are the one that abandoned Belle Reve, not I. I stayed and fought for it, bled for it, almost died for it!

STELLA: Stop this hysterical outburst and tell me what's happened? What do you mean fought and bled? What kind of—

BLANCHE: I knew you would, Stella. I knew you would take this attitude about it.

STELLA: About—what? Please!

BLANCHE [slowly]: The loss—the loss ...

STELLA: Belle Reve? Lost, is it? No!

---

① reproachful：表示责备的

BLANCHE: Yes, Stella. [They stare at each other across the yellow-checked linoleum① of the table. Blanche slowly nods her head and Stella looks slowly down at her hands folded on the table. The music of the ("blue piano" grows louder. Blanche touches her handkerchief to her forehead.]

STELLA: But how did it go? What happened?

BLANCHE [springing up]: You're a fine one to ask me how it went!

STELLA: Blanche!

BLANCHE: You're a fine one to sit there accusing me of it!

STELLA: Blanche!

BLANCHE: I, I, I took the blows in my face and my body! All of those deaths! The long parade to the graveyard! Father, mother! Margaret, that dreadful way! So big with it, it couldn't be put in a coffin! But had to be burned like rubbish! You just came home in time for the funerals, Stella. And funerals are pretty compared to deaths. Funerals are quiet, but deaths—not always. Sometimes the air breathing is hoarse, and sometimes it rattles, and sometimes they even cry out to you, "Don't let me go!" Even the old, sometimes, say, "Don't let me go." As if you were able to stop them! But funerals are quiet, with pretty flowers. And, oh, what gorgeous boxes they pack them away in! Unless you were there at the bed when they cried out, "Hold me!" you'd never suspect there was the struggle for breath and bleeding. You didn't dream, but I saw! Saw! Saw! And now you sit there telling me with your eyes that I let the place go! How in hell do you think all that sickness and dying was paid for? Death is expensive, Miss Stella! And old Cousin Jessie's right after Margaret's, hers! Why, the Grim Reaper had put up his tent on our doorstep! ... Stella. Belle Reve was his headquarters! Honey—that's how it slipped through my fingers! Which of them left us a fortune? Which of them left a cent of insurance even? Only poor Jessie—one hundred to pay for her coffin. That was all, Stella! And I with my pitiful salary at the school. Yes, accuse me! Sit there and stare at me, thinking I let the place go! I let the place go? Where were you! In bed with your—Polack!

STELLA [springing]: Blanche! You be still! That's enough! [She starts out.]

BLANCHE: Where are you going?

STELLA: I'm going into the bathroom to wash my face.

BLANCHE: Oh, Stella, Stella, you're crying!

STELLA: Does that surprise you?

BLANCHE: Forgive me—I didn't mean to—[The sound of men's voices is heard. Stella goes into the bathroom, closing the door behind her. The men appear, and

---

① linoleum: 油地毡

[Blanche realizes it must be Stanley returning, she moves uncertainly from the bathroom door to the dressing table, looking apprehensively towards the front door. Stanley enters, followed by Steve and Mitch. Stanley pauses near his door, Steve by the foot of the Spiral stair, and Mitch is slightly above and to the right of them, about to go out. As the men enter, we hear some of the following dialogue.]

STANLEY: Is that how he got it?

STEVE: Sure that's how he got it. He hit the old weather-bird for 300 bucks on a six-number-ticket.

MITCH: Don't tell him those things; he'll believe it. [Mitch starts out.]

STANLEY [restraining Mitch]: Hey, Mitch—come back here. [Blanche, at the sound of voices, retires in the bedroom. She picks up Stanley's photo from dressing table, looks at it, puts it down. When Stanley enters the apartment, she darts① and hides behind the screen at the head of bed.]

STEVE [to Stanley and Mitch]: Hey, are we playin' poker tomorrow?

STANLEY: Sure—at Mitch's.

MITCH [hearing this, returns quickly to the stair rail]: No—not at my place. My mother's still sick.

STANLEY: Okay, at my place ... [Mitch starts out again] But you bring the beer! [Mitch pretends not to hear, calls out "Goodnight all," and goes out, singing. Eunice's voice is heard, above] Break it up down there! I made the spaghetti dish and ate it myself.

STEVE [going upstairs]: I told you and phoned you we were playing. [To the men] Jax beer!

EUNICE: You never phoned me once.

STEVE: I told you at breakfast—and phoned you at lunch ...

EUNICE: Well, never mind about that. You just get yourself home here once in a while.

STEVE: You want it in the papers? [More laughter and shouts of parting come from the men. Stanley throws the screen door of the kitchen open and comes in. He is of medium height, about five feet eight or nine, and strongly, compactly built. Animal joy in his being is implicit in all his movements and attitudes. Since earliest manhood the center of his life has been pleasure with women, the giving and taking of it, not with weak indulgence, dependently, but with the power and pride of a richly feathered male bird among hens. Branching out from this complete and satisfying center are all the auxiliary② channels of his life, such as his heartiness with men, his appreciation of rough humor, his love of good drink and food and games, his car, his radio, everything that is his,

---

① dart: 猛冲
② auxiliary: 辅助的,备用的

that bears his emblem① of the gaudy seed-bearer. He sizes women up at a glance, with sexual classifications, crude images flashing into his mind and determining the way he smiles at them.]

BLANCHE [drawing involuntarily back from his stare]: You must be Stanley. I'm Blanche.

STANLEY: Stella's sister?

BLANCHE: Yes.

STANLEY: H'lo. Where's the little woman?

BLANCHE: In the bathroom.

STANLEY: Oh. Didn't know you were coming in town

BLANCHE: I—uh—

STANLEY: Where you from, Blanche?

BLANCHE: Why, I—live in Laurel. [He has crossed to the closet and removed the whiskey bottle.]

STANLEY: In Laurel, huh? Oh, yeah. Yeah, in Laurel, that's right. Not in my territory. Liquor goes fast in hot weather. [He holds the bottle to the light to observe its depletion②.] Have a shot?

BLANCHE: No, I—rarely touch it.

STANLEY: Some people rarely touch it, but it touches them often.

BLANCHE [faintly]: Ha~ha.

STANLEY: My clothes're stickin' to me. Do you mind if I make myself comfortable? [He starts to remove his shirt.]

BLANCHE: Please, please do.

STANLEY: Be comfortable is my motto.

BLANCHE: It's mine, too. It's hard to stay looking fresh. I haven't washed or even powdered my face and—here you are!

STANLEY: You know you can catch cold sitting around in damp things, especially when you been exercising hard like bowling is. You're a teacher, aren't you?

BLANCHE: Yes.

STANLEY: What do you teach, Blanche?

BLANCHE: English.

STANLEY: I never was a very good English student. How long you here for, Blanche?

BLANCHE: I—don't know yet.

STANLEY: You going to shack up here?

BLANCHE: I thought I would if it's not inconvenient for you all.

STANLEY: Good.

BLANCHE: Traveling wears me out.

---

① emblem: 徽章
② depletion: 耗尽

STANLEY: Well, take it easy. [A cat screeches near the window. Blanche springs up.]
BLANCHE: What's that?
STANLEY: Cats ... Hey, Stella!
STELLA [faintly, from the bathroom]: Yes, Stanley.
STANLEY: Haven't fallen in, have you? [He grins at Blanche. She tries unsuccessfully to smile back. There is a silence.] I'm afraid I'll strike you as being the unrefined type. Stella's spoke of you a good deal. You were married once, weren't you? [The music of the polka① rises up, faint in the distance.]
BLANCHE: Yes. When I was quite young.
STANLEY: What happened?
BLANCHE: The boy—the boy died. [She sinks back down] I'm afraid I'm—going to be sick! [Her head falls on her arms.]

Questions for discussion
1. What does the title of the play stand for?
2. What is expected of a woman in today's society? Consider career, marriage, family. And what is expected of a man?
3. From your perspective, what causes Blanche's tragedy?
4. Do you think Blanche is a southern lady or a wanton woman?

文学术语(Definition of Literary Terms)

Tragedy, according to Aristotle, is "the imitation of an action that is serious and also, as having magnitude, complete in itself," in the medium of poetic language and in the manner of dramatic rather than of narrative presentation, involving "incidents arousing pity and fear, wherewith to accomplish the catharsis of such emotions."

Section B Cultural Notes

Before You Read

1. Try to search on the Internet or in the library about homophobia in the United States and the related information. Give a 3-minute classroom presentation.
2. Do you agree that homophobia should be legalized? Why?

---

① polka：波尔卡舞

Start to Read

Homophobia[①]

Homophobia encompasses a range of negative attitudes and feelings toward homosexuality or people who are identified or perceived as being lesbian, gay, bisexual or transgender (LGBT). It can be expressed as antipathy, contempt, prejudice, aversion[②], or hatred, may be based on irrational fear, and is sometimes related to religious beliefs.

Homophobia is observable in critical and hostile behavior such as discrimination and violence on the basis of sexual orientations that are non-heterosexual[③]. According to the 2010 Hate Crimes Statistics released by the FBI National Press Office, 19.3 percent of hate crimes across the United States "were motivated by a sexual orientation bias." Moreover, in a Southern Poverty Law Center 2010 Intelligence Report extrapolating[④] data from fourteen years (1995-2008), which had complete data available at the time, of the FBI's national hate crime statistics found that LGBT people were "far more likely than any other minority group in the United States to be victimized by violent hate crime."

Recognized types of homophobia include institutionalized homophobia, e.g. religious homophobia and state-sponsored homophobia, and internalized homophobia, experienced by people who have same-sex attractions, regardless of how they identify. Forms of homophobia toward identifiable LGBT social groups have similar yet specific names: lesbophobia—the intersection of homophobia and sexism directed against lesbians, biphobia—towards bisexuality and bisexual people, and transphobia, which targets transsexualism, transsexual and transgender people, and gender variance or gender role nonconformity.

Homophobia manifests in different forms, and a number of different types have been postulated[⑤], among which are internalized homophobia, social homophobia, emotional homophobia, rationalized homophobia, and others. There were also ideas to classify homophobia, racism, and sexism as an intolerant personality disorder.

In 1992, the American Psychiatric Association, recognizing the power of the stigma against homosexuality, issued the following statement, reaffirmed by the Board of Trustees, July 2011: "Whereas homosexuality per se implies no impairment in judgment, stability, reliability, or general social or vocational capabilities, the American Psychiatric Association (APA) calls on all international health organizations, psychiatric

---

① homophobia: 对同性恋者的厌恶和恐惧
② aversion: 厌恶
③ heterosexual: 异性恋
④ extrapolate: 推断,判定
⑤ postulate: 假设

organizations, and individual psychiatrists in other countries to urge the repeal in their own countries of legislation that penalizes homosexual acts by consenting adults in private. Further, APA calls on these organizations and individuals to do all that is possible to decrease the stigma related to homosexuality wherever and whenever it may occur."

The Bible, especially the Old Testament, contains some passages commonly interpreted ascondemning homosexuality or same-gender sexual relations. Leviticus 18:22, says "Thou shalt not lie with mankind, as with womankind: it is abomination①." The destruction of Sodom and Gomorrah is also commonly seen as a condemnation② of **homosexuality.** Christians and Jews who oppose homosexuality often cite such passages; historical context and interpretation is more complicated. Scholarly debate over the interpretation of these passages has focused on placing them in proper historical context, for instance pointing out that Sodom's sins are historically interpreted as being other than homosexuality, and on the translation of rare or unusual words in the passages in question. In *Religion Dispatches* magazine, Candace Chellew-Hodge argues that the six or so verses that are often cited to condemn LGBT people are referring instead to "abusive sex." She states that the Bible has no condemnation for "loving, committed, gay and lesbian relationships" and that Jesus was silent on the subject.

In the United States, attitudes about people who are homosexual may vary on the basis of partisan identification. Republicans are far more likely than Democrats to have negative attitudes about people who are gay and lesbian, according to surveys conducted by the National Election Studies from 2000 through 2004. This disparity is shown in the graph on the right, which is from a 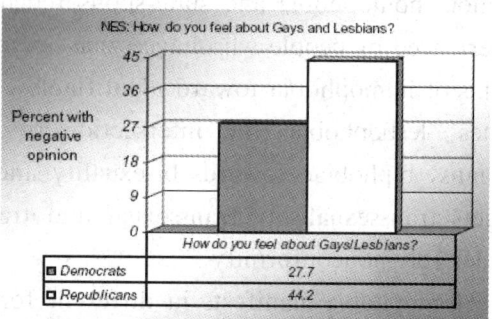 book published in 2008 by Joseph Fried. The tendency of Republicans to view gay and lesbian people negatively could be based on homophobia, religious beliefs, or conservatism with respect to the traditional family. Homophobia also varies by region; statistics show that the Southern United States has more reports of anti-gay prejudice than any other region in the US.

After You Read

I. Questions for discussion

1. What is the definition of homophobia?

---

① abomination: 憎恶
② condemnation: 谴责,指责

2. How many types of homophobia are there?
3. What was the percentage of hate crimes across the United States motivated by a sexual orientation bias?
4. What strategies has APA applied to assist homosexuality?
5. What was the attitude of Jesus towards homosexuality?
6. Why do Republicans view gay and lesbian people negatively?

II. True or false
1. Homophobia is observable in critical and hostile behavior such as discrimination and violence on the basis of sexual orientations that are non-heterosexual. (   )
2. Biphobia is the intersection of homophobia and sexism directed against lesbians. (   )
3. APA tries hard to increase the stigma related to homosexuality wherever and whenever it may occur. (   )
4. Christians and Jews who oppose homosexuality often cite such passages; historical context and interpretation is more complicated. (   )
5. In the United States, attitudes about people who are homosexual do not vary on the basis of partisan identification. (   )
6. Statistics show that the Southern United States has more reports of anti-gay prejudice than any other region in the US. (   )

For Fun

I. Movies to see

A Streetcar Named Desire (1951): It is a 1951 American drama film, with elements of film noir, an adaptation of Tennessee Williams's Pulitzer Prize-winning 1947 play of the same name. It is the story of a southern belle, Blanche Dubois, who, after encountering a series of personal losses, leaves her aristocratic background seeking refuge with her sister and brother-in-law in a dilapidated New Orleans tenement.

II. Websites to visit
1. http://vivien-leigh.info/
2. http://www.theguardian.com/culture/tennesseewilliams

III. Writing

Someone believes that people have benefited from modern communication technology, while others believe that some people do not benefit at all. Which opinion do you agree with?

Arthur Miller (1915–2005)
阿瑟·米勒

Section A Literary Focus

作者简介(About the Author)

【生平】 阿瑟·米勒是美国最杰出的戏剧大师之一,被誉为"美国戏剧的良心",出生于美国纽约一个犹太商人家庭。30 年代初美国经济的大萧条时期,他的父亲破产,家里生计维艰。中学毕业后,米勒一边打工一边在密歇根大学新闻系和英文系学习,并开始创作剧本。1947 年,阿瑟·米勒的成名作《都是我的儿子》上演。两年后,《推销员之死》在百老汇连续上演了 742 场,一举囊括了托尼奖、普利策奖和纽约剧评界奖,从而使阿瑟·米勒赢得国际声誉。另外,米勒还创作了《萨勒姆女巫》、《桥头眺望》《美国时钟》等剧,均针砭时弊,对社会现实和戏剧技巧作了深刻的探索,体现了米勒对社会问题的直面追问,以及对人性、理智、社会正义等问题的犀利见解。自传体剧本《堕落之后》记述了他与好莱坞名演员玛丽莲·梦露一段并不成功的婚姻生活,也深刻剖析了左翼知识分子的内心。1978 年,米勒来华访问,回国后出版《访问中国》一书。1981 年,《萨勒姆女巫》在华上演,获得很大成功。1983 年,米勒再度来华,亲自执导《推销员之死》,次年出版《"推销员"在北京》一书,从此他和中国结下了不解之缘。

【主要作品】 《都是我的儿子》(*All My Sons*,1947),《推销员之死》(*Death of a Salesman*,1949),《萨勒姆的女巫》(*The Crucible*,1953),《代价》(*The Price*,1968)等。

作品选读(Selected Writings)

Death of a Salesman

《推销员之死》是米勒于 1949 年写的揭露美国梦瑕疵的一本书,该书使米勒成为一代大师,获得若干奖项,被称为 20 世纪美国戏剧的里程碑。作品通过两代人的失败,否定了人人都能成功的"美国神话",在结构安排、时空处理、人物形象刻画和内心复杂情感的描写上都取得了很高的成就。该书被誉为"美国梦不再"的代表作。作品在百老汇首演后获得巨大成功,震惊了美国剧坛,为 33 岁的米勒在美国戏剧界奠定了大师的地位。

《推销员之死》讲述了年逾花甲的推销员威利·洛曼悲剧性的经历。壮年时代的威利精明强干,两个儿子比夫和哈皮,是他的骄傲。尽管比夫的学习成绩不及格,也没有引起做父亲的重视,因为,他确认比夫将来完全可以当一名体育明星。然而,事与愿违,大儿子比夫多次离家出走,不愿留在充满竞争与欺诈的大城市里。在沉重的压力下,威利的精神恍惚不定。为了拯救威利,老伴儿林达把威利要自杀的企图告诉了儿子们。小儿子哈皮想出一个办法,让比夫向朋友借钱,由洛曼兄弟独立经营,干出一番事业。为了预祝未来理想的实现,父子们约定在餐馆中聚会。而就在他们见面时,双方带来的都是不幸的消息:比夫没有借到钱,威利也被公司开除了。这使得父子间又发生了激烈的争吵。最终,为了死后的保险赔偿给家人带来福利,威利还是自杀了。

Act II (Excerpt)

[*The knocking is heard again. He takes a few steps away from her, and she vanishes*① *into the wing. The light follows him, and now he is facing* YOUNG BIFF, *who carries a suitcase.* BIFF *steps toward him. The music is gone.*]

Biff: Why didn't you answer?

Willy: Biff! What are you doing in Boston?

Biff: Why didn't you answer! I've been knocking for five minutes, I called you on the phone—

Willy: I just heard you. I was in the bathroom and had the door shut. Did anything happen home?

Biff: Dad—I let you down.

Willy: What do you mean?

Biff: Dad ...

Willy: Biff, what's this about? [*Putting his arm around* BIFF] Come on, let's go downstairs and get you a malted②.

Biff: Dad, I flunked③ math.

Willy: Not for the term?

Biff: The term. I haven't got enough credits to graduate.

Willy: You mean to say Bernard wouldn't give you the answers?

Biff: He did, he tried, but I only got a sixty-one.

Willy: And they wouldn't give you four points?

Biff: Birnbaum refused absolutely. I begged him, Pop, but he won't give me those points. You gotta talk to him before they close the school. Because if he saw the kind of man you are, and you just talked to him in your way, I'm sure he'd come through for me. The class came right before practice, see, and I didn't go enough. Would you talk to him? He'd like you, Pop. You know the way you could talk.

---

① vanish:消失
② malted:麦乳精
③ flunk:不及格

Willy: You're on. We'll drive right back.

Biff: Oh, Dad, good work! I'm sure he'll change it for you!

Willy: Go downstairs and tell the clerk I'm checkin' out. Go right down.

Biff: Yes, sir! See, the reason he hates me, Pop—one day he was late for class so I got up at the blackboard and imitated him. I crossed my eyes and talked with a lithp①.

Willy [*laughing*]: You did? The kids like it?

Biff: They nearly died laughing!

Willy: Yeah? What'd you do?

Biff: The thquare root of thixthy twee is … [WILLY *bursts out laughing*; BIFF *joins him*] And in the middle of it he walked in!

[WILLY *laughs and the* WOMAN *joins in offstage.*]

Willy [*without hesitation*]: Hurry downstairs and—

Biff: Somebody in there?

Willy: No, that was next door.

[*The* WOMAN *laughs offstage.*]

Biff: Somebody got in your bathroom!

Willy: No, it's the next room, there's a party—

The Woman [*enters, laughing. She lisps this*]: Can I come in? There's something in the bathtub, Willy, and its moving!

[WILLY *looks at* BIFF, *who is staring open-mouthed and horrified at the* WOMAN.]

Willy: Ah—you better go back to your room. They must be finished painting by now. They're painting her room so I let her take a shower here. Go back, go back … [*He pushes her.*]

The Woman [*resisting*]: But I've got to get dressed, Willy, I can't—

Willy: Get out of here! Go back, go back … [*Suddenly striving for the ordinary.*] This is Miss Francis, Biff, she's a buyer. They're painting her room. Go back, Miss Francis, go back …

The Woman: But my clothes, I can't go out naked in the hall!

Willy [*pushing her offstage*]: Get outa here! Go back, go back!

[BIFF *slowly sits down on his suitcase as the argument continues offstage.*]

The Woman: Where's my stockings? You promised me stockings, Willy!

Willy: I have no stockings here!

The Woman: You had two boxes of size nine sheers for me, and I want them!

Willy: Here, for God's sake, will you get outa here!

The Woman [*enters holding a box of stockings*]: I just hope there's nobody in the hall. That's all I hope. [*To* BIFF] Are you football or baseball?

---

① lithp：lisp 咬舌发音

Biff: Football.

The Woman [*angry, humiliated*]: That's me too. G'night. [*She snatches her clothes from* WILLY, *and walks out.*]

Willy [*after a pause*]: Well, better get going. I want to get to the school first thing in the morning. Get my suits out of the closet. I'll get my valise①. [BIFF *doesn't move.*] What's the matter? [BIFF *remains motionless, tears falling.*] She's a buyer. Buys for J. H. Simmons. She lives down the hall—they're painting. You don't imagine—[*He breaks off. After a pause.*] Now listen, pal, she's just a buyer. She sees merchandise in her room and they have to keep it looking just so ... [*Pause. Assuming command.*] All right, get my suits. [BIFF *doesn't move.*] Now stop crying and do as I say. I gave you an *order*. Biff, I gave you an order! Is that what you do when I give you an order? How dare you cry? [*Putting his arm around* BIFF.] Now look, Biff, when you grow up you'll understand about these things. You mustn't—you mustn't overemphasize a thing like this. I'll see Birnbaum first thing in the morning.

Biff: Never mind.

Willy [*getting down beside* BIFF]: Never mind! He's going to give you those points. I'll see to it.

Biff: He wouldn't listen to you.

Willy: He certainly will listen to me. You need those points for the U of Virginia.

Biff: I'm not going there.

Willy: Heh? If I can't get him to change that mark you'll make it up in Summer school. You've got all summer to—

Biff [*his weeping breaking from him*]: Dad ...

Willy [*infected by it*]: Oh, my boy ...

Biff: Dad ...

Willy: She's nothing to me, Biff. I was lonely, I was terribly lonely.

Biff: You—you gave her Mama's stockings! [*His tears break through and he rises* to go.]

Willy [*grabbing for* BIFF]: I gave you an order!

Biff: Don't touch me, you—liar!

Willy: Apologize for that!

Biff: You fake! You phony② little fake! You fake! [*Overcome, he turns quickly and weeping fully goes* out *with his suitcase.* WILLY *is left on the floor on his knees.*]

Willy: I gave you an order! Biff, come back here or I'll beat you! Come back here! I'll whip you!

---

① valise：旅行箱
② phony：欺骗的

[STANLEY *comes quickly in from the right and stands in front of* WILLY.]

Willy [*shouts at* STANLEY]: I gave you an order ...

Stanley: Hey, let's pick it up, pick it up, Mr Loman. [*He helps* WILLY *to his feet*.] Your boys left with the chippies①. They said they'll see you home.

[*A second waiter watches some distance away*.]

Willy: But we were supposed to have dinner together.

[*Music is heard*, WILLY'S *theme*.]

Stanley: Can you make it?

Willy: I'll—sure, I can make it. [*Suddenly concerned about his clothes*] Do I—I look all right?

Stanley: Sure, you look all right. [*He flicks a speck off* WILLY'S *lapel*②.]

Willy: Here—here's a dollar.

Stanley: Oh, your son paid me. It's all right.

Willy [*putting it in* STANLEY'S *hand*]: No, take it. You're a good boy.

Stanley: Oh, no, you don't have to ...

Willy: Here—here's some more. I don't need it any more. [*After a slight pause*] Tell me—is there a seed store in the neighbourhood?

Stanley: Seeds? You mean like to plant?

[*As* WILLY *turns*, STANLEY *slips the money back into his jacket pocket*.]

Willy: Yes. Carrots, peas ...

Stanley: Well, there's hardware stores on Sixth Avenue, but it may be too late now.

Willy [*anxiously*]: Oh, I'd better hurry. I've got to get some seeds. [*He starts off to the right*.] I've got to get some seeds, right away. Nothing's planted. I don't have a thing in the ground.

[WILLY *hurries out as the light goes down*. STANLEY *moves over to the right after him, watches him off. The other waiter has been staring at* WILLY.]

Stanley [*to the waiter*]: Well, whatta you looking at?

[*The waiter picks up the chairs and moves off right*. STANLEY *takes the table and follows him. The light fades on this area. There is a long pause, the sound of the flute coming over. The light gradually rises on the kitchen, which is empty*. HAPPY *appears at the door of the house, followed by* BIFF. HAPPY *is carrying a large bunch of long-stemmed roses. He enters the kitchen, looks around for* LINDA. *Not seeing her, he turns to* BIFF, *who is just outside the house door, and makes a gesture with his hands, indicating* 'Not here, I guess'. *He looks into the living-room and freezes. Inside*, LINDA, *unseen, is seated*, WILLY'S *coat on her lap. She rises ominously*③ *and quietly moves*

---

① chippy：放浪女子
② lapel：西服上的翻领
③ ominously：不吉利地

toward HAPPY, who backs up into the kitchen, afraid.]

Happy: Hey, what're you doing up? [LINDA *says nothing but moves toward him implacably.*] Where's Pop? [*He keeps backing to the right, and now* LINDA *is in full view in the doorway to the living-room.*] Is he sleeping?

Linda: Where were you?

Happy [*trying to laugh it off*]: We met two girls, Mom, very fine types. Here, we brought you some flowers. [*Offering them to her*] Put them in your room, Ma.

[She knocks them to the floor at BIFF'S feet. He has now come inside and closed the door behind him. She stares at BIFF, silent.]

Happy: Now what'd you do that for? Mom, I want you to have some flowers—

Linda [*cutting* HAPPY *off, violently to* BIFF]: Don't you care whether he lives or dies?

Happy [*going to the stairs*]: Come upstairs, Biff.

Biff [*with a flare of disgust, to* HAPPY]: Go away from me! [*To* LINDA] What do you mean, lives or dies? Nobody's dying around here, pal.

Linda: Get out of my sight! Get out of here!

Biff: I wanna see the boss.

Linda: You're not going near him!

Biff: Where is *he*? [*He moves into the living-room and* LINDA *follows.*]

Linda [*shouting after* BIFF]: You invite him to dinner. He looks forward to it all day—[BIFF *appears in his parents' bedroom, looks around, and exits*]—and then you desert him there. There's no stranger you'd do that to!

Happy: Why? He had a swell time with us. Listen, when I—[LINDA *comes back into the kitchen*]—desert him I hope I don't outlive the day!

Linda: Get out of here!

Happy: Now look, Mom ...

Linda: Did you have to go to women tonight? You and your lousy① rotten whores②!

[BIFF *re-enters the kitchen.*]

Happy: Mom, all we did was follow Biff around trying to cheer him up! [*To* BIFF] Boy, what a night you gave me!

Linda: Get out of here, both of you, and don't come back! I don't want you tormenting him any more. Go on now, get your things together! [*To* BIFF] You can sleep in his apartment. [*She starts to pick up the flowers and stops herself.*] Pick up this stuff, I'm not your maid any more. Pick it up, you bum③, you!

[HAPPY *turns his back to her in refusal.* BIFF *slowly moves over and gets down on*

---

① lousy: 讨厌的
② whore: 荡妇,娼妓
③ bum: 流浪汉,无赖

his knees, picking up the flowers.]

Linda: You're a pair of animals! Not one, not another living soul would have had the cruelty to walk out on that man in a restaurant!

Biff [*not looking at her*]: Is that what he said?

Linda: He didn't have to say anything. He was so humiliated he nearly limped when he came in.

Happy: But, Mom, he had a great time with us—

Biff [*cutting him off violently*]: Shut up!

[*Without another word*, HAPPY *goes upstairs.*]

Linda: You! You didn't even go in to see if he was all right!

Biff [*still on the floor in front of* LINDA, *the flowers in his hand; with self-loathing*①]: No. Didn't. Didn't do a damned thing. How do you like that, heh? Left him babbling in a toilet.

Linda: You louse. You ...

Biff: Now you hit it on the nose! [*He gets up, throws the flowers in the wastebasket.*] The scum of the earth, and you're looking at him!

Linda: Get out of here!

Biff: I gotta talk to the boss, Mom. Where is he?

Linda: You're not going near him. Get out of this house!

Biff [*with absolute assurance, determination*]: No. We're gonna have an abrupt conversation, him and me.

Linda: You're not talking to him!

[*Hammering is heard from outside the house, off right.* BIFF *turns toward the noise.*]

Linda [*suddenly pleading*]: Will you please leave him alone?

Biff: What's he doing out there?

Linda: He's planting the garden!

Biff [*quietly*]: Now? Oh, my God!

[BIFF *moves outside,* LINDA *following. The light dies down on them and comes up on the centre of the apron as* WILLY *walks into it. He is carrying a flashlight, a hoe, and a handful of seed packets. He raps the top of the hoe sharply to fix it firmly, and then moves to the left, measuring off the distance with his foot. He holds the flashlight to look at the seed packets, reading off the instructions. He is in the blue of night.*]

Willy: Carrots ... quarter-inch apart. Rows ... one-foot rows. [*He measures it off.*] One foot. [*He puts down a package and measures off.*] Beets. [*He puts down another package, and measures again.*] Lettuce. [*He reads the package, puts it down.*] One foot—[*He breaks off as* BEN *appears at the right and moves slowly

---

① self-loathing: 自我讨厌的

down to him.] What a proposition, ts, ts. Terrific, terrific. 'Cause she's suffered, Ben, the woman has suffered. You understand me? A man can't go out the way he came in, Ben, a man has got to add up to something. You can't, you can't—[BEN *moves toward him as though to interrupt.*] You gotta consider, now. Don't answer so quick. Remember, it's a guaranteed twenty-thousand-dollar proposition. Now look, Ben, I want you to go through the ins and outs of this thing with me. I've got nobody to talk to, Ben, and the woman has suffered, you hear me?

Ben [*standing still, considering*]: What's the proposition?

Willy: It's twenty thousand dollars on the barrelhead. Guaranteed, gilt-edged①, you understand?

Ben: You don't want to make a fool of yourself. They might not honour the policy.

Willy: How can they dare refuse? Didn't I work like a coolie to meet every premium on the nose? And now they don't pay off! Impossible!

Ben: It's called a cowardly thing, William.

Willy: Why? Does it take more guts to stand here the rest of my life ringing up a zero?

Ben [*yielding*]: That's a point, William. [*He moves, thinking, turns.*] And twenty thousand—that is something one can feel with the hand, it is there.

Willy [*now assured, with rising power*]: Oh, Ben, that's the whole beauty of it! I see it like a diamond, shining in the dark, hard and rough, that I can pick up and touch in my hand. Not like—like an appointment! This would not be another damned-fool appointment, Ben, and it changes all the aspects. Because he thinks I'm nothing, see, and so he spites me. But the funeral—[*Straightening up*] Ben, that funeral will be massive! They'll come from Maine, Massachusetts, Vermont, New Hampshire! All the old-timers② with the strange licence plates—that boy will be thunderstruck, Ben, because he never realized—I am known! Rhode Island, New York, New Jersey—I am known, Ben, and he'll see it with his eyes once and for all. He'll see what I am, Ben! He's in for a shock, that boy!

Ben [*coming down to the edge of the garden*]: He'll call you a coward.

Willy [*suddenly fearful*]: No, that would be terrible.

Ben: Yes. And a damned fool.

Willy: No, no, he mustn't, I won't have that! [*He is broken and desperate.*]

Ben: He'll hate you, William.

[*The gay music of the boys is heard.*]

Willy: Oh, Ben, how do we get back to all the great times? Used to be so full of light,

---

① gilt-edged: 最上等的
② old-timer: 老资格的人，老前辈

and comradeship, the sleigh-riding① in winter, and the ruddiness on his cheeks. And always some kind of good news coming up, always something nice coming up ahead. And never even let me carry the valises in the house, and simonizing, simonizing that little red car! Why, why can't I give him something and not have him hate me?

Ben: Let me think about it. [*He glances at his watch.*] I still have a little time. Remarkable proposition, but you've got to be sure you're not making a fool of yourself.

[BEN *drifts off upstage and goes out of sight*. BIFF *comes down from the left*.]

Willy [*suddenly conscious of* BIFF, *turns and looks up at him, then begins picking up the packages of seeds in confusion*]: Where the hell is that seed? [*Indignantly*] You can't see nothing out here! They boxed in the whole goddamn neighbourhood!

Biff: There are people all around here. Don't you realize that?

Willy: I'm busy. Don't bother me.

Biff [*taking the hoe from* WILLY]: I'm saying good-bye to you, Pop. [WILLY *looks at him, silent, unable to move.*] I'm not coming back any more.

Willy: You're not going to see Oliver tomorrow?

Biff: I've got no appointment, Dad.

Willy: He put his arm around you, and you've got no appointment?

Biff: Pop, get this now, will you? Everytime I've left it's been a fight that sent me out of here. Today I realized something about myself and I tried to explain it to you and I—I think I'm just not smart enough to make any sense out of it for you. To hell with whose fault it is or anything like that. [*He takes* WILLY'S *arm.*] Let's just wrap it up, heh? Come on in, we'll tell Mom. [*He gently tries to pull* WILLY *to left.*]

Willy [*frozen, immobile, with guilt in his voice*]: No, I don't want to see her.

Biff: Come on! [*He pulls again, and* WILLY *tries to pull away.*]

Willy [*highly nervous*]: No, no, I don't want to see her.

Biff [*tries to look into* WILLY'S *face, as if to find the answer there*]: Why don't you want to see her?

Willy [*more harshly now*]: Don't bother me, will you?

Biff: What do you mean, you don't want to see her? You don't want them calling you yellow, do you? This isn't your fault; it's me, I'm a bum. Now come inside! [WILLY *strains to get away.*] Did you hear what I said to you?

[WILLY *pulls away and quickly goes by himself into the house.* BIFF *follows.*]

Linda [*to* WILLY]: Did you plant, dear?

Biff [*at the door, to* LINDA]: All right, we had it out. I'm going and I'm not

---

① sleigh-riding: 骗局

writing any more.

Linda [*going to* WILLY *in the kitchen*]: I think that's the best way, dear. 'Cause there's no use drawing it out, you'll just *never* get along.

[WILLY *doesn't respond.*]

Biff: People ask where I am and what I'm doing, you don't know, and you don't care. That way it'll be off your mind and you can start brightening up again. All right? That clears it, doesn't it? [WILLY *is silent, and* BIFF *goes to him.*] You gonna wish me luck, scout! [H*e extends his hand*] What do you say?

Linda: Shake his hand, Willy.

Willy [*turning to her, seething with hurt*]: There's no necessity to mention the pen at all, y'know.

Biff [*gently*]: I've got no appointment, Dad.

Willy [*erupting fiercely*]: He put his arm around ... ?

Biff: Dad, you're never going to see what I am, so what's the use of arguing? If I strike oil① I'll send you a cheque. Meantime forget I'm alive.

Willy [*to* LINDA]: Spite, see?

Biff: Shake hands, Dad.

Willy: Not my hand.

Biff: I was hoping not go this way.

Willy: Well, this is the way you're going. Good-bye.

[BIFF *looks at him a moment, then turns sharply and goes to the stairs.*]

Willy [*stops him with*]: May you rot in hell if you leave this house!

Biff [*turning*]: Exactly what is it that you want from me?

Willy: I want you to know, on the train, in the mountains, in the valleys, wherever you go, that you cut down your life for spite!

Biff: No, no.

Willy: Spite, spite, is the word of your undoing! And when you're down and out, remember what did it. When you're rotting somewhere beside the railroad tracks, remember, and don't you dare blame it on me!

Biff: I'm not blaming it on you!

Willy: I won't take the rap for this, you hear?

[HAPPY *comes down the stairs and stands on the bottom step, watching.*]

Biff: That's just what I'm telling you!

Willy [*sinking into a chair at the table, with full accusation*]: You're trying to put a knife in me—don't think I don't know what you're doing!

Biff: All right, phony! Then let's lay it on the line. [*He whips the rubber tube out of his pocket and puts it on the table.*]

---

① strike oil: 飞黄腾达

Happy: You crazy—

Linda: Biff! [*She moves to grab the hose, but* BIFF *holds it down with his hand.*]

Biff: Leave it there! Don't move it!

Willy [*not looking at it*]: What is that?

Biff: You know goddam well what that is.

Willy [*caged, wanting to escape*]: I never saw that.

Biff: You saw it. The mice didn't bring it into the cellar! What is this supposed to do, make a hero out of you? This supposed to make me sorry for you?

Willy: Never heard of it.

Biff: There'll be no pity for you, you hear it? No pity!

Willy [*to* LINDA]: You hear the spite!

Biff: No, you're going to hear the truth—what you are and what I am!

Linda: Stop it!

Willy: Spite!

Happy [*coming down toward* BIFF]: You cut it now!

Biff [*to* HAPPY]: The man don't know who we are! The man is gonna know! [*To* WILLY] —We never told the truth for ten minutes in this house!

Happy: We always told the truth!

Biff [*turning on him*]: You big blow, are you the assistant buyer? You're one of the two assistants to the assistant, aren't you?

Happy: Well, I'm practically—

Biff: You're practically full of it! We all are! And I'm through with It. [*To* WILLY] Now hear this, Willy, this is me.

Willy: I know you!

Biff: You know why I had no address for three months? I stole a suit in Kansas City and I was in jail. [*To* LINDA, *who is sobbing*] Stop crying. I'm through with it.

[LINDA *turns away from them, her hands covering her face.*]

Willy: I suppose that's my fault!

Biff: I stole myself out of every good job since high school!

Willy: And whose fault is that?

Biff: And I never got anywhere because you blew me so full of hot air I could never stand taking orders from anybody! That's whose fault it is!

Willy: I hear that!

Linda: Don't, Biff!

Biff: It's goddam time you heard that! I had to be boss big shot in two weeks and I'm through with it!

Willy: Then hang yourself! For spite, hang yourself!

Biff: No! Nobody's hanging himself, Willy! I ran down eleven flights with a pen in my hand today. And suddenly I stopped, you hear me? And in the middle of that office building, do you hear this? I stopped in the middle of that building and I saw—the sky. I saw the things that I love in this world. The work and the food and time to sit and smoke. And I looked at the pen and said to myself, what the hell am I grabbing this for? Why am I trying to become what I don't want to be? What am I doing in an office, making a contemptuous①, begging fool of myself, when all I want is out there, waiting for me the minute I say I know who I am! Why can't I say that, Willy? [*He tries to make* WILLY *face him, but* WILLY *pulls away and moves to the left.*]

Willy [*with hatred, threateningly*]: The door of your life is wide open!

Biff: Pop! I'm a dime a dozen, and so are you!

Willy [*turning on him now in an uncontrolled outburst*]: I am not a dime a dozen! I am Willy Loman, and you are Biff Loman!

[BIFF *starts for* WILLY, *but is blocked by* HAPPY. *In his fury,* BIFF *seems on the verge of attacking his father.*]

Biff: I am not a leader of men, Willy, and neither are you. You were never anything but a hard-working drummer② who landed in the ash-can like all the rest of them! I'm one dollar an hour, Willy! I tried seven states and couldn't raise it. A buck an hour! Do you gather my meaning? I'm not bringing home any prizes any more, and you're going to stop waiting for me to bring them home!

Willy [*directly to* BIFF]: You vengeful, spiteful mut!

[BIFF *breaks from* HAPPY. WILLY, *in fright, starts up the stairs.* BIFF *grabs him.*]

Biff [*at the peak of his fury*]: Pop, I'm nothing! I'm nothing! Pop. Can't you understand that? There's no spite in it any more, I'm just what I am, that's all.

[BIFF's *fury has spent itself, and he breaks down, sobbing, holding on to* WILLY, *who dumbly fumbles for* BIFF's *face.*]

Willy [*astonished*]: What're you doing? What're you doing? [*To* LINDA] Why is he crying?

Biff [*crying, broken*]: Will you let me go, for Christ's sake? Will you take that phony dream and burn it before something happens? [*Struggling to contain himself, he pulls away and moves to the stairs.*] I'll go in the morning. Put him—put him to bed. [*Exhausted,* BIFF *moves up the stairs to his room.*]

Willy [*after a long pause, astonished, elevated*]: Isn't that—isn't that remarkable? Biff—he likes me!

Linda: He loves you, Willy!

Happy [*deeply moved*]: Always did, Pop.

Willy: Oh, Biff! [*Staring wildly*] He cried! Cried to me. [*He is choking with his*

---

① contemptuous: 轻蔑的
② drummer: 旅行推销员

love, and now cries out his promise] That boy—that boy is going to be magnificent①!

[BEN *appears in the light just outside the kitchen.*]

Ben: Yes, outstanding, with twenty thousand behind him

Linda [*sensing the racing of his mind, fearfully, carefully*]: Now come to bed, Willy. It's all settled now.

Willy [*finding it difficult not to rush out of the house*]: Yes, we'll sleep. Come on. Go to sleep, Hap.

Ben: And it does take a great kind of a man to crack the jungle.

[*In accents of dread*, BEN's *idyllic music starts up.*]

Happy [*his arm around* LINDA]: I'm getting married, Pop, don't forget it. I'm changing everything. I'm gonna run that department before the year is up. You'll see, Mom. [*He kisses her.*]

Ben: The jungle is dark but full of diamonds, Willy.

[WILLY *turns, moves, listening to* BEN.]

Linda: Be good. You're both good boys, just act that way, that's all.

Happy: 'Night, Pop. [*He goes upstairs.*]

Linda [*to* WILLY]: Come, dear.

Ben [*with greater force*]: One must go in to fetch a diamond out.

Willy [*to* LINDA, *as he moves slowly along the edge of the kitchen, toward the door*]: I just want to get settled down, Linda. Let me sit alone for a little.

Linda [*almost uttering her fear*]: I want you upstairs.

Willy [*taking her in his arms*]: In a few minutes, Linda. I couldn't sleep right now. Go on, you look awful tired. [*He kisses her.*]

Ben: Not like an appointment at all. A diamond is rough and hard to the touch.

Willy: Go on now. I'll be right up.

Linda: I think this is the only way, Willy.

Willy: Sure, it's the best thing.

Ben: Best thing!

Willy: The only way. Everything is gonna be—go on, kid, get to bed. You look so tired.

Linda: Come right up.

Willy: Two minutes.

[LINDA *goes into the living-room, then reappears in her bedroom.* WILLY *moves just outside the kitchen door.*]

Willy: Loves *me.* [*Wonderingly*] Always loved me. Isn't that a remarkable thing? Ben, he'll worship me for it!

Ben [*with promise*]: It's dark there, but full of diamonds.

---

① magnificent：杰出的

Willy:	Can you imagine that magnificence with twenty thousand dollars in his pocket?
Linda	[*calling from her room*]: Willy! Come up!
Willy	[*calling into the kitchen*]: Yes! Yes. Coming! It's very smart, you realize that, don't you, sweetheart? Even Ben sees it. I gotta go, baby. 'Bye! 'Bye! [*Going over to BEN, almost dancing*] Imagine? When the mail comes he'll be ahead of Bernard again!
Ben:	A perfect proposition all around.
Willy:	Did you see how he cried to me? Oh, if I could kiss him, Ben!
Ben:	Time, William, time!
Willy:	Oh, Ben, I always knew one way or another we were gonna make it, Biff and I!
Ben	[*looking at his watch*]: The boat. We'll be late. [*He moves slowly off into the darkness.*]
Willy	[*elegiacally, turning to the house*]: Now when you kick off, boy, I want a seventy-yard boot, and get right down the field under the ball, and when you hit, hit low and hit hard, because it's important, boy. [*He swings around and faces the audience.*] There's all kinds of important people in the stands, and the first thing you know ... [*Suddenly realizing he is alone*] Ben! Ben, where do I ... ? [*He makes a sudden movement of search.*] Ben, how do I ... ?
Linda	[*calling*]: Willy, you coming up?
Willy	[*uttering a gasp of fear, whirling about as if to quiet her*]: Sh! [*He turns around as if to find his way; sounds, faces, voices, seem to be swarming in upon him and he flicks at them, crying, 'Sh! Sh!' Suddenly music, faint and high, stops him. It rises in intensity, almost to an unbearable scream. He goes up and down on his toes, and rushes off around the house*] Shhh!
Linda:	Willy?
	[*There is no answer. LINDA waits. BIFF gets up off his bed. He is still in his clothes. HAPPY sits up. BIFF stands listening.*]
Linda	[*with real fear*]: Willy, answer me! Willy!
	[*There is the sound of a car starting and moving away at full speed.*]
Linda:	No!
Biff	[*rushing down the stairs*]: Pop!
	[As the car speeds off, the music crashes down in a frenzy of sound, which becomes the soft pulsation① of a single cello string. BIFF slowly returns to his bedroom. He and HAPPY gravely don their jackets. LINDA slowly walks out of her room. The music has developed into a dead march. The leaves of day are appearing over everything. CHARLEY and BERNARD, sombrely② dressed,

---

① pulsation: 脉动
② sombrely: 忧郁地

appear and knock on the kitchen door. BIFF and HAPPY slowly descend the stairs to the kitchen as CHARLEY and BERNARD enter. All stop a moment when LINDA, in clothes of mourning, bearing a little bunch of roses, comes through the draped doorway into the kitchen. She goes to CHARLEY and takes his arm. Now all move toward the audience, through the wall-line of the kitchen. At the limit of the *apron*, LINDA *lays down the flowers, kneels, and sits back on her heels. All stare down at the grave.*]

Questions for discussion
1. What are the causes that make Willy commit suicide?
2. What role does Ben play in Willy's final decision to kill himself for the insurance money?

文学术语(Definition of Literary Terms)

The American Dream is a national ethos of the United States, a set of ideals in which freedom includes the opportunity for prosperity and success, and an upward social mobility achieved through hard work.

Section B   Cultural Notes

Before You Read

1. Try to search on the Internet or in the library about the American Dream and the related information. Give a 3-minute classroom presentation.
2. Do you know anything about drama? Share your information with your partners.
3. Do you know Marilyn Monroe? Briefly summarize her life.

Start to Read

Marilyn Monroe

Norma Jean Baker, better known as Marilyn Monroe, experienced a disrupted, loveless childhood that included two years at an orphanage. When Norma Jean, born on June 1, 1926, was seven years old her mother, Gladys (Monroe) Baker Mortenson, was diagnosed as a paranoid schizophrenic and hospitalized. Norma was left to a series of foster homes and the Los Angeles Orphans' Home Society. She opted for an early marriage on June 19, 1942, and her husband, James Dougherty, joined the U. S. Merchant Marine in 1943.

During the war years Norma Jean worked at the Radio Plane Company in Van

Nuys, California, but she was soon discovered by photographers. She enrolled in a 3-month modeling course, and in 1946, aware of her considerable charm and the potential it had for a career in films, Norma obtained a divorce. She headed for Hollywood, where Ben Lyon, head of casting at Twentieth Century Fox, arranged a screen test. On August 26, 1946, she signed a $125 a week, one-year contract with the studio. Ben Lyon was the one who suggested a new name for the **fledgling** actress—Marilyn Monroe.

During her first year at Fox Monroe did not appear in any films, and her contract was not renewed. In the spring of 1948 Columbia Pictures hired her for a small part in *Ladies of the Chorus*. In 1950 John Huston cast her in *Asphalt Jungle*, a tiny part which landed her a role in *All About Eve*. She was now given a seven-year contract with Twentieth Century Fox and appeared in *The Fireball*, *Let's Make It Legal*, *Love Nest*, and *As Young as You Feel*.

In 1952, after an extensive publicity campaign, Monroe appeared in *Don't Bother to Knock*, *Full House*, *Clash by Night*, *We're Not Married*, *Niagara*, and *Monkey Business*. After this the magazine Photoplay termed her the "most promising actress", and she was earning top dollars for Twentieth Century Fox.

On January 14, 1954, she married Yankee baseball player Joe DiMaggio. But the pressures created by her billing as a screen sex symbol caused the marriage to founder, and the couple divorced on October 27, 1954.

Continually cast as a dumb blond, Monroe made *Seven Year Itch* in 1954. Growing weary of the stereotyping, she broke her contract with Fox and moved to New York City. There she studied at the Actors Studio with Lee and Paula Strasberg. Gloria Steinem recalls a conversation with Monroe during that time in which Monroe referred to her own opinion of her abilities compared to a group of notables at the Actors Studio. "I admire all these people so much. I'm just not good enough."

In 1955 she formed her own studio, Marilyn Monroe Productions, and re-negotiated a contract with Twentieth Century Fox. She appeared in *Bus Stop* in 1956 and married playwright Arthur Miller on July 1, 1956.

Critics described Monroe in the film *The Prince and the Showgirl*, produced by her own company, as "a **sparkling** light comedienne." Monroe won the Italian David di Donatello award for "best foreign actress of 1958," and in 1959 she appeared in *Some Like It Hot*. In 1961 she starred in *The Misfits*, for which Arthur Miller did the screenplay.

The couple was divorced on January 24, 1961, and later that year Monroe entered a New York psychiatric clinic. After her brief hospitalization there she returned to the Fox studio to work on a film, but her **erratic** behavior betrayed severe emotional disturbance, and the studio **discharged** her in June 1962.

Marilyn Monroe was found dead in her Los Angeles bungalow on August 5, 1962, an empty bottle of sleeping pills by her side.

After You Read

I. Vocabulary

1. paranoid   A. awkward   B. suffer
               C. extremely suspicious   D. indifference
2. fledgling   A. callow   B. mature   C. capable   D. successful
3. sparkling   A. artificial B. glittering C. free   D. slight
4. erratic   A. regular   B. surprising   C. terrible   D. odd
5. discharge   A. fire   B. abandon   C. resume   D. pour

II. True or false

1. Marilyn Monroe experienced a happy and loving childhood with her mother.   (   )
2. Marilyn Monroe had three failed marriages and her last husband was Arthur Miller.   (   )
3. In the spring of 1948 Columbia Pictures hired her for a small part in *As Young as You Feel*.   (   )
4. Monroe still made an image as a dumb blond in *Seven Year Itch* in 1954. Growing weary of the stereotyping, she broke her contract with Fox and moved to New York City.   (   )
5. She appeared in *Bus Stop* in 1956 and married playwright Arthur Miller in the same year.   (   )
6. Marilyn Monroe was found dead in her Los Angeles bungalow on August 5, 1962, an empty bottle of sleeping pills by her side.   (   )

For Fun

I. Movies to see

Death of a Salesman (1951): It is a 1951 film adapted from the play of the same name by Arthur Miller. It was directed by László Benedek.

II. Websites to visit

1. http://www.doc88.com/p-997218549756.html
2. www.americandream.com
3. http://www.answers.com/topic/marilyn-monroe#ixzz3BlKyx0cF

III. Writing

The gap between the poor and rich is getting larger and larger. What do you think is the cause of the phenomenon? What are possible solutions to this problem? Write a composition to express your ideas within 300 words.

Chapter 16

Joseph Heller (1923–1999)
约瑟夫·海勒

Section A Literary Focus

作者简介(About the Author)

【生平】 约瑟夫·海勒 1923 年 5 月出生于纽约布鲁克林的科尼岛区,父母是俄国犹太移民。5 岁时,父亲去世,他和哥哥、母亲只好自谋生路,艰难度日。1941 年海勒毕业于亚伯拉罕·林肯高中,1942 年 10 月参加美国空军第 12 军团,驻防科西嘉,并作为侧翼投弹手执行轰炸任务共 60 次。1945 年海勒作为空军上尉退役;同年 9 月 3 日与雪莉·海尔德结婚,并按美国兵役法就读于南卡罗莱纳大学,不久转入纽约大学,1948 年获英语学士学位。1949 年又于哥伦比亚大学获硕士学位,并作为 1949-1950 年度的富布莱特学者赴牛津大学访学。此后,他曾先后在宾夕法尼亚州立大学、耶鲁大学和纽约市大学任教,并当选为美国艺术文学院成员。

约瑟夫·海勒于 1999 年 12 月 12 日在纽约东汉普敦的家里由于心脏病突发不幸逝世,享年 76 岁。海勒是黑色幽默文学的代表人物,其作品在黑色幽默文学中影响最大,成为这一流派最具代表性的作品之一。

【主要作品】 长篇小说《第 22 条军规》(*Catch-22*, 1961),长篇小说《出了毛病》(*Something Happened*, 1974),长篇小说《像高尔德一样好》(*Good as Gold*, 1979),短篇小说集《多多益善》(*Catch as Catch Can*: *The Collected Stories and Other Writings*, 2003)等。

作品选读(Selected Writings)

Catch-22

约瑟夫·海勒的长篇小说《第 22 条军规》讲述了第二次世界大战末,在意大利厄尔巴岛以南八英里的地中海的一个美国空军基地——皮亚诺萨小岛上,轰炸手约塞连上尉像只惊弓之鸟,在一片混乱、荒谬与恐怖中,置一切权威、信条于不顾,为保存自己的性命而进行着几近疯狂的努力。在这个岛上,他生活的唯一目的就是逃避作战飞行。于是,他一次又一次地装病住进医院,因为他发现唯有这里才是最好的藏身之地。最后,他终于开了小差,逃到了瑞典。

《第22条军规》是一部严肃的、讽刺性极强的小说。通过这部小说,约瑟夫·海勒将他眼中的美国社会展现在读者眼前。这个社会处于一种有组织的混乱、一种制度化了的疯狂之中,这个社会的一切只服从"第二十二条军规"的荒诞逻辑。这样一种病态的、荒诞的社会只有海勒的想象力才能够包容它,只有"黑色幽默"这样的创作手法才能够较好地表现它。通过"第二十二条军规"这个象征,读者也可以看到战争、美国社会及其官僚机构的荒诞、疯狂和不可理喻。

40. CATCH-22

There was, of course, a catch.

"Catch-22?" inquired Yossarian.

"Of course," Colonel Korn answered pleasantly, after he had chased the mighty guard of massive M.P.s out with an insouciant① flick of his hand and a slightly contemptuous nod—most relaxed, as always, when he could be most cynical. His rimless square eyeglasses glinted with sly amusement as he gazed at Yossarian. "After all, we can't simply send you home for refusing to fly more missions and keep the rest of the men here, can we? That would hardly be fair to them."

"You're goddam right!" Colonel Cathcart blurted out, lumbering back and forth gracelessly like a winded bull, puffing and pouting angrily. "I'd like to tie him up hand and foot and throw him aboard a plane on every mission. That's what I'd like to do." Colonel Korn motioned Colonel Cathcart to be silent and smiled at Yossarian. "You know, you really have been making things terribly difficult for Colonel Cathcart," he observed with flip good humor, as though the fact did not displease him at all. "The men are unhappy and morale is beginning to deteriorate. And it's all your fault."

"It's your fault," Yossarian argued, "for raising the number of missions."

"No, it's your fault for refusing to fly them," Colonel Korn retorted. "The men were perfectly content to fly as many missions as we asked as long as they thought they had no alternative. Now you've given them hope, and they're unhappy. So the blame is all yours."

"Doesn't he know there's a war going on?" Colonel Cathcart, still stamping back and forth, demanded morosely② without looking at Yossarian.

"I'm quite sure he does," Colonel Korn answered. "That's probably why he refuses to fly them."

"Doesn't it make any difference to him?"

"Will the knowledge that there's a war going on weaken your decision to refuse to participate in it?" Colonel Korn inquired with sarcastic seriousness, mocking Colonel

---

① insouciant: 漫不经心的,无忧无虑的

② morosely: 忧郁地

Cathcart.

"No, sir," Yossarian replied, almost returning Colonel Korn's smile.

"I was afraid of that," Colonel Korn remarked with an elaborate sigh, locking his fingers together comfortably on top of his smooth, bald, broad, shiny brown head. "You know, in all fairness, we really haven't treated you too badly, have we? We've fed you and paid you on time. We gave you a medal and even made you a captain."

"I never should have made him a captain," Colonel Cathcart exclaimed bitterly. "I should have given him a court-martial after he loused up that Ferrara mission and went around twice."

"I told you not to promote him," said Colonel Korn, "but you wouldn't listen to me."

"No you didn't. You told me to promote him, didn't you?"

"I told you not to promote him. But you just wouldn't listen."

"I should have listened."

"You never listen to me," Colonel Korn persisted with relish. "That's the reason we're in this spot."

"All right, gee whiz. Stop rubbing it in, will you?" Colonel Cathcart burrowed① his fists down deep inside his pockets and turned away in a slouch. "Instead of picking on me, why don't you figure out what we're going to do about him?"

"We're going to send him home, I'm afraid." Colonel Korn was chuckling triumphantly when he turned away from Colonel Cathcart to face Yossarian. "Yossarian, the war is over for you. We're going to send you home. You really don't deserve it, you know, which is one of the reasons I don't mind doing it. Since there's nothing else we can risk doing to you at this time, we've decided to return you to the States. We've worked out this little deal to—"

"What kind of deal?" Yossarian demanded with defiant mistrust.

Colonel Korn tossed his head back and laughed. "Oh, a thoroughly despicable② deal, make no mistake about that. It's absolutely revolting. But you'll accept it quickly enough."

"Don't be too sure."

"I haven't the slightest doubt you will, even though it stinks to high heaven. Oh, by the way. You haven't told any of the men you've refused to fly more missions, have you?"

"No, sir," Yossarian answered promptly.

Colonel Korn nodded approvingly. "That's good. I like the way you lie. You'll go far in this world if you ever acquire some decent ambition."

"Doesn't he know there's a war going on?" Colonel Cathcart yelled out suddenly,

---

① burrow: 躲藏起来
② despicable: 卑劣的,可鄙的

and blew with vigorous disbelief into the open end of his cigarette holder.

"I'm quite sure he does," Colonel Korn replied acidly, "since you brought that identical point to his attention just a moment ago." Colonel Korn frowned wearily for Yossarian's benefit, his eyes twinkling swarthily[①] with sly and daring scorn. Gripping the edge of Colonel Cathcart's desk with both hands, he lifted his flaccid haunches far back on the corner to sit with both short legs dangling freely. His shoes kicked lightly against the yellow oak wood, his sludge-brown socks, garterless, collapsed in sagging circles below ankles that were surprisingly small and white. "You know, Yossarian," he mused affably[②] in a manner of casual reflection that seemed both derisive and sincere, "I really do admire you a bit. You're an intelligent person of great moral character who has taken a very courageous stand. I'm an intelligent person with no moral character at all, so I'm in an ideal position to appreciate it."

"These are very critical times," Colonel Cathcart asserted petulantly[③] from a far corner of the office, paying no attention to Colonel Korn.

"Very critical times indeed," Colonel Korn agreed with a placid nod. "We've just had a change of command above, and we can't afford a situation that might put us in a bad light with either General Scheisskopf or General Peckem. Isn't that what you mean, Colonel?"

"Hasn't he got any patriotism?"

"Won't you fight for your country?" Colonel Korn demanded, emulating Colonel Cathcart's harsh, self-righteous tone. "Won't you give up your life for Colonel Cathcart and me?" Yossarian tensed with alert astonishment when he heard Colonel Korn's concluding words. "What's that?" he exclaimed. "What have you and Colonel Cathcart got to do with my country? You're not the same." "How can you separate us?" Colonel Korn inquired with ironical tranquillity[④].

"That's right," Colonel Cathcart cried emphatically. "You're either for us or against us. There's no two ways about it."

"I'm afraid he's got you," added Colonel Korn. "You're either for us or against your country. It's as simple as that."

"Oh, no, Colonel. I don't buy that." Colonel Korn was unrufled. "Neither do I, frankly, but everyone else will. So there you are."

"You're a disgrace to your uniform!" Colonel Cathcart declared with blustering wrath, whirling to confront Yossarian for the first time. "I'd like to know how you ever got to be a captain, anyway."

"You promoted him," Colonel Korn reminded sweetly, stifling a snicker. "Don't

---

① swarthily：黑黝黝地
② affably：友好地，殷勤地
③ petulantly：脾气坏地
④ tranquillity：心神稳定

you remember?"

"Well, I never should have done it."

"I told you not to do it," Colonel Korn said. "But you just wouldn't listen to me."

"Gee whiz, will you stop rubbing it in?" Colonel Cathcart cried. He furrowed his brow and glowered at Colonel Korn through eyes narrow with suspicion, his fists clenched on his hips. "Say, whose side are you on, anyway?"

"Your side, Colonel. What other side could I be on?"

"Then stop picking on me, will you? Get off my back, will you?"

"I'm on your side, Colonel. I'm just loaded with patriotism."

"Well, just make sure you don't forget that." Colonel Cathcart turned away grudgingly① after another moment, incompletely reassured, and began striding the floor, his hands kneading his long cigarette holder. He jerked a thumb toward Yossarian. "Let's settle with him. I know what I'd like to do with him. I'd like to take him outside and shoot him. That's what I'd like to do with him. That's what General Dreedle would do with him."

"But General Dreedle isn't with us any more," said Colonel Korn, "so we can't take him outside and shoot him." Now that his moment of tension with Colonel Cathcart had passed, Colonel Korn relaxed again and resumed kicking softly against Colonel Cathcart's desk. He returned to Yossarian. "So we're going to send you home instead. It took a bit of thinking, but we finally worked out this horrible little plan for sending you home without causing too much dissatisfaction among the friends you'll leave behind. Doesn't that make you happy?"

"What kind of plan? I'm not sure I'm going to like it."

"I know you're not going to like it." Colonel Korn laughed, locking his hands contentedly on top of his head again. "You're going to loathe② it. It really is odious and certainly will offend your conscience. But you'll agree to it quickly enough. You'll agree to it because it will send you home safe and sound in two weeks, and because you have no choice. It's that or a court-martial. Take it or leave it." Yossarian snorted. "Stop bluffing, Colonel. You can't court-martial me for desertion in the face of the enemy. It would make you look bad and you probably couldn't get a conviction." "But we can court-martial you now for desertion from duty, since you went to Rome without a pass. And we could make it stick. If you think about it a minute, you'll see that you'd leave us no alternative. We can't simply let you keep walking around in open insubordination without punishing you. All the other men would stop flying missions, too. No, you have my word for it. We will court-martial you if you turn our deal down, even though it would raise a lot of questions and be a terrible black eye for Colonel Cathcart." Colonel

---

① grudgingly: 勉强地,不情愿地
② loathe: 讨厌,厌恶

Cathcart winced at the words "black eye" and, without any apparent premeditation①, hurled his slender onyx-and-ivory② cigarette holder down viciously on the wooden surface on his desk. "Jesus Christ!" he shouted unexpectedly. "I hate this goddam cigarette holder!" The cigarette holder bounced off the desk to the wall, ricocheted③ across the window sill to the floor and came to a stop almost where he was standing. Colonel Cathcart stared down at it with an irascible scowl. "I wonder if it's really doing me any good."

"It's a feather in your cap with General Peckem, but a black eye for you with General Scheisskopf," Colonel Korn informed him with a mischievous look of innocence.

"Well, which one am I supposed to please?"

"Both."

"How can I please them both? They hate each other. How am I ever going to get a feather in my cap from General Scheisskopf without getting a black eye from General Peckem?"

"March."

"Yeah, march. That's the only way to please him. March. March." Colonel Cathcart grimaced sullenly. "Some generals! They're a disgrace to their uniforms. If people like those two can make general, I don't see how I can miss."

"You're going to go far." Colonel Korn assured him with a flat lack of conviction, and turned back chuckling to Yossarian, his disdainful merriment increasing at the sight of Yossarian's unyielding expression of antagonism and distrust. "And there you have the crux of the situation. Colonel Cathcart wants to be a general and I want to be a colonel, and that's why we have to send you home."

"Why does he want to be a general?"

"Why? For the same reason that I want to be a colonel. What else have we got to do? Everyone teaches us to aspire to higher things. A general is higher than a colonel, and a colonel is higher than a lieutenant④ colonel. So we're both aspiring. And you know, Yossarian, it's a lucky thing for you that we are. Your timing on this is absolutely perfect, but I suppose you took that factor into account in your calculations."

"I haven't been doing any calculating," Yossarian retorted.

"Yes, I really do enjoy the way you lie," Colonel Korn answered. "Won't it make you proud to have your commanding officer promoted to general—to know you served in an outfit that averaged more combat missions per person than any other? Don't you want to earn more unit citations and more oak leaf clusters for your Air Medal? Where's your

---

① premeditation：预先设想
② onyx-and-ivory：象牙红玛瑙
③ ricochet：跳弹
④ lieutenant：中尉

esprit de corps? Don't you want to contribute further to this great record by flying more combat missions? It's your last chance to answer yes."

"No."

"In that case, you have us over a barrel—" said Colonel Korn without rancor.

"He ought to be ashamed of himself!"

"—and we have to send you home. Just do a few little things for us, and—"

"What sort of things?" Yossarian interrupted with belligerent① misgiving.

"Oh, tiny, insignificant things. Really, this is a very generous deal we're making with you. We will issue orders returning you to the States—really, we will—and all you have to do in return is ... " "What? What must I do?" Colonel Korn laughed curtly. "Like us." Yossarian blinked. "Like you?" "Like us."

"Like you?"

"That's right," said Colonel Korn, nodding, gratified immeasurably by Yossarian's guileless surprise and bewilderment. "Like us. Join us. Be our pal. Say nice things about us here and back in the States. Become one of the boys. Now, that isn't asking too much, is it?"

"You just want me to like you? Is that all?"

"That's all."

"That's all?"

"Just find it in your heart to like us." Yossarian wanted to laugh confidently when he saw with amazement that Colonel Korn was telling the truth. "That isn't going to be too easy," he sneered. "Oh, it will be a lot easier than you think," Colonel Korn taunted② in return, undismayed by Yossarian's barb. "You'll be surprised at how easy you'll find it to like us once you begin." Colonel Korn hitched up the waist of his loose, voluminous trousers. The deep black grooves isolating his square chin from his jowls were bent again in a kind of jeering and reprehensible mirth③. "You see, Yossarian, we're going to put you on easy street. We're going to promote you to major and even give you another medal. Captain Flume is already working on glowing press releases describing your valor over Ferrara, your deep and abiding loyalty to your outfit and your consummate dedication to duty. Those phrases are all actual quotations, by the way. We're going to glorify you and send you home a hero, recalled by the Pentagon for morale and public-relations purposes. You'll live like a millionaire. Everyone will lionize you. You'll have parades in your honor and make speeches to raise money for war bonds. A whole new world of luxury awaits you once you become our pal. Isn't it lovely?" Yossarian found himself listening intently to the fascinating elucidation④ of

---

① belligerent: 好战的
② taunt: 奚落
③ mirth: 欢乐,高兴
④ elucidation: 说明,阐释

details. "I'm not sure I want to make speeches."

"Then we'll forget the speeches. The important thing is what you say to people here." Colonel Korn leaned forward earnestly, no longer smiling. "We don't want any of the men in the group to know that we're sending you home as a result of your refusal to fly more missions. And we don't want General Peckem or General Scheisskopf to get wind of any friction between us, either. That's why we're going to become such good pals."

"What will I say to the men who asked me why I refused to fly more missions?"

"Tell them you had been informed in confidence that you were being returned to the States and that you were unwilling to risk your life for another mission or two. Just a minor disagreement between pals, that's all."

"Will they believe it?"

"Of course they'll believe it, once they see what great friends we've become and when they see the press releases and read the flattering things you have to say about me and Colonel Cathcart. Don't worry about the men. They'll be easy enough to discipline and control when you've gone. It's only while you're still here that they may prove troublesome. You know, one good apple can spoil the rest," Colonel Korn concluded with conscious irony. "You know—this would really be wonderful—you might even serve as an inspiration to them to fly more missions."

"Suppose I denounce you when I get back to the States?"

"After you've accepted our medal and promotion and all the fanfare①? No one would believe you, the Army wouldn't let you, and why in the world should you want to? You're going to be one of the boys, remember? You'll enjoy a rich, rewarding, luxurious, privileged existence. You'd have to be a fool to throw it all away just for a moral principle, and you're not a fool. Is it a deal?" "I don't know."

"It's that or a court-martial."

"That's a pretty scummy trick I'd be playing on the men in the squadron②, isn't it?"

"Odious," Colonel Korn agreed amiably, and waited, watching Yossarian patiently with a glimmer of private delight.

"But what the hell!" Yossarian exclaimed. "If they don't want to fly more missions, let them stand up and do something about it the way I did. Right?"

"Of course," said Colonel Korn.

"There's no reason I have to risk my life for them, is there?"

"Of course not." Yossarian arrived at his decision with a swift grin. "It's a deal!" he announced jubilantly③.

"Great," said Colonel Korn with somewhat less cordiality than Yossarian had

---

① fanfare: 宣传,炫耀
② squadron: 空军中队
③ jubilantly: 欢欣地

expected, and he slid himself off Colonel Cathcart's desk to stand on the floor. He tugged the folds of cloth of his pants and undershorts free from his crotch① and gave Yossarian a limp hand to shake. "Welcome aboard."

"Thanks, Colonel. I—"

"Call me Blackie, John. We're pals now."

"Sure, Blackie. My friends call me Yo-Yo. Blackie, I—"

"His friends call him Yo-Yo," Colonel Korn sang out to Colonel Cathcart. "Why don't you congratulate Yo-Yo on what a sensible move he's making?"

"That's a real sensible move you're making, Yo-Yo," Colonel Cathcart said, pumping Yossarian's hand with clumsy zeal.

"Thank you, Colonel, I—"

"Call him Chuck," said Colonel Korn.

"Sure, call me Chuck," said Colonel Cathcart with a laugh that was hearty and awkward. "We're all pals now."

"Sure, Chuck."

"Exit smiling," said Colonel Korn, his hands on both their shoulders as the three of them moved to the door.

"Come on over for dinner with us some night, Yo-Yo," Colonel Cathcart invited hospitably. "How about tonight? In the group dining room."

"I'd love to, sir."

"Chuck," Colonel Korn corrected reprovingly.

"I'm sorry, Blackie. Chuck. I can't get used to it."

"That's all right, pal."

"Sure, pal."

"Thanks, pal."

"Don't mention it, pal."

"So long, pal." Yossarian waved goodbye fondly to his new pals and sauntered② out onto the balcony corridor, almost bursting into song the instant he was alone. He was home free: he had pulled it off; his act of rebellion had succeeded; he was safe, and he had nothing to be ashamed of to anyone. He started toward the staircase with a jaunty and exhilarated air. A private in green fatigues saluted him. Yossarian returned the salute happily, staring at the private with curiosity. He looked strangely familiar. When Yossarian returned the salute, the private in green fatigues turned suddenly into Nately's whore and lunged at him murderously with a bone-handled kitchen knife that caught him in the side below his upraised arm. Yossarian sank to the floor with a shriek, shutting his eyes in overwhelming terror as he saw the girl lift the knife to strike at him again. He was already unconscious when Colonel Korn and Colonel Cathcart dashed out of the

---

① crotch: 胯部

② saunter: 闲逛,漫步

office and saved his life by frightening her away.

41. Snowden

"Cut," said a doctor.

"You cut," said another.

"No cuts," said Yossarian with a thick, unwieldy tongue.

"Now look who's butting in," complained one of the doctors. "Another county heard from. Are we going to operate or aren't we?"

"He doesn't need an operation," complained the other. "It's a small wound. All we have to do is stop the bleeding, clean it out and put a few stitches in."

"But I've never had a chance to operate before. Which one is the scalpel①? Is this one the scalpel?"

"No, the other one is the scalpel. Well, go ahead and cut already if you're going to. Make the incision."

"Like this?"

"Not there, you dope!"

"No incisions," Yossarian said, perceiving through the lifting fog of insensibility that the two strangers were ready to begin cutting him.

"Another county heard from," complained the first doctor sarcastically. "Is he going to keep talking that way while I operate on him?"

"You can't operate on him until I admit him," said a clerk.

"You can't admit him until I clear him," said a fat, gruff colonel with a mustache and an enormous pink face that pressed down very close to Yossarian and radiated scorching heat like the bottom of a huge frying pan. "Where were you born?" The fat, gruff colonel reminded Yossarian of the fat, gruff colonel who had interrogated② the chaplain③ and found him guilty. Yossarian stared up at him through a glassy film. The cloying scents of formaldehyde④ and alcohol sweetened the air.

"On a battlefield," he answered.

"No, no. In what state were you born?"

"In a state of innocence."

"No, no, you don't understand."

"Let me handle him," urged a hatchet-faced man with sunken acrimonious eyes and a thin, malevolent mouth. "Are you a smart aleck or something?" he asked Yossarian.

"He's delirious⑤," one of the doctors said. "Why don't you let us take him back

---

① scalpel：手术刀
② interrogate：审问
③ chaplain：牧师
④ formaldehyde：甲醛
⑤ delirious：发狂的，精神错乱的

inside and treat him?"

"Leave him right here if he's delirious. He might say something incriminating."

"But he's still bleeding profusely. Can't you see? He might even die."

"Good for him!"

"It would serve the finky bastard right," said the fat, gruff colonel. "All right, John, let's speak out. We want to get to the truth."

"Everyone calls me Yo-Yo."

"We want you to co-operate with us, Yo-Yo. We're your friends and we want you to trust us. We're here to help you. We're not going to hurt you."

"Let's jab our thumbs down inside his wound and gouge it," suggested the hatchet-faced① man. Yossarian let his eyes fall closed and hoped they would think he was unconscious.

"He's fainted," he heard a doctor say. "Can't we treat him now before it's too late? He really might die."

"All right, take him. I hope the bastard does die."

"You can't treat him until I admit him," the clerk said.

Yossarian played dead with his eyes shut while the clerk admitted him by shuffling some papers, and then he was rolled away slowly into a stuffy, dark room with searing spotlights overhead in which the cloying smell of formaldehyde and sweet alcohol was even stronger. The pleasant, permeating stink was intoxicating. He smelled ether too and heard glass tinkling. He listened with secret, egotistical② mirth to the husky breathing of the two doctors. It delighted him that they thought he was unconscious and did not know he was listening. It all seemed very silly to him until one of the doctors said, "Well, do you think we should save his life? They might be sore at us if we do."

"Let's operate," said the other doctor. "Let's cut him open and get to the inside of things once and for all. He keeps complaining about his liver. His liver looks pretty small on this X ray." "That's his pancreas, you dope. This is his liver."

"No it isn't. That's his heart. I'll bet you a nickel this is his liver. I'm going to operate and find out. Should I wash my hands first?"

"No operations," Yossarian said, opening his eyes and trying to sit up.

"Another county heard from," scoffed one of the doctors indignantly. "Can't we make him shut up?"

"We could give him a total. The ether's right here."

"No totals," said Yossarian.

"Another county heard from," said a doctor.

"Let's give him a total and knock him out. Then we can do what we want with

---

① hatchet-faced: 瘦削脸型的

② egotistical: 自我本位的，傲慢自尊的

him." They gave Yossarian total anesthesia① and knocked him out. He woke up thirsty in a private room, drowning in ether fumes. Colonel Korn was there at his bedside, waiting calmly in a chair in his baggy, wool, olive-drab shirt and trousers. A bland, phlegmatic smile hung on his brown face with its heavy-bearded cheeks, and he was buffing the facets of his bald head gently with the palms of both hands. He bent forward chuckling when Yossarian awoke, and assured him in the friendliest tones that the deal they had made was still on if Yossarian didn't die. Yossarian vomited, and Colonel Korn shot to his feet at the first cough and fled in disgust, so it seemed indeed that there was a silver lining to every cloud, Yossarian reflected, as he drifted back into a suffocating daze. A hand with sharp fingers shook him awake roughly. He turned and opened his eyes and saw a strange man with a mean face who curled his lip at him in a spiteful scowl and bragged, "We've got your pal, buddy. We've got your pal." Yossarian turned cold and faint and broke into a sweat. "Who's my pal?" he asked when he saw the chaplain sitting where Colonel Korn had been sitting. "Maybe I'm your pal," the chaplain answered.

But Yossarian couldn't hear him and closed his eyes. Someone gave him water to sip and tiptoed away. He slept and woke up feeling great until he turned his head to smile at the chaplain and saw Aarfy there instead. Yossarian moaned instinctively and screwed his face up with excruciating② irritability when Aarfy chortled and asked how he was feeling. Aarfy looked puzzled when Yossarian inquired why he was not in jail. Yossarian shut his eyes to make him go away. When he opened them, Aarfy was gone and the chaplain was there. Yossarian broke into laughter when he spied the chaplain's cheerful grin and asked him what in the hell he was so happy about.

"I'm happy about you," the chaplain replied with excited candor and joy. "I heard at Group that you were very seriously injured and that you would have to be sent home if you lived. Colonel Korn said your condition was critical. But I've just learned from one of the doctors that your wound is really a very slight one and that you'll probably be able to leave in a day or two. You're in no danger. It isn't bad at all." Yossarian listened to the chaplain's news with enormous relief. "That's good."

"Yes," said the chaplain, a pink flush of impish③ pleasure creeping into his cheeks. "Yes, that is good." Yossarian laughed, recalling his first conversation with the chaplain. "You know, the first time I met you was in the hospital. And now I'm in the hospital again. Just about the only time I see you lately is in the hospital. Where've you been keeping yourself?" The chaplain shrugged. "I've been praying a lot," he confessed. "I try to stay in my tent as much as I can, and I pray every time Sergeant Whitcomb leaves the area, so that he won't catch me."

---

① anesthesia: 麻醉
② excruciating: 折磨人的,使人烦恼的
③ impish: 顽皮的,恶作剧的

"Does it do any good?"

"It takes my mind off my troubles," the chaplain answered with another shrug. "And it gives me something to do."

"Well that's good, then, isn't it?"

"Yes," agreed the chaplain enthusiastically, as though the idea had not occurred to him before. "Yes, I guess that is good." He bent forward impulsively with awkward solicitude. "Yossarian, is there anything I can do for you while you're here, anything I can get you?" Yossarian teased him jovially①. "Like toys, or candy, or chewing gum?" The chaplain blushed again, grinning self-consciously, and then turned very respectful. "Like books, perhaps, or anything at all. I wish there was something I could do to make you happy. You know, Yossarian, we're all very proud of you."

"Proud?"

"Yes, of course. For risking your life to stop that Nazi assassin. It was a very noble thing to do." "What Nazi assassin?"

"The one that came here to murder Colonel Cathcart and Colonel Korn. And you saved them. He might have stabbed you to death as you grappled with him on the balcony. It's a lucky thing you're alive!" Yossarian snickered sardonically when he understood. "That was no Nazi assassin." "Certainly it was. Colonel Korn said it was."

"That was Nately's girl friend. And she was after me, not Colonel Cathcart and Colonel Korn. She's been trying to kill me ever since I broke the news to her that Nately was dead."

"But how could that be?" the chaplain protested in livid and resentful confusion. "Colonel Cathcart and Colonel Korn both saw him as he ran away. The official report says you stopped a Nazi assassin from killing them."

"Don't believe the official report," Yossarian advised dryly. "It's part of the deal."

"What deal?"

"The deal I made with Colonel Cathcart and Colonel Korn. They'll let me go home a big hero if I say nice things about them to everybody and never criticize them to anyone for making the rest of the men fly more missions." The chaplain was appalled and rose halfway out of his chair. He bristled with bellicose② dismay. "But that's terrible! That's a shameful, scandalous deal, isn't it?" "Odious," Yossarian answered, staring up woodenly at the ceiling with just the back of his head resting on the pillow. "I think 'odious' is the word we decided on."

"Then how could you agree to it?"

"It's that or a court-martial, Chaplain."

"Oh," the chaplain exclaimed with a look of stark remorse, the back of his hand covering his mouth. He lowered himself into his chair uneasily. "I shouldn't have said

---

① jovially: 愉快地,高兴地
② bellicose: 好战的,好斗的

anything."

"They'd lock me in prison with a bunch of criminals."

"Of course. You must do whatever you think is right, then." The chaplain nodded to himself as though deciding the argument and lapsed into embarrassed silence.

"Don't worry," Yossarian said with a sorrowful laugh after several moments had passed. "I'm not going to do it."

"But you must do it," the chaplain insisted, bending forward with concern. "Really, you must. I had no right to influence you. I really had no right to say anything."

"You didn't influence me." Yossarian hauled himself over onto his side and shook his head in solemn mockery. "Christ, Chaplain! Can you imagine that for a sin? Saving Colonel Cathcart's life! That's one crime I don't want on my record." The chaplain returned to the subject with caution. "What will you do instead? You can't let them put you in prison."

"I'll fly more missions. Or maybe I really will desert and let them catch me. They probably would."

"And they'd put you in prison. You don't want to go to prison."

"Then I'll just keep flying missions until the war ends, I guess. Some of us have to survive." "But you might get killed."

"Then I guess I won't fly any more missions."

"What will you do?"

"I don't know."

"Will you let them send you home?"

"I don't know. Is it hot out? It's very warm in here."

"It's very cold out," the chaplain said.

"You know," Yossarian remembered, "a very funny thing happened—maybe I dreamed it. I think a strange man came in here before and told me he's got my pal. I wonder if I imagined it." "I don't think you did," the chaplain informed him. "You started to tell me about him when I dropped in earlier."

"Then he really did say it. 'We've got your pal, buddy,' he said. 'We've got your pal.' He had the most malignant manner I ever saw. I wonder who my pal is."

"I like to think that I'm your pal, Yossarian," the chaplain said with humble sincerity. "And they certainly have got me. They've got my number and they've got me under surveillance①, and they've got me right where they want me. That's what they told me at my interrogation."

"No, I don't think it's you he meant," Yossarian decided. "I think it must be someone like Nately or Dunbar. You know, someone who was killed in the war, like Clevinger, Orr, Dobbs, Kid Sampson or McWatt." Yossarian emitted a startled gasp

---

① surveillance: 监督, 监视

and shook his head. "I just realized it," he exclaimed. "They've got all my pals, haven't they? The only ones left are me and Hungry Joe." He tingled with dread as he saw the chaplain's face go pale. "Chaplain, what is it?"

"Hungry Joe was killed."

"God, no! On a mission?"

"He died in his sleep while having a dream. They found a cat on his face."

"Poor bastard," Yossarian said, and began to cry, hiding his tears in the crook of his shoulder. The chaplain left without saying goodbye. Yossarian ate something and went to sleep. A hand shook him awake in the middle of the night. He opened his eyes and saw a thin, mean man in a patient's bathrobe and pajamas who looked at him with a nasty smirk and jeered.

"We've got your pal, buddy. We've got your pal." Yossarian was unnerved. "What the hell are you talking about?" he pleaded in incipient① panic.

"You'll find out, buddy. You'll find out." Yossarian lunged for his tormentor's throat with one hand, but the man glided out of reach effortlessly and vanished into the corridor with a malicious laugh. Yossarian lay there trembling with a pounding pulse. He was bathed in icy sweat. He wondered who his pal was. It was dark in the hospital and perfectly quiet. He had no watch to tell him the time. He was wide-awake, and he knew he was a prisoner in one of those sleepless, bedridden nights that would take an eternity to dissolve into dawn. A throbbing chill oozed up his legs. He was cold, and he thought of Snowden, who had never been his pal but was a vaguely familiar kid who was badly wounded and freezing to death in the puddle of harsh yellow sunlight splashing into his face through the side gunport when Yossarian crawled into the rear section of the plane over the bomb bay after Dobbs had beseeched him on the intercom to help the gunner, please help the gunner. Yossarian's stomach turned over when his eyes first beheld the macabre scene; he was absolutely revolted, and he paused in fright a few moments before descending, crouched on his hands and knees in the narrow tunnel over the bomb bay beside the sealed corrugated carton containing the first-aid kit. Snowden was lying on his back on the floor with his legs stretched out, still burdened cumbersomely by his flak suit, his flak helmet, his parachute harness and his Mae West. Not far away on the floor lay the small tail-gunner in a dead faint. The wound Yossarian saw was in the outside of Snowden's thigh, as large and deep as a football, it seemed. It was impossible to tell where the shreds of his saturated② coveralls ended and the ragged flesh began.

There was no morphine③ in the first-aid kit, no protection for Snowden against pain but the numbing shock of the gaping wound itself. The twelve syrettes of morphine had

---

① incipient：起初的，初始的

② saturated：渗透的

③ morphine：吗啡

been stolen from their case and replaced by a cleanly lettered note that said: "What's good for M&M Enterprises is good for the country. Milo Minderbinder." Yossarian swore at Milo and held two aspirins out to ashen lips unable to receive them. But first he hastily drew a tourniquet① around Snowden's thigh because he could not think what else to do in those first tumultuous moments when his senses were in turmoil, when he knew he must act competently at once and feared he might go to pieces completely. Snowden watched him steadily, saying nothing. No artery was spurting, but Yossarian pretended to absorb himself entirely into the fashioning of a tourniquet, because applying a tourniquet was something he did know how to do. He worked with simulated skill and composure, feeling Snowden's lack-luster gaze resting upon him. He recovered possession of himself before the tourniquet was finished and loosened it immediately to lessen the danger of gangrene②. His mind was clear now, and he knew how to proceed. He rummaged through the first-aid kit for scissors.

"I'm cold," Snowden said softly. "I'm cold."

"You're going to be all right, kid," Yossarian reassured him with a grin. "You're going to be all right."

"I'm cold," Snowden said again in a frail, childlike voice. "I'm cold."

"There, there," Yossarian said, because he did not know what else to say. "There, there." "I'm cold," Snowden whimpered. "I'm cold."

"There, there. There, there." Yossarian was frightened and moved more swiftly. He found a pair of scissors at last and began cutting carefully through Snowden's coveralls high up above the wound, just below the groin③. He cut through the heavy gabardine cloth all the way around the thigh in a straight line. The tiny tail gunner④ woke up while Yossarian was cutting with the scissors, saw him, and fainted again. Snowden rolled his head to the other side of his neck in order to stare at Yossarian more directly. A dim, sunken light glowed in his weak and listless eyes. Yossarian, puzzled, tried not to look at him. He began cutting downward through the coveralls along the inside seam. The yawning wound—was that a tube of slimy bone he saw running deep inside the gory scarlet flow behind the twitching, startling fibers of weird muscle?—was dripping blood in several trickles, like snow melting on eaves, but viscous and red, already thickening as it dropped. Yossarian kept cutting through the coveralls to the bottom and peeled open the severed leg of the garment. It fell to the floor with a plop, exposing the hem of khaki undershorts that were soaking up blotches of blood on one side as though in thirst. Yossarian was stunned at how waxen and ghastly Snowden's bare

---

① tourniquet: 止血带
② gangrene: 坏疽
③ groin: 腹股沟
④ tail gunner: 机尾炮射击员

leg looked, how loathsome, how lifeless and esoteric① the downy, fine, curled blond hairs on his odd white shin and calf. The wound, he saw now, was not nearly as large as a football, but as long and wide as his hand and too raw and deep to see into clearly. The raw muscles inside twitched like live hamburger meat. A long sigh of relief escaped slowly through Yossarian's mouth when he saw that Snowden was not in danger of dying. The blood was already coagulating② inside the wound, and it was simply a matter of bandaging him up and keeping him calm until the plane landed. He removed some packets of sulfanilamide③ from the first-aid kit. Snowden quivered when Yossarian pressed against him gently to turn him up slightly on his side. "Did I hurt you?"

"I'm cold," Snowden whimpered. "I'm cold."

"There, there," Yossarian said. "There, there."

"I'm cold. I'm cold."

"There, there. There, there."

"It's starting to hurt me," Snowden cried out suddenly with a plaintive, urgent wince. Yossarian scrambled frantically through the first-aid kit in search of morphine again and found only Milo's note and a bottle of aspirin. He cursed Milo and held two aspirin tablets out to Snowden. He had no water to offer. Snowden rejected the aspirin with an almost imperceptible shake of his head. His face was pale and pasty. Yossarian removed Snowden's flak helmet and lowered his head to the floor.

"I'm cold," Snowden moaned with half-closed eyes. "I'm cold." The edges of his mouth were turning blue. Yossarian was petrified. He wondered whether to pull the rip cord of Snowden's parachute and cover him with the nylon folds. It was very warm in the plane. Glancing up unexpectedly, Snowden gave him a wan, co-operative smile and shifted the position of his hips a bit so that Yossarian could begin salting the wound with sulfanilamide. Yossarian worked with renewed confidence and optimism. The plane bounced hard inside an air pocket, and he remembered with a start that he had left his own parachute up front in the nose. There was nothing to be done about that. He poured envelope after envelope of the white crystalline powder into the bloody oval wound until nothing red could be seen and then drew a deep, apprehensive breath, steeling himself with gritted teeth as he touched his bare hand to the dangling shreds of drying flesh to tuck them up inside the wound. Quickly he covered the whole wound with a large cotton compress and jerked his hand away. He smiled nervously when his brief ordeal had ended. The actual contact with the dead flesh had not been nearly as repulsive as he had anticipated, and he found an excuse to caress the wound with his fingers again and again to convince himself of his own courage.

---

① esoteric: 秘传的
② coagulate: 凝结
③ sulfanilamide: 磺胺

Next he began binding the compress in place with a roll of gauze①. The second time around Snowden's thigh with the bandage, he spotted the small hole on the inside through which the piece of flak had entered, a round, crinkled wound the size of a quarter with blue edges and a black core inside where the blood had crusted. Yossarian sprinkled this one with sulfanilamide too and continued unwinding the gauze around Snowden's leg until the compress was secure. Then he snipped off the roll with the scissors and slit the end down the center. He made the whole thing fast with a tidy square knot. It was a good bandage, he knew, and he sat back on his heels with pride, wiping the perspiration② from his brow, and grinned at Snowden with spontaneous friendliness.

"I'm cold," Snowden moaned. "I'm cold."

"You're going to be all right, kid," Yossarian assured him, patting his arm comfortingly.

"Everything's under control." Snowden shook his head feebly. "I'm cold," he repeated, with eyes as dull and blind as stone. "I'm cold."

"There, there," said Yossarian, with growing doubt and trepidation③. "There, there. In a little while we'll be back on the ground and Doc Daneeka will take care of you." But Snowden kept shaking his head and pointed at last, with just the barest movement of his chin, down toward his armpit④. Yossarian bent forward to peer and saw a strangely colored stain seeping through the coveralls just above the armhole of Snowden's flak suit. Yossarian felt his heart stop, then pound so violently he found it difficult to breathe. Snowden was wounded inside his flak suit. Yossarian ripped open the snaps of Snowden's flak suit and heard himself scream wildly as Snowden's insides slithered down to the floor in a soggy pile and just kept dripping out. A chunk of flak more than three inches big had shot into his other side just underneath the arm and blasted all the way through, drawing whole mottled quarts of Snowden along with it through the gigantic hole in his ribs it made as it blasted out. Yossarian screamed a second time and squeezed both hands over his eyes. His teeth were chattering in horror. He forced himself to look again. Here was God's plenty, all right, he thought bitterly as he stared—liver, lungs, kidneys, ribs, stomach and bits of the stewed tomatoes Snowden had eaten that day for lunch. Yossarian hated stewed tomatoes and turned away dizzily and began to vomit, clutching his burning throat. The tail gunner woke up while Yossarian was vomiting, saw him, and fainted again. Yossarian was limp with exhaustion, pain and despair when he finished. He turned back weakly to Snowden, whose breath had grown softer and more rapid, and whose face had grown paler. He

---

① gauze：纱布
② perspiration：汗水
③ trepidation：恐惧,惊恐
④ armpit：腋窝

wondered how in the world to begin to save him.

"I'm cold," Snowden whimpered. "I'm cold."

"There, there," Yossarian mumbled mechanically in a voice too low to be heard. "There, there." Yossarian was cold, too, and shivering uncontrollably. He felt goose pimples clacking all over him as he gazed down despondently at the grim secret Snowden had spilled all over the messy floor. It was easy to read the message in his entrails. Man was matter, that was Snowden's secret. Drop him out a window and he'll fall. Set fire to him and he'll burn. Bury him and he'll rot, like other kinds of garbage. The spirit gone, man is garbage. That was Snowden's secret. Ripeness was all. "I'm cold," Snowden said. "I'm cold."

"There, there," said Yossarian. "There, there." He pulled the rip cord of Snowden's parachute and covered his body with the white nylon sheets.

"I'm cold."

"There, there."

Questions for discussion
1. How does *Catch-22* differ from other war stories?
2. What does Snowden's death mean to Yossarian?
3. Could you find some examples in the text to illustrate the technique of Black Humor?
4. What do you think of the protagonist Yossarian? Is he a hero?

文学术语(Definition of Literary Terms)

Black Humor, in literature, drama, and film, grotesque or morbid humor used to express the absurdity, insensitivity, paradox, and cruelty of the modern world. Ordinary characters or situations are usually exaggerated far beyond the limits of normal satire or irony. Black humor uses devices often associated with tragedy and is sometimes equated with tragic farce.

Section B Cultural Notes

Before You Read

1. Try to search the Internet or in the library about World War II and the related information. Give a 3-minute classroom presentation.
2. Do you know Pearl Harbor? Briefly summarize the event.

Start to Read

World War II and the United States

The United States emerged from World War I an isolationist nation. Even though American President Woodrow Wilson was among the main pillars in the founding of the League of Nations, the United States Senate never allowed the North American power, geographically separated from the rest of the world in its views, to join the organization. Overall, the top political leaders of the US feared to become entangled in European politics, or worse, future European wars.

The Great Depression that began with the stock market crash in 1929 brought a difficult period to the United States, while American farmers further suffered from catastrophic dust storms collectively known as the Dust Bowl. President Franklin Roosevelt, elected in 1932, instituted several socialist programs that effectively responded to the economic and social issues that resulted from the depression. As a result, Roosevelt began to earn a deep-rooted respect from the American people.

In the mid-1930s, Roosevelt began to think that "he could buy peace for a generation of Americans, but the more he pondered the character of the regime in Berlin, the more convinced he became that the next U.S. generation would lie at Hitler's mercy." Bypassing the appeaser British Prime Minister Neville Chamberlain's office, he contacted Winston Churchill directly via telephone and established what was to become one of the most important working relationships during the war. As much as the American people respected him, however, Roosevelt was unable to sway the public to openly support a war against Nazi Germany, but he was able to convince the Congress to support Britain via Lend-Lease①. That all changed in Dec 1941 when Japan attacked Pearl Harbor and declared war in the United States. With this event, Roosevelt was able to play his political cards and change the American public opinion nearly overnight, changing the isolationist attitude into a patriotic fervor.

World War II turned out to be the costliest war in American history in terms of spending, but the spending also played a key part in lifting the United States out of economic depression. The increasing need for war goods not only wiped out the unemployment but also drew women into the work force in large numbers for the first time.

On the political front, gradually during the course of war between 1941 to 1945, United States stepped onto the world stage as a superpower. Her ability to carry on a multi-front war against both Germany and Japan with her expansive industrial capabilities was the main reason.

At the end of the war, United States unleashed② two atomic weapons against Japan.

---

① Lend-Lease: 平等租借交换
② unleash: 发动;释放

President Harry Truman's decision that led to the utter destruction of Hiroshima and Nagasaki remains a controversial topic until today.

On January 22, 1917, the German government gave notice that unrestricted submarine warfare would be resumed. When five U.S. vessels had been sunk by April, Wilson asked Congress for a declaration of war. Immediately, the government set about mobilizing its military resources, industry, labor and agriculture. By October 1918, on the eve of Allied victory, a U.S. army of over 1,750,000 soldiers had been deployed in France.

The U.S. Navy was crucial in helping the British break the submarine blockade, and in the summer of 1918, during a long-awaited German offensive, fresh American troops, under the command of General John J. Pershing, played a decisive role on land. In November, for example, American forces took an important part in the vast Meuse-Argonne offensive, which cracked Germany's vaunted Hindenburg Line.

President Wilson contributed greatly to an early end to the war by defining the war aims of the Allies, and by insisting that the struggle was being waged not against the German people but against their autocratic① government. His famous Fourteen Points, submitted to the Senate in January 1918 as the basis for a just peace, called for abandonment of secret international agreements, a guarantee of freedom of the seas, the removal of tariff barriers between nations, reductions in national armaments, and an adjustment of colonial claims with due regard to the interests of the inhabitants affected. Other points sought to ensure self-rule and unhampered economic development for European nationalities. The Fourteenth Point constituted the keystone of Wilson's arch of peace—the formation of an association of nations to afford "mutual guarantees of political independence and territorial integrity to great and small states alike."

By the summer of 1918, when Germany's armies were being beaten back, the German government appealed to Wilson to negotiate on the basis of the Fourteen Points. The president conferred with the Allies, who acceded② to the German proposal. An armistice was concluded on November 11.

After You Read

I. Discuss the following questions based on the text.
1. When did the Great Depression begin with the stock market crash?
2. Why did Roosevelt begin to earn a deep-rooted respect from the American people?
3. What motivated Roosevelt to try to convince the Congress to support Britain via Lend-Lease?
4. How did American people come out of the Great Depression in the World War II?

---

① autocratic: 专制的,独裁的
② accede: 同意,接受

5. Who contributed greatly to an early end to the war by defining the war aims of the Allies?
6. When were Germany's armies being beaten back?

II. True or false

1. Overall, the top political leaders of the US were afraid of becoming entangled in European politics, or worse, future European wars. ( )
2. The Great Depression resulted in lots of economic and social issues, such as the well-known Dust Bowl. ( )
3. Roosevelt contacted Winston Churchill directly via telephone and rejected the suggestion of becoming the working partner during the war. ( )
4. The United States gradually became a superpower because she could carry on a multi-front war against both Germany and Japan with her expansive industrial capabilities. ( )
5. There is no controversy about the utter destruction of Hiroshima and Nagasaki. ( )
6. The Fourteenth Point constituted the keystone of Roosevelt's arch of peace—the formation of an association of nations to afford "mutual guarantees of political independence and territorial integrity to great and small states alike." ( )

For Fun

I. Movies to see

Catch-22 (1970): It is a 1970 satirical comedy-drama war film adapted from the novel of the same name by Joseph Heller. In creating a black comedy revolving around the "lunatic characters" of Heller's satirical anti-war novel set at a fictional World War II Mediterranean base, director Mike Nichols and screenwriter Buck Henry (also in the cast) worked on the film script for two years, converting Heller's complex novel to the medium of film.

II. Websites to visit

1. http://www.notablebiographies.com/He-Ho/Heller-Joseph.html
2. http://www.world-war-2.info/
3. http://ww2db.com/country/united_states)

III. Writing

There are many people spreading Confucianism in different countries of the world. What do you think of those efforts? Could you find a better way to spread Chinese culture? Write about 250 words to express your ideas.

Chapter 17

The Twentieth Century American Poets (II) Allen Ginsberg (1926-1997)
艾伦·金斯伯格

Section A Literary Focus

作者简介(About the Author)

【生平】 艾伦·金斯伯格,美国诗人。他生于新泽西州的纽华克城,在纽约哥伦比亚大学求学期间曾一度被开除,却于1955年在旧金山的一次朗诵会上,以其《嚎叫》获得轰动性成功。作为一首诗和一部文献,《嚎叫》可以同艾略特的《荒原》相提并论,成为金斯伯格和他的同时代人的里程碑。他在《嚎叫及其他诗》(1956年)中的标题诗确立了其在避世运动中的领袖诗人地位。金斯伯格后来参与了20世纪60年代的"嬉皮士"运动,一度宣扬使用毒品的自由。在越南战争期间,他是一名主要的反战激进分子。金斯伯格被奉为"垮掉的一代"之父,他集诗人、文学运动领袖、激进的无政府主义者、旅行家、预言家和宗教徒于一身。不论在生活方式或在诗歌风格上,他均与众不同,自成一格,创立了美国新的一代诗风。他是同性恋者,吸过毒,又改信佛教,成了一名"信仰佛教的犹太人"。他的诗无情地揭露了美国社会的阴暗面,在对社会诅咒的背后体现的是他深切的人文关怀。金斯伯格在1954年遇见了他那位当时年仅21岁的同性爱人彼得·奥洛夫斯基(Peter Orlovsky),奥洛夫斯基作为金斯伯格一生的爱人和伴侣直到1997年金斯伯格去世。

【主要作品】 诗集《嚎叫及其他》(*Howl and Other Poems*,1956),诗集《卡迪什及其他》(*Kaddish and Other Poems*,1960),诗集《美国的衰弱》(*The Fall of America*:*Poems of These States*,1973),诗集《诗选:1947-1995》(*Selected Poems*:1947-1995,1996)等。

作品选读(Selected Writings)

Howl(*Selected*)①

艾伦·金斯堡最出名的作品是长诗《嚎叫》,在这首诗中他赞扬了垮掉派的伙伴们,对当时在美国泛滥的物质主义与墨守成规做出了猛烈批判;他无所顾忌地讴歌了性能量的各种表现形态,包括同性爱。《嚎叫》曾被旧金山警方以"淫秽"罪名控告,经文学界出面辩护,警方败诉。诗集售出30万册,影响了整整一代人。

For Carl Solomon

  Ⅲ

  Carl Solomon! I'm with you in Rockland
  where you're madder than I am
  I'm with you in Rockland
  where you must feel strange
  I'm with you in Rockland
  where you imitate the shade of my mother
  I'm with you in Rockland
  where you've murdered your twelve secretaries
  I'm with you in Rockland
  where you laugh at this invisible humor
  I'm with you in Rockland
  where we are great writers on the same dreadful② typewriter
  I'm with you in Rockland
  where your condition has become serious and is reported on the radio
  I'm with you in Rockland
  where the faculties of the skull③ no longer admit the worms of the senses
  I'm with you in Rockland
  where you drink the tea of the breasts of the spinsters of Utica④
  I'm with you in Rockland
  where you pun on the bodies of your nurses the harpies of the Bronx⑤
  I'm with you in Rockland
  where you scream in a straight jacket that you're losing the game of actual pingpong

---

① 《嚎叫》发表后,作为反映金斯伯格反主流声音最精湛的作品,立即取得巨大成功。初读诗歌,会感到它不是诗,而是淫秽词语的堆积。诚然,诗歌中语言淫秽,包括令人尴尬的字词,但仔细阅读,会发现《嚎叫》是一篇充满批判精神的优秀作品。
② dreadful:糟糕的
③ skull:头脑
④ spinsters of Utica:尤提卡老处女
⑤ harpies of the Bronx:布隆克斯的女人岛

of the abyss①

I'm with you in Rockland

where you bang on the catatonic② piano the soul is innocent and immortal it should never die ungodly in an armed mad house

I'm with you in Rockland

where fifty more shocks will never return your soul to its body again from its pilgrimage③ to a cross in the void

I'm with you in Rockland

where you accuse your doctors of insanity and plot the Hebrew socialist revolution against the fascist national Golgotha④

I'm with you in Rockland

where you will split the heavens of Long Island and resurrect⑤ your living human Jesus from the superhuman tomb

I'm with you in Rockland

where there are twenty-five-thousand mad comrades all together singing the final stanzas of the Internationale⑥

I'm with you in Rockland

where we hug and kiss the United States under our bed sheets the United States that coughs all night and won't let us sleep

I'm with you in Rockland

where we wake up electrified out of the coma by our own souls' airplanes roaring over the roof they've come to drop angelic bombs the hospital illuminates itself imaginary walls collapse O skinny legions run outside O starry-spangled⑦ shock of mercy the eternal war is here O victory forget your underwear we're free

I'm with you in Rockland

in my dreams you walk dripping from a sea-journey on the highway across America in tears to the door of my cottage⑧ in the Western night

Questions for discussion
1. What is the function of repetition in the poem?
2. Apart from repetition, can you find other figure(s) of speech used in the poem? Please list them.

---

① abyss：深渊
② catatonic：紧张症
③ pilgrimage：朝圣
④ Golgotha：骷髅地
⑤ resurrect：复活
⑥ Internationale：国际歌
⑦ starry-spangled：星光灿烂的
⑧ cottage：村舍

3. Can you make a comparison between the poem and traditional poems?
4. Some people regard the poem as an unconventional response to the distorted irrational society. Do you agree?

文学术语 (Definition of Literary Terms)

The Beat Generation was a group of American Post-World War II writers who came to prominence in the 1950s, as well as the cultural phenomena that they both documented and inspired. Central elements of "Beat" culture included experimentation with drugs, alternative forms of sexuality, an interest in Eastern religion, a rejection of materialism, and the idealizing of exuberant, unexpurgated means of expression and being.

Section B Cultural Notes

Before You Read

1. Try to search on the Internet or in the library about the Cold War and the related information. Give a 3-minute classroom presentation.
2. Do you know John F. Kennedy? Briefly summarize his life.
3. How do you understand the relation between war and peace?

Start to Read

The Cold War

During World War II, the United States and the Soviet Union fought together as allies against the Axis powers. However, the relationship between the two nations was a tense one. Americans had long been wary of Soviet communism and concerned about Russian leader Joseph Stalin's tyrannical①, blood-thirsty rule of his own country. For their part, the Soviets resented the Americans' decades-long refusal to treat the USSR as a legitimate part of the international community as well as their delayed entry into World War II, which resulted in the deaths of tens of millions of Russians. After the war ended, these grievances ripened into an overwhelming sense of mutual distrust and enmity②. Postwar Soviet expansionism in Eastern Europe fueled many Americans' fears of a Russian plan to control the world. Meanwhile, the USSR came to resent what they

---

① tyrannical: 暴君的, 专横的
② enmity: 敌意, 敌对

perceived as American officials' bellicose rhetoric, arms buildup and interventionist① approach to international relations. In such a hostile atmosphere, no single party was entirely to blame for the Cold War; in fact, some historians believe it was inevitable.

The Cold War: Containment

By the time World War II ended, most American officials agreed that the best defense against the Soviet threat was a strategy called "containment." In 1946, in his famous "Long Telegram," the diplomat George Kennan (1904-2005) explained this policy: The Soviet Union, he wrote, was "a political force committed fanatically② to the belief that with the U.S. there can be no permanent modus Vivendi [agreement between parties that disagree]"; as a result, America's only choice was the "long-term, patient but firm and vigilant containment of Russian expansive tendencies." President Harry Truman (1884-1972) agreed. "It must be the policy of the United States," he declared before Congress in 1947, "to support free peoples who are resisting attempted subjugation③ ... by outside pressures." This way of thinking would shape American foreign policy for the next four decades.

The Cold War: The Atomic Age

The containment strategy also provided the rationale for an unprecedented arms buildup in the United States. In 1950, a National Security Council Report known as NSC-68 had echoed Truman's recommendation that the country use military force to "contain" communist expansionism anywhere it seemed to be occurring. To that end, the report called for a four-fold increase in defense spending.

In particular, American officials encouraged the development of atomic weapons like the ones that had ended World War II. Thus began a deadly "arms race." In 1949, the Soviets tested an atom bomb of their own. In response, President Truman announced that the United States would build an even more destructive atomic weapon: the hydrogen④ bomb, or "superbomb." Stalin followed suit.

As a result, the stakes of the Cold War were perilously high. The first H-bomb test, in the Eniwetok atoll in the Marshall Islands, showed just how fearsome the nuclear age could be. It created a 25-square-mile fireball that vaporized an island, blew a huge hole in the ocean floor and had the power to destroy half of Manhattan. Subsequent American and Soviet tests spewed poisonous radioactive waste into the atmosphere.

The ever-present threat of nuclear annihilation⑤ had a great impact on American domestic life as well. People built bomb shelters in their backyards. They practiced attack drills in schools and other public places. The 1950s and 1960s saw an epidemic of

---

① interventionist: 内政干涉者
② fanatically: 狂热的
③ subjugation: 征服,镇压
④ hydrogen: 氢
⑤ annihilation: 覆灭,消灭

popular films that horrified moviegoers with depictions of nuclear devastation and mutant creatures. In these and other ways, the Cold War was a constant presence in Americans' everyday lives.

After You Read

I. Discuss the following questions based on the text.

1. What did the United States and the Soviet Union fight together as allies against during World War II?
2. What were the reasons why the Soviets resented the United States of America?
3. Which party was entirely to blame for the Cold War?
4. What is the best defense strategy against the Soviet threat just after the World War II?
5. According to George Kennan, what is the explanation of "containment"?
6. How many years would the way of Harry Truman's thinking shape American foreign policy?
7. What was the major military force of the United States to "contain" communist expansionism?
8. What threats are posed by the Cold War on present American society?

II. True or false

1. After the World War II, the relationship between the Soviet Union and the United States was a tense one. (   )
2. As the Americans see it, Russian leader Joseph Stalin is a tyrannical but benignant ruler of the country. (   )
3. The situation of the Cold War could be easily tackled by both countries. (   )
4. American officials discouraged the development of atomic weapons like the ones that had ended World War II. (   )
5. The first H-bomb test created a 25-square-mile fireball that vaporized an island, blew a huge hole in the ocean floor and had the power to destroy half of Manhattan. (   )
6. Subsequent American and Soviet tests released harmful and poisonous radioactive waste into the atmosphere. (   )
7. Although the Cold War lasted for a long time, it had no giant impact on the domestic life of both countries. (   )

For Fun

I. Websites to visit

1. http://en.wikipedia.org/wiki/The_cold_war
2. http://www.jfklibrary.org/

3. http://www.history.com/topics/cold-war

II. Writing

Someone believes that a country should help its local residents, while others believe that the help should be given to the most needed. Discuss both of opinions and present your opinion within 250 words.

Sylvia Plath (1932–1963)
西尔维娅·普拉斯

Section A Literary Focus

作者简介 (About the Author)

【生平】 西尔维娅·普拉斯,美国自白派诗人的代表,出生于美国马萨诸塞州的波士顿地区,她8岁时父亲去世,她和弟弟由母亲抚养大。1955年,普拉斯以优异成绩毕业于著名的史密斯女子学院,之后获得富布赖特奖学金去英国剑桥大学深造。在那里,她遇到了后来成为桂冠诗人的特德·休斯(1930—1998),两人于1956年6月结为连理。在与休斯育有一子一女后,两人婚姻出现裂痕并于1962年9月分居,普拉斯独自抚养两个孩子。1963年2月11日,她在伦敦的寓所自杀。普拉斯的小说创作有非常突出的自传性特色,几乎每一篇都能从作者本人的生活经历中找到影子。作为诗人的普拉斯也曾非常投入地学习过绘画,这些特点都鲜明地体现在她的作品中:感情细致入微,用词不俗而且准确,描摹景物富于色彩感,因此赋予她的诗一种独特的阅读快感。

【主要作品】 诗集《巨人及其他诗歌》(*The Colossus and Other Poems*, 1972),诗集《爱丽尔》(*Ariel*, 1965),诗集《冬树》(*Winter Trees*, 1971),小说《钟形罩》(*The Bell Jar*, 1963)等。

作品选读(Selected Writings)

Poppies[1] in October

Even the sun-clouds this morning cannot manage such skirts.
Nor the woman in the ambulance
Whose red heart blooms through her coat so astoundingly—

A gift, a love gift
Utterly unasked for
By a sky

Palely and flamingly[2]
Igniting its carbon monoxides[3], by eyes
Dulled to a halt[4] under bowlers[5].

O my God, what am I
That these late mouths should cry open
In a forest of frost, in dawn of cornflowers[6].

Questions for discussion
1. What is the image of the woman and what has she gone through in the poem?
2. What is the poet's intention to mention poppies and cornflowers in the poem?

Fever 103°

Pure? What does it mean?
The tongues of hell
Are dull, dull as the triple

Tongues of dull, fat Cerberus[7]
Who wheezes[8] at the gate. Incapable
Of licking clean

---

[1] poppy：罂粟花
[2] flamingly：火热地
[3] carbon monoxide：一氧化碳
[4] halt：犹豫，踌躇，停止
[5] bowler：圆顶礼帽
[6] cornflower：矢车菊
[7] Cerberus：冥府看门狗
[8] wheeze：呼哧呼哧地响

The aguey tendon, the sin, the sin.
The tinder① cries.
The indelible② smell

Of a snuffed candle!
Love, love, the low smokes roll
From me like Isadora's③ scarves, I'm in a fright

One scarf will catch and anchor in the wheel.
Such yellow sullen④ smokes
Make their own element. They will not rise,

But trundle⑤ round the globe
Choking the aged and the meek,
The weak

Hothouse baby in its crib⑥,
The ghastly orchid
Hanging its hanging garden in the air,

Devilish leopard⑦!
Radiation turned it white
And killed it in an hour.

Greasing the bodies of adulterers
Like Hiroshima ash and eating in.
The sin. The sin.

Darling, all night
I have been flickering, off, on, off, on.
The sheets grow heavy as a lecher's kiss.

Three days. Three nights.

---

① tinder：易燃物
② indelible：难忘的，不散的
③ Isadora：依莎多拉·邓肯(1877—1927)，美国舞蹈家，因围巾卷入辐条外露的车轮而断颈身亡
④ sullen：缓慢的，停滞的
⑤ trundle：转动
⑥ crib：婴儿床
⑦ leopard：豹子

Lemon water, chicken
Water, water make me retch①.

I am too pure for you or anyone.
Your body
Hurts me as the world hurts God. I am a lantern—

My head a moon
Of Japanese paper, my gold beaten skin
Infinitely delicate and infinitely expensive.

Does not my heat astound you. And my light.
All by myself I am a huge camellia②
Glowing and coming and going, flush on flush.

I think I am going up,
I think I may rise—
The beads of hot metal fly, and I, love, I

Am a pure acetylene③
Virgin
Attended by roses,

By kisses, by cherubim④,
By whatever these pink things mean.
Not you, nor him

Not him, nor him
(My selves dissolving, old whore petticoats⑤)—
To Paradise.

Questions for discussion

1. What is the symbolic meaning of "Fever 103°"?
2. What is the attitude of Sylvia Plath towards love?

---

① retch: 作呕
② camellia: 山茶花
③ acetylene: 乙炔
④ cherubim: 小天使
⑤ petticoat: 衬裙

Metaphors

I'm a riddle① in nine syllables.
An elephant, a ponderous② house,
A melon strolling on two tendrils③.
O red fruit, ivory, fine timbers④!
This loaf's big with its yeasty rising.
Money's new-minted⑤ in this fat purse.
I'm a means, a stage, a cow in calf.
I've eaten a bag of green apples,
Boarded the train there's no getting off.

Questions for discussion
1. What is the answer to the riddle in "Metaphors"?
2. What is your attitude towards pregnancy?

文学术语(Definition of Literary Terms)

Confessional poetry is a style of poetry that emerged in the United States during the 1950s. It has been described as poetry "of the personal," focusing on extreme moments of individual experience, the psyche, and personal trauma, including previously taboo matter such as mental illness, sexuality, and suicide, often set in relation to broader social themes.

Section B Cultural Notes

Before You Read

1. Try to search the Internet or in the library about Confessional Poetry and the related information. Give a 3-minute classroom presentation.
2. Do you know Sylvia Plath? Briefly summarize her life.

---

① riddle：谜语
② ponderous：笨重的,呆板的
③ tendril：藤蔓,卷须
④ timber：木材,木料
⑤ new-minted：新铸造的

Start to Read

Confessional Poetry

Confessional poetry is being redefined. The term has always been ambiguous. Sometimes it has been taken to describe the work of the small circle of Robert Lowell and three of his students—Sylvia Plath, Anne Sexton and W. D. Snodgrass—and at other times the poetry of intimacy and crisis famously defined by M. L. Rosenthal in a 1959 article, a delineation① which incorporates a wider range of writers, such as Adrienne Rich and John Berryman, or even more broadly younger writers like Sharon Olds and Mark Doty. But over the last decade the very validity of the name has come into question, and the poets traditionally read through a confessional paradigm② are being approached in new ways.

There are two main challenges to the confessional paradigm. One is mounted in works of literary history such as Thomas Travisano's 1999 *Midcentury Quartet: Bishop, Lowell, Jarrell, Berryman, and the Making of a Postmodern Aesthetic* and Adam Kirsch's 2005 *The Wounded Surgeon: Confession and Transformation in Six American Poets*. Both Travisano and Kirsch reject the term confessional outright, Travisano rigorously and Kirsch dismissively. "In confession found a bad metaphor for what the most gifted of these poets were doing," Kirsch writes, sketching instead a case for the metaphor that gives his book its title, taken from a line by T. S. Eliot—that of the wounded surgeon. Travisano devotes an early chapter of his study to an attack on what he names the "confessional paradigm," developing five lines of argument against the term. What Kirsch and Travisano have most clearly in common is their objection to what Travisano identifies in the first of his objections as "how the confessional paradigm has prejudiced, and is still prejudicing, artistic evaluation." An emphasis on the matter of the confessions of the poetry has obscured, according to this line of argument, its creators' artistic achievements.

A slightly older but still forceful approach has taken what amounts to an opposing stance to this distinction between artistry and autobiography. Participating in the rise of critical histories and theoretical works emphasizing the connections between autobiography and gender, a number of critics have approached the genre of confessional writing more broadly as women's writing, exploring how writing works with and works out issues of women's experience and gender identity. The editors of the recent volume of essays *After Confession: Poetry as Autobiography*, Kate Sontag and David Graham, have counterbalanced a section on "Ethical & Aesthetic Considerations" with a section on "Women & Autobiography." Deborah Nelson's 2002 *Pursuing Privacy in Cold War America* discusses the representation of domestic space by Sexton and Rich

---

① delineation：描写，叙述
② paradigm：范例

as a response to the gendering of the home as a masculine enclosure, arguing that both poets "redefine the home, the location of autonomy①, adulthood, and citizenship, as the womb." And in a 2006 essay on confessional poetry and "the gendered poetics of the real," Elizabeth Gregory argues that the ambitious American poets of the 1950s can be seen as "embracing the 'feminine' confessional position," so that Berryman and Lowell, as well as Plath and Sexton, ought to be understood as exploring new terrain of feminine writing.

The argument I would like to make in this essay is that we can also revisit confessional poetry as men's autobiographical writing. Neither rushing to make evaluative judgments about the poetry on the one hand, nor following a critical tendency to feminize autobiographical writing on the other, I suggest here that we read important poems of this now canonical body of work for the light that they cast on the experience of masculinity in the period. This is hardly an eccentric② suggestion. Critical studies of masculinity have abounded over the last decade, and various shapes of homosocialism in the poetry of the period—though not in the confessional school itself—have been explored in Michael Davidson's *Guys Like Us: Citing Masculinity in Cold War Poetics*. Though conversation has been started, there remains a good deal to be said on this subject.

I take my lead in this respect from Diane Wood Middlebrook's remark in her 1993 essay, "What Was Confessional Poetry?", that among the characteristics uniting the four indisputably confessional poets is the fact that "all four poets had become parents—of daughters, as it happens—not long before writing their confessional poems." We have in Snodgrass and Lowell a pair of poets writing with a truly unaccustomed level of personal candor and detail about the experience of being a father generally and of being the father of a daughter more specifically. No critical work has been done at this particular intersection of gender and autobiographical or life writing.

There are a number of interesting questions raised by this confluence③, and this essay will not be an attempt to answer them all. My focus is on what confessional poets reveal about the experience of fatherhood—specifically of fathering daughters—in their historical period. And the argument that I will make is that despite the similarity of their work with earlier poetry of fatherhood, these poets are remarkable for being consistently attuned to the quality of the relationship between themselves and their daughters, and that they experience through this attunement④ a sense of loneliness. What they show, in a way that the plays and movies of the period do not capture as pointedly, is that for the men committed to writing about the experience of fathering in

---

① autonomy：自治，自主权
② eccentric：古怪的
③ confluence：交汇处
④ attunement：点化，协调

postwar America fathering a daughter meant sustaining a relationship that made their own masculinity into an occasion of loneliness.

After You Read

I. Questions for discussion

1. Why has the term "Confessional Poetry" always been ambiguous?
2. What are two main challenges to the confessional paradigm?
3. What have Kirsch and Travisano most clearly in common?
4. According to a 2006 essay, what should Berryman and Lowell, as well as Plath and Sexton, be understood as?
5. What is the main argument of the writer of this essay?
6. What is the relationship between father and daughter revealed in the confessional poetry from the perspective of the essay?

II. True or false

1. Over the last decade the very validity of the name has come into question, and the poets traditionally read through a confessional paradigm are being approached in new ways. ( )
2. Travisano devotes an early chapter of his study to an attack on what he names the "confessional paradigm," developing five lines to support the term. ( )
3. An old approach has taken what amounts to an opposing stance to this distinction between antique and autobiography. ( )
4. Deborah Nelson's 2002 *Pursuing Privacy in Cold War America* discusses the representation of domestic space by Sexton and Rich as a response to the gendering of the home as a masculine enclosure. ( )
5. Over the last decade, critical studies of masculinity on confessional poetry have abounded over. ( )
6. A sense of loneliness is the only subject unveiled in the confessional poetry, according to the writer of the essay. ( )

For Fun

I. Movies to see

The Bell Jar (1979): It is a 1979 film directed by Larry Peerce and based on the novel by Sylvia Plath. It stars Marilyn Hassett and Julie Harris. The story follows a young woman's summer in New York City working for a women's magazine, her return home to New England, and her subsequent psychological breakdown within the context of the difficulties of the 1950s—ranging from the Rosenberg execution, to the disturbing aspects of pop culture, to the distraction of predatory college boys.

II. Websites to visit

1. http://www.poets.org/poetsorg/text/brief-guide-confessional-poetry
2. http://www.neuroticpoets.com/plath/
3. http://www.freepatentsonline.com/article/College-Literature/211454294.html

III. Writing

Someone believes that a taxpayer has done his or her part as a citizen. However, someone believes that a citizen should assume other responsibilities. Discuss both of opinions and present your opinion within 250 words.

Chapter 18
Toni Morrison(1931-   )
托尼·莫里森

Section A　Literary Focus

作者简介(About the Author)

【生平】　托尼·莫里森,美国非洲裔女作家。生于俄亥俄州钢城洛里恩。1949 年她以优异成绩考入当时专为黑人开设的霍华德大学,攻读英语和古典文学。大学毕业后,又进入康奈尔大学专攻福克纳和沃尔夫的小说,并以此获硕士学位。此后,她在德克萨斯南方大学和霍德华大学任教。1966 年,她在纽约兰多姆出版社担任高级编辑,曾为拳王穆罕默德·阿里自传和一些青年黑人作家的作品的出版竭尽全力。她所主编的《黑人之书》,记叙了美国黑人三百年历史,被称为美国黑人史的百科全书。70 年代起,她先后在纽约州立大学、耶鲁大学和巴尔德学院讲授美国黑人文学,并为《纽约时报书评周报》撰写过 30 篇高质量的书评文章,1987 年起出任普林斯顿大学教授,讲授文学创作。莫里森可以说是一位学者型的小说家。她的作品均以美国的黑人生活为主要内容,笔触细腻,人物、语言及故事情节生动逼真,想象力丰富。1993 年,由于她"在小说中以丰富的想象力和富有诗意的表达方式使美国现实的一个极其重要方面充满活力",莫里森获诺贝尔文学奖。

【主要作品】　《最蓝的眼睛》(*The Bluest Eye*,1970)、《所罗门之歌》(*Song of Solomon*,1977)、《秀拉》(*Sula*,1973)、《宠儿》(*Beloved*,1987)、《恩惠》(*A Mercy*,2008)、《家园》(*Home*,2012)等。

作品选读(Selected Writings)

托尼·莫里森的短篇小说《宣叙》发表于 1983 年,讲述了儿童时代相识的两个不同种族的小女孩的成长故事。故事的叙事者是其中一个女孩特怀拉,通过她的回忆讲述了残疾黑人玛吉遭受种族和性别歧视的残酷事实,凸显了性别、种族和文化的问题。独特的叙述者、不同的叙述声音、细腻的描写手法是这篇小说的特色。

Recitatif

My mother danced all night and Roberta's was sick. That's why we were taken to St. Bonny's. People want to put their arms around you when you tell them you were in a shelter, but it really wasn't bad. No big long room with one hundred beds like Bellevue. There were four to a room, and when Roberta and me came, there was a shortage of state kids, so we were the only ones assigned to 406 and could go from bed to bed if we wanted to. And we wanted to, too. We changed beds every night and for the whole four months we were there we never picked one out as our own permanent bed.

It didn't start out that way. The minute I walked in and the Big Bozo introduced us, I got sick to my stomach. It was one thing to be taken out of your own bed early in the morning—it was something else to be stuck in a strange place with a girl from a whole other race. And Mary, that's my mother, she was right. Every now and then she would stop dancing long enough to tell me something important and one of the things she said was that they never washed their hair and they smelled funny. Roberta sure did. Smell funny, I mean. So when the Big Bozo (nobody ever called her Mrs. Itkin, just like nobody ever said St. Bonaventure)—when she said, "Twyla, this is Roberta. Roberta, this is Twyla. Make each other welcome." I said, "My mother won't like you putting me in here."

"Good," said Bozo. "Maybe then she'll come and take you home."

How's that for mean? If Roberta had laughed I would have killed her, but she didn't. She just walked over to the window and stood with her back to us.

"Turn around," said the Bozo. "Don't be rude. Now Twyla. Roberta. When you hear a loud buzzer, that's the call for dinner. Come down to the first floor. Any fights and no movie." And then, just to make sure we knew what we would be missing. "*The Wizard of Oz*.①"

Roberta must have thought I meant that my mother would be mad about my being put in the shelter. Not about rooming with her, because as soon as Bozo left she came over to me and said, "Is your mother sick too?"

"No," I said. "She just likes to dance all night."

"Oh," she nodded her head and I liked the way she understood things so fast. So for the moment it didn't matter that we looked like salt and pepper standing there and that's what the other kids called us sometimes. We were eight years old and got F's all the time. Me because I couldn't remember what I read or what the teacher said. And Roberta because she couldn't read at all and didn't even listen to the teacher. She wasn't good at anything except jacks, at which she was a killer: pow scoop pow scoop pow scoop.

We didn't like each other all that much at first, but nobody else wanted to play with us because we weren't real orphans with beautiful dead parents in the sky. We were

---

① *The Wizard of Oz*:《绿野仙踪》

dumped. Even the New York City Puerto Ricans① and the upstate Indians ignored us. All kinds of kids were in there, black ones, white ones, even two Koreans. The food was good, though. At least I thought so. Roberta hated it and left whole pieces of things on her plate: Spam, Salisbury steak②—even jello③ with fruit cocktail in it, and she didn't care if I ate what she wouldn't. Mary's idea of supper was popcorn and a can of YooHoo④. Hot mashed potatoes and two weenies was like Thanksgiving for me.

It really wasn't bad, St. Bonny's. The big girls on the second floor pushed us around now and then. But that was all. They wore lipstick and eyebrow pencil land wobbled⑤ their knees while they watched TV. Fifteen, sixteen, even, some of them were. They were put-out girls, scared runaways most of them. Poor little girls who fought their uncles off but looked tough to us, and mean. God did they look mean. The staff tried to keep them separate from the younger children, but sometimes they caught us watching them in the orchard where they played radios and danced with each other. They'd light out after us and pull our hair or twist our arms. We were scared of them, Roberta and me, but neither of us wanted the other one to know it. So we got a good list of dirty names we could shout back when we ran from them through the orchard. I used to dream a lot and almost always the orchard was there. Two acres, four maybe, of these little apple trees. Hundreds of them. Empty and crooked like beggar women when I first came to St. Bonny's but fat with flowers when I left. I don't know why I dreamt about that orchard so much. Nothing really happened there. Nothing all that important, I mean. Just the big girls dancing and playing the radio. Roberta and me watching. Maggie fell down there once. The kitchen woman with legs like parentheses⑥. And the big girls laughed at her. We should have helped her up, I know, but we were scared of those girls with lipstick and eyebrow pencil. Maggie couldn't talk. The kids said she had her tongue cut out, but I think she was just born that way: mute. She was old and sandy-colored and she worked in the kitchen. I don't know if she was nice or not. I just remember her legs like parentheses and how she rocked when she walked. She worked from early in the morning till two o'clock, and if she was late, if she had too much cleaning and didn't get out till two-fifteen or so, she'd cut through the orchard so she wouldn't miss her bus and have to wait another hour. She wore this really stupid little hat—a kid's hat with ear flaps—and she wasn't much taller than we were. A really awful little hat. Even for a mute, it was dumb—dressing like a kid and never saying anything at all."

---

① Puerto Ricans：波多黎各人
② Salisbury steak：疏利士巴利牛肉饼
③ jello：凝胶物
④ YooHoo：一种巧克力软饮料
⑤ wobble：摇摆，晃动
⑥ parentheses：parenthesis 复数，圆括号

"But what about if somebody tries to kill her?" I used to wonder about that. "Or what if she wants to cry? Can she cry?"

"Sure," Roberta said. "But just tears. No sounds come out."

"She can't scream?"

"Nope. Nothing."

"Can she hear?"

"I guess."

"Let's call her," I said. And we did.

"Dummy! Dummy!" She never turned her head.

"Bow legs! Bow legs!" Nothing. She just rocked on, the chin straps of her baby-boy hat swaying from side to side. I think we were wrong. I think she could hear and didn't let on. And it shames me even now to think there was somebody in there after all who heard us call her those names and couldn't tell on us.

We got along all right, Roberta and me. Changed beds every night, got F's in civics and communication skills and gym. The Bozo was disappointed in us, she said. Out of 130 of us state cases, 90 were under twelve. Almost all were real orphans with beautiful dead parents in the sky. We were the only ones dumped and the only ones with F's in three classes including gym. So we got along—what with her leaving whole pieces of things on her plate and being nice about not asking questions.

I think it was the day before Maggie fell down that we found out our mothers were coming to visit us on the same Sunday. We had been at the shelter twenty-eight days (Roberta twenty-eight and a half) and this was their first visit with us. Our mothers would come at ten o'clock in time for chapel, then lunch with us in the teachers' lounge①. I thought if my dancing mother met her sick mother it might be good for her. And Roberta thought her sick mother would get a big bang out of a dancing one. We got excited about it and curled each other's hair. After breakfast we sat on the bed watching the road from the window. Roberta's socks were still wet. She washed them the night before and put them on the radiator to dry. They hadn't, but she put them on anyway because their tops were so pretty—scalloped② in pink. Each of us had a purple construction—paper basket that we had made in craft class. Mine had a yellow crayon rabbit on it. Roberta's had eggs with wiggly lines of color. Inside were cellophane grass and just the jelly beans because I'd eaten the two marshmallow③ eggs they gave us. The Big Bozo came herself to get us. Smiling she told us we looked very nice and to come downstairs. We were so surprised by the smile we'd never seen before, neither of us moved.

"Don't you want to see your mommies?"

---

① lounge：休息室

② scalloped：扇形的

③ marshmallow：棉花糖

I stood up first and spilled the jelly beans all over the floor. Bozo's smile disappeared while we scrambled to get the candy up off the floor and put it back in the grass.

She escorted us downstairs to the first floor, where the other girls were lining up to file into the chapel. A bunch of grown-ups stood to one side. Viewers mostly. The old biddies who wanted servants and the fags who wanted company looking for children they might want to adopt. Once in a while a grandmother. Almost never anybody young or anybody whose face wouldn't scare you in the night. Because if any of the real orphans had young relatives they wouldn't be real orphans. I saw Mary right away. She had on those green slacks I hated and hated even more now because didn't she know we were going to chapel? And that fur jacket with the pocket linings so ripped she had to pull to get her hands out of them. But her face was pretty—like always, and she smiled and waved like she was the little girl looking for her mother—not me.

I walked slowly, trying not to drop the jelly beans and hoping the paper handle would hold. I had to use my last Chiclet because by the time I finished cutting everything out, all the Elmer's was gone. I am left-handed and the scissors never worked for me. It didn't matter, though; I might just as well have chewed the gum. Mary dropped to her knees and grabbed me, mashing the basket, the jelly beans, and the grass into her ratty fur jacket.

"Twyla, baby. Twyla, baby!"

I could have killed her. Already I heard the big girls in the orchard the next time saying, "Twyyyyyla, baby!" But I couldn't stay mad at Mary while she was smiling and hugging me and smelling of Lady Esther dusting powder. I wanted to stay buried in her fur all day.

To tell the truth I forgot about Roberta. Mary and I got in line for the traipse① into chapel and I was feeling proud because she looked so beautiful even in those ugly green slacks② that made her behind stick out. A pretty mother on earth is better than a beautiful dead one in the sky even if she did leave you all alone to go dancing.

I felt a tap on my shoulder, turned, and saw Roberta smiling. I smiled back, but not too much lest somebody think this visit was the biggest thing that ever happened in my life. Then Roberta said, "Mother, I want you to meet my roommate, Twyla. And that's Twyla's mother."

I looked up it seemed for miles. She was big. Bigger than any man and on her chest was the biggest cross I'd ever seen. I swear it was six inches long each way. And in the crook of her arm was the biggest Bible ever made.

Mary, simple-minded as ever, grinned and tried to yank her hand out of the pocket with the raggedy lining—to shake hands, I guess. Roberta's mother looked down at me

---

① traipse: 闲荡,漫步
② slacks: 女裤

and then looked down at Mary too. She didn't say anything, just grabbed Roberta with her Bible-free hand and stepped tout of line, walking quickly to the rear of it. Mary was still grinning because she's not too swift when it comes to what's really going on. Then this light bulb goes off in her head and she says "That bitch!" really loud and us almost in the chapel now. Organ music whining; the Bonny Angels singing sweetly. Everybody in the world turned around to look. And Mary would have kept it up—kept calling names if I hadn't squeezed her hand as hard as I could. That helped a little, but she still twitched and crossed and uncrossed her legs all through service. Even groaned a couple of times. Why did I think she would come there and act right? Slacks. No hat like the grandmothers and viewers, and groaning all the while. When we stood for hymns she kept her mouth shut. Wouldn't even look at the words on the page. She actually reached in her purse for a mirror to check her lipstick. All I could think of was that she really needed to be killed. The sermon lasted a year, and I knew the real orphans were looking smug again.

We were supposed to have lunch in the teachers' lounge, but Mary didn't bring anything, so we picked fur and cellophane grass off the mashed jelly beans and ate them. I could have killed her. I sneaked a look at Roberta. Her mother had brought chicken legs and ham sandwiches and oranges and a whole box of chocolate-covered grahams. Roberta drank milk from a thermos while her mother read the Bible to her.

Things are not right. The wrong food is always with the wrong people. Maybe that's why I got into waitress work later—to match up the right people with the right food. Roberta just let those chicken legs sit there, but she did bring a stack of grahams up to me later when the visit was over. I think she was sorry that her mother would not shake my mother's hand. And I liked that and I liked the fact that she didn't say a word about Mary groaning all the way through the service and not bringing any lunch.

Roberta left in May when the apple trees were heavy and white. On her last day we went to the orchard to watch the big girls smoke and dance by the radio. It didn't matter that they said, "Twyyyyyla, baby." We sat on the ground and breathed. Lady Esther. Apple blossoms. I still go soft when I smell one or the other. Roberta was going home. The big cross and the big Bible was coming to get her and she seemed sort of glad and sort of not. I thought I would die in that room of four beds without her and I knew Bozo had plans to move some other dumped kid in there with me. Roberta promised to write every day, which was really sweet of her because she couldn't read a lick so how could she write anybody. I would have drawn pictures and sent them to her but she never gave me her address. Little by little she faded. Her wet socks with the pink scalloped tops and her big serious-looking eyes—that's all I could catch when I tried to bring her to mind.

I was working behind the counter at the Howard Johnson's on the Thruway just before the Kingston exit. Not a bad job. Kind of a long ride from Newburgh, but okay once I got there. Mine was the second night shift—eleven to seven. Very light until a Greyhound checked in for breakfast around six-thirty. At that hour the sun was all the way clear of the hills behind the restaurant. The place looked better at night—more like shelter—but I loved it when the sun broke in, even if it did show all the cracks in the vinyl① and the speckled floor looked dirty no matter what the mop boy did.

It was August and a bus crowd was just unloading. They would stand around a long while: going to the john, and looking at gifts and junk-for-sale machines, reluctant to sit down so soon. Even to eat. I was trying to fill the coffee pots and get them all situated on the electric burners when I saw her. She was sitting in a booth smoking a cigarette with two guys smothered in head and facial hair. Her own hair was so big and wild I could hardly see her face. But the eyes. I would know them anywhere. She had on a powder-blue halter and shorts outfit and earrings the size of bracelets. Talk about lipstick and eyebrow pencil. She made the big girls look like nuns. I couldn't get off the counter until seven o'clock, but I kept watching the booth in case they got up to leave before that. My replacement was on time for a change, so I counted and stacked my receipts as fast as I could and signed off. I walked over to the booths, smiling and wondering if she would remember me. Or even if she wanted to remember me. Maybe she didn't want to be reminded of St. Bonny's or to have anybody know she was ever there. I know I never talked about it to anybody.

I put my hands in my apron pockets and leaned against the back of the booth facing them.

"Roberta? Roberta Fisk?"

She looked up. "Yeah?"

"Twyla."

She squinted② for a second and then said, "Wow."

"Remember me?"

"Sure. Hey. Wow."

"It's been a while," I said, and gave a smile to the two hairy guys.

"Yeah. Wow. You work here?"

"Yeah," I said. "I live in Newburgh."

"Newburgh? No kidding?" She laughed then a private laugh that included the guys but only the guys, and they laughed with her. What could I do but laugh too and wonder why I was standing there with my knees showing out from under that uniform. Without looking I could see the blue and white triangle on my head, my hair shapeless in a net, my ankles thick in white oxfords. Nothing could have been less sheer than my stockings. There was this silence that came downright after I laughed. A silence it was her turn to fill up. With introductions, maybe, to her boyfriends or an invitation to sit down and have a Coke. Instead she lit a cigarette off the one she'd just finished and said, "We're on our way to the Coast. He's got an appointment with Hendrix."

---

① vinyl: 乙烯基
② squint: 眯眼看

She gestured casually toward the boy next to her.

"Hendrix Fantastic," I said. "Really fantastic. What's she doing now?"

Roberta coughed on her cigarette and the two guys rolled their eyes up at the ceiling."

Hendrix. Jimi Hendrix, asshole. He's only the biggest—Oh, wow. Forget it."

I was dismissed without anyone saying goodbye, so I thought I would do it for her.

"How's your mother?" I asked. Her grin cracked her whole face. She swallowed. "Fine," she said. "How's yours?"

"Pretty as a picture," I said and turned away. The backs of my knees were damp. Howard Johnson's really was a dump in the sunlight.

James is as comfortable as a house slipper. He liked my cooking and I liked his big loud family. They have lived in Newburgh all of their lives and talk about it the way people do who have always known a home. His grandmother is a porch swing older than his father and when they talk about streets and avenues and buildings they call them names they no longer have. They still call the A & P Rico's because it stands on property once a mom and pop store owned by Mr. Rico. And they call the new community college Town Hall because it once was. My mother-in-law puts up jelly and cucumbers and buys butter wrapped in cloth from a dairy. James and his father talk about fishing and baseball and I can see them all together on the Hudson in a raggedy skiff. Half the population of Newburgh is on welfare now, but to my husband's family it was still some upstate paradise of a time long past. A time of ice houses and vegetable wagons, coal furnaces① and children weeding gardens. When our son was born my mother-in-law gave me the crib② blanket that had been hers.

But the town they remembered had changed. Something quick was in the air. Magnificent old houses, so ruined they had become shelter for squatters and rent risks, were bought and renovated. Smart IBM people moved out of their suburbs back into the city and put shutters up and herb gardens in their backyards. A brochure came in the mail announcing the opening of a Food Emporium③. Gourmet food it said—and listed items the rich IBM crowd would want. It was located in a new mall at the edge of town and I drove out to shop there one day—just to see. It was late in June. After the tulips④ were gone and the Queen Elizabeth roses were open everywhere. It railed my cart along the aisle tossing in smoked oysters and Robert's sauce and things I knew would sit in my cupboard for years. Only when I found some Klondike ice cream bars did I feel less guilty about spending James's fireman's salary so foolishly. My father-in-law ate them

---

① furnace: 火炉
② crib: 婴儿床
③ emporium: 商场
④ tulip: 郁金香

with the same gusto① little Joseph did.

  Waiting in the check-out line I heard a voice say, "Twyla!"

  The classical music piped over the aisles had affected me and the woman leaning toward me was dressed to kill. Diamonds on her hand, a smart white summer dress. "I'm Mrs. Benson," I said.

  "Ho. Ho. The Big Bozo," she sang.

  For a split second I didn't know what she was talking about. She had a bunch of asparagus② and two cartons of fancy water.

  "Roberta!"

  "Right."

  "For heaven's sake. Roberta."

  "You look great," she said.

  "So do you. Where are you? Here? In Newburgh?"

  "Yes. Over in Annandale."

  I was opening my mouth to say more when the cashier called my attention to her empty counter.

  "Meet you outside." Roberta pointed her finger and went into the express line.

  I placed the groceries and kept myself from glancing around to check Roberta's progress. I remembered Howard Johnson's and looking for a chance to speak only to be greeted with a stingy③ "wow". But she was waiting for me and her huge hair was sleek④ now, smooth around a small, nicely shaped head. Shoes, dress, everything lovely and summery and rich. I was dying to know what happened to her, how she got from Jimi Hendrix to Annandale, a neighborhood full of doctors and IBM executives. Easy, I thought. Everything is so easy for them. They think they own the world.

  "How long," I asked her. "How long have you been here?"

  "A year. I got married to a man who lives here. And you, you're married too, right? Benson, you said."

  "Yeah. James Benson."

  "And is he nice?"

  "Oh, is he nice?"

  "Well, is he?" Roberta's eyes were steady as though she really meant the question and wanted an answer."

  He's wonderful, Roberta. Wonderful."

  "So you're happy."

  "Very."

---

① gusto：爱好，嗜好

② asparagus：芦笋

③ stingy：尖酸的，吝啬的

④ sleek：光滑的

"That's good," she said and nodded her head. "I always hoped you'd be happy. Any kids? I know you have kids."

"One. A boy. How about you?"

"Four."

"Four?"

She laughed. "Step kids. He's a widower."

"Oh."

"Got a minute? Let's have a coffee."

I thought about the Klondikes melting and the inconvenience of going all the way to my car and putting the bags in the trunk. Served me right for buying all that stuff I didn't need. Roberta was ahead of me."

Put them in my car. It's right here."

And then I saw the dark blue limousine①.

"You married a Chinaman?"

"No," she laughed. "He's the driver."

"Oh, my. If the Big Bozo could see you now."

We both giggled②. Really giggled. Suddenly, in just a pulse beat, twenty years disappeared and all of it came rushing back. The big girls (whom we called gar girls-Roberta's misheard word for the evil stone faces described in a civics class) there dancing in the orchard, the ploppy mashed potatoes, the double weenies, the Spam with pineapple. We went into the coffee shop holding onto one another and I tried to think why we were glad to see each other this time and not before. Once, twelve years ago, we passed like strangers. A black girl and a white girl meeting in a Howard Johnson's on the road and having nothing to say. One in a blue and white triangle waitress hat—the other on her way to see, Hendrix. Now we were behaving like sisters separated for much too long. Those four short months were nothing in time. Maybe it was the thing itself. Just being there, together. Two little girls who knew what nobody else in the world knew—how not to ask questions. How to believe what had to be believed. There was politeness in that reluctance and generosity as well. Is your mother sick too? No, she dances all night. Oh—and an understanding nod.

We sat in a booth by the window and fell into recollection like veterans.

"Did you ever learn to read?"

"Watch." She picked up the menu. "Special of the day. Cream of corn soup. Entrees. Two dots and a wriggly line. Quiche③. Chef salad, scallops ..."

I was laughing and applauding when the waitress came up.

"Remember the Easter baskets?"

---

① limousine: 豪华轿车

② giggle: 傻笑,咯咯地笑

③ quiche: 乳蛋饼

"And how we tried to introduce them?"

"Your mother with that cross like two telephone poles."

"And yours with those tight slacks."

We laughed so loudly heads turned and made the laughter harder to suppress.

"What happened to the Jimi Hendrix date?"

Roberta made a blow-out sound with her lips.

"When he died I thought about you."

"Oh, you heard about him finally?"

"Finally. Come on, I was a small-town country waitress."

"And I was a small-town country dropout. God, were we wild. I still don't know how I got out of there alive."

"But you did."

"I did. I really did. Now I'm Mrs. Kenneth Norton."

"Sounds like a mouthful."

"It is."

"Servants and all?"

Roberta held up two fingers.

"Ow! What does he do?"

"Computers and stuff. What do I know?"

"I don't remember a hell of a lot from those days, but Lord, St. Bonny's is as clear as daylight. Remember Maggie? The day she fell down and those gar girls laughed at her?"

Roberta looked up from her salad and stared at me. "Maggie didn't fall," she said.

"Yes, she did. You remember."

"No, Twyla. They knocked her down. Those girls pushed her down and tore her clothes. In the orchard."

"I don't—that's not what happened."

"Sure it is. In the orchard. Remember how scared we were?"

"Wait a minute. I don't remember any of that."

"And Bozo was fired."

"You're crazy. She was there when I left. You left before me."

"I went back. You weren't there when they fired Bozo."

"What?"

"Twice. Once for a year when I was about ten, another for two months when I was fourteen. That's when I ran away."

"You ran away from St. Bonny's?"

"I had to. What do you want? Me dancing in that orchard?"

"Are you sure about Maggie?"

"Of course I'm sure. You've blocked it, Twyla. It happened. Those girls had behavior problems, you know."

"Didn't they, though. But why can't I remember the Maggie thing?"

"Believe me. It happened. And we were there."

"Who did you room with when you went back?" I asked her as if I would know her. The Maggie thing was troubling me."

"Creeps. They tickled① themselves in the night."

My ears were itching and I wanted to go home suddenly. This was all very well but she couldn't just comb her hair, wash her face and pretend everything was hunky-dory②. After the Howard Johnson's snub③. And no apology. Nothing.

"Were you on dope or what that time at Howard Johnson's?" I tried to make my voice sound friendlier than I felt.

"Maybe, a little. I never did drugs much. Why?"

"I don't know; you acted sort of like you didn't want to know me then."

"Oh, Twyla, you know how it was in those days: black-white. You know how everything was."

But I didn't know. I thought it was just the opposite. Bus loads of blacks and whites came into Howard Johnson's together. They roamed together then: students, musicians, lovers, protesters. You got to see everything at Howard Johnson's and blacks were very friendly with whites in those days. But sitting there with nothing on my plate but two hard tomato wedges wondering about the melting Klondikes it seemed childish remembering the slight. We went to her car, and with the help of the driver, got my stuff into my station wagon.

"We'll keep in touch this time," she said.

"Sure," I said. "Sure. Give me a call."

"I will," she said, and then just as I was sliding behind the wheel, she leaned into the window. "By the way. Your mother. Did she ever stop dancing?"

I shook my head. "No. Never."

Roberta nodded.

"And yours? Did she ever get well?"

She smiled a tiny sad smile. "No. She never did. Look, call me, okay?"

"Okay," I said, but I knew I wouldn't. Roberta had messed up my past somehow with that business about Maggie. I wouldn't forget a thing like that. Would I?

Strife came to us that fall. At least that's what the paper called it. Strife. Racial strife. The word made me think of a bird—a big shrieking bird out of 1,000,000,000 B. C. flapping its wings and cawing. Its eye with no lid always bearing down on you. All day it screeched④ and at night it slept on the roof-tops. It woke you in the morning and

---

① tickle: 挠痒痒
② hunky-dory: 没问题
③ snub: 斥责,冷落
④ screech: 尖叫

from the Today show to the eleven o'clock news it kept you an awful company. I couldn't figure it out from one day to the next. I knew I was supposed to feel something strong, but I didn't know what, and James wasn't any help. Joseph was on the list of kids to be transferred from the junior high school to another one at some far-out-of-the-way place and I thought it was a good thing until I heard it was a bad thing. I mean I didn't know. All the schools seemed dumps to me, and the fact that one was nicer looking didn't hold much weight. But the papers were full of it and then the kids began to get jumpy. In August, mind you. Schools weren't even open yet. I thought Joseph might be frightened to go over there, but he didn't seem scared so I forgot about it, until I found myself driving along Hudson Street out there by the school they were trying to integrate and saw a line of women marching. And who do you suppose was in line, big as life, holding a sign in front of her bigger than her mother's cross? MOTHERS HAVE RIGHTS TOO! It said.

I drove on, and then changed my mind. I circled the block, slowed down and honked① my horn.

Roberta looked over and when she saw me she waved. I didn't wave back, but I didn't move either. She handed her sign to another woman and came over to where I was parked.

"Hi."

"What are you doing?"

"Picketing. What's it look like?"

"What for?"

"What do you mean 'What for?' They want to take my kids and send them out of the neighborhood. They don't want to go."

"So what if they go to another school? My boy's being bussed too, and I don't mind. Why should you?"

"It's not about us, Twyla. Me and you. It's about our kids."

"What's more us than that?"

"Well, it is a free country."

"Not yet, but it will be."

"What the hell does that mean? I'm not doing anything to you."

"You really think that?"

"I know it."

"I wonder what made me think you were different."

"I wonder what made me think you were different."

"Look at them," I said. "Just look. Who do they think they are? Swarming② all over the place like they own it. And now they think they can decide where my child goes

---

① honk：按喇叭

② swarm：挤满

to school. Look at them, Roberta. They're Bozos."

Roberta turned around and looked at the women. Almost all of them were standing still now, waiting. Some were even edging toward us. Roberta looked at me out of some refrigerator behind her eyes. "No, they're not. They're just mothers."

"And what am I? Swiss cheese?"

"I used to curl your hair."

I hated your hands in my hair.

The women were moving. Our faces looked mean to them of course and they looked as though they could not wait to throw themselves in front of a police car, or better yet, into my car and drag me away by my ankles. Now they surrounded my car and gently, gently began to rock it. I swayed back and forth like a sideways yo-yo. Automatically I reached for Roberta, like the old days in the orchard when they saw us watching them and we had to get out of there, and if one of us fell the other pulled her up and if one of us was caught the other stayed to kick and scratch, and neither would leave the other behind. My arm short out of the car window but no receiving hand was there. Roberta was looking at me sway from side to side in the car and her face was still. My purse slid from the car seat down under the dashboard①. The four policemen who had been drinking Tab in their car finally got the message and strolled over, forcing their way through the women. Quietly, firmly they spoke. "Okay, ladies. Back in line or off the streets."

Some of them went away willingly; others had to be urged away from the car doors and the hood. Roberta didn't move. She was looking steadily at me. I was fumbling to turn on the ignition, which wouldn't catch because the gearshift② was still in drive. The seats of the car were a mess because the swaying had thrown my grocery coupons all over it and my purse was sprawled③ on the floor.

"Maybe I am different now, Twyla. But you're not. You're the same little state kid who kicked a poor old black lady when she was down on the ground. You kicked a black lady and you have the nerve to call me a bigot④."

The coupons were everywhere and the guts of my purse were bunched under the dashboard. What was she saying? Black? Maggie wasn't black.

"She wasn't black," I said.

"Like hell she wasn't, and you kicked her. We both did. You kicked a black lady who couldn't even scream."

"Liar!"

"You're the liar! Why don't you just go on home and leave us alone, huh?"

---

① dashboard: 汽车等仪表板
② gearshift: 换挡杆
③ sprawl: 躺卧
④ bigot: 偏执的人

She turned away and I skidded away from the curb.

The next morning I went into the garage and cut the side out of the carton our portable TV had come in. it wasn't nearly big enough, but after a while I had a decent sign: red spray-painted① letters on a while background—AND SO DO CHILDREN. I meant just to go down to the school and tack it up somewhere so those cows on the picket line across the street could see it, but when I got there, some ten or so others had already assemble—protesting the cows across the street. Police permits and everything. I got in line and we strutted② in time on our side while Roberta's group strutted on theirs. That first day we were all dignified, pretending the other side didn't exist. The second day there was name calling and finger gestures. But that was about all. People changed signs from time to time, but Roberta never did and neither did I. Actually my sign didn't make sense without Roberta's. "And so do children what?" one of the women on my side asked me. Have right, I said, as though it was obvious.

Roberta didn't acknowledge my presence in any way and I got to thinking maybe she didn't know I was there. I began to pace myself in the line, jostling③ people one minute and lagging behind the next, so Roberta and I could reach the end of our respective lines at the same time and there would be a moment in our turn when we would face each other. Still, I couldn't tell whether she saw me and knew my sign was for her. The next day I went early before we were scheduled to assemble. I waited until she got there before I exposed my new creation. As soon as she hoisted her MOTHERS HAVE RIGHTS TOO I began to wave my new one, which said, HOW WOULD YOU KNOW? I know she saw that one, but I had gotten addicted now. My signs got crazier each day, and the women on my side decided that I was a kook④. They couldn't make heads or tails out of my brilliant screaming posters.

I brought a painted sign in queenly red with huge black letters that said IS YOUR MOTHER WELL? Roberta took her lunch break and didn't come back for the rest of the day or any day after. Two days later I stopped going too and couldn't have been missed because nobody understood my signs anyway.

It was a nasty six weeks. Classes were suspended and Joseph didn't go to anybody's school until October. The children—everyone's children—soon got bored with that extended vacation they thought was going to be so great. They looked at TV until their eyes flattened. I spent a couple of mornings tutoring my son, as the other mothers said we should. Twice I opened a text from last year that he had never turned in. Twice he yawned in my face. Other mothers organized living room sessions so the kids would keep up. None of the kids could concentrate so they drifted back to *The Price Is Right* and

---

① spray-painted: 喷漆的
② strut: 趾高气扬地走
③ jostle: 推挤
④ kook: 疯子

The Brady Bunch. When the school finally opened there were fights once or twice and some sirens roared through the streets every once in a while. There were a lot of photographers from Albany. And just when ABC was about to send up a news crew, the kids settled down like nothing in the world had happened. Joseph hung my HOW WOULD YOU KNOW? sign in his bedroom. I don't know what became of AND SO DO CHILDREN. I think my father-in-law cleaned some fish on it. He was always puttering around in our garage. Each of his five children lived in Newburgh and he acted as though he had five extra homes.

I couldn't help looking for Roberta when Joseph graduated from high school, but I didn't see her. It didn't trouble me much what she had said to me in the car. I mean the kicking part. I know I didn't do that, I couldn't do that. But I was puzzled by her telling me Maggie was black. When I thought about it I actually couldn't be certain. She wasn't pitch-black①, I know, or I would have remembered that. What I remember was the kiddie hat, and the semicircle legs②. I tried to reassure myself about the race thing for a long time until it dawned on me that the truth was already there, and Roberta knew it. I didn't kick her; I didn't join in with the gar girls and kick that lady, but I sure did want to. We watched and never tried to help her and never called for help. Maggie was my dancing mother. Deaf, I thought, and dumb. Nobody inside. Nobody who would hear you if you cried in the night. Nobody who could tell you anything important that you could use. Rocking, dancing, swaying as she walked. And when the gar girls pushed her down, and started roughhousing③, I knew she wouldn't scream, couldn't—just like me—and I was glad about that.

We decided not to have a tree, because Christmas would be at my mother-in-law's house, so why have a tree at both places? Joseph was at SUNY New Paltz and we had to economize, we said. But at the last minute, I changed my mind. Nothing could be that bad. So I rushed around town looking for a tree, something small but wide. By the time I found a place, it was snowing and very late. I dawdled like it was the most important purchase in the world and the tree man was fed up with me. Finally I chose one and had it tied onto the trunk of the car. I drove away slowly because the sand trucks were not out yet and the streets could be murder at the beginning of a snowfall. Downtown the streets were wide and rather empty except for a cluster of people coming out of the Newburgh Hotel. The one hotel in town that wasn't built out of cardboard and Plexiglas④. A party, probably. The men huddled in the snow were dressed in tails and the women had on furs. Shiny things glittered from underneath their coats. It made me

---

① pitch-black：极黑的，漆黑的
② semicircle legs：罗圈腿
③ roughhouse：粗暴对待
④ Plexiglas：树脂玻璃

tired to look at them. Tired, tired, tired. On the next corner was a small diner with loops and loops of paper bells in the window. I stopped the car and went in. Just for a cup of coffee and twenty minutes of peace before I went home and tried to finish everything before Christmas Eve.

"Twyla?"

There she was. In a silvery evening gown and dark fur coat. A man and another woman were with her, the man fumbling for change to put in the cigarette machine. The woman was humming and tapping on the counter with her fingernails. They all looked a little bit drunk.

"Well. It's you."

"How are you?"

I shrugged. "Pretty good. Frazzled①. Christmas and all."

"Regular?" called the woman from the counter.

"Fine," Roberta called back and then, "Wait for me in the car."

She slipped into the booth beside me. "I have to tell you something, Twyla. I made up my mind if I ever saw you again, I'd tell you."

"I'd just as soon not hear anything, Roberta. It doesn't matter now, anyway."

"No," she said. "Not about that."

"Don't be long," said the woman. She carried two regulars to go and the man peeled his cigarette pack as they left.

"It's about St. Bonny's and Maggie."

"Oh, please."

"Listen to me. I really did think she was black. I didn't make that up. I really thought so. But now I can't be sure. I just remember her as old, so old. And because she couldn't talk—well, you know, I thought she was crazy. She'd been brought up in an institution like my mother was and like I thought I would be too. And you were right. We didn't kick her. It was the gar girls. Only them. But, well, I wanted to. I really wanted them to hurt her. I said we did it, too. You and me, but that's not true. And I don't want you to carry that around. It was just that I wanted to do it so bad that day—wanting to is doing it."

Her eyes were watery from the drinks she'd had, I guess. I know it's that way with me. One glass of wine and I start bawling over the littlest thing.

"We were kids, Roberta."

"Yeah. Yeah. I know, just kids."

"Eight."

"Eight."

"And lonely."

"Scared, too."

---

① frazzled: 疲惫的

She wiped her cheeks with the heel of her hand and smiled. "Well, that's all I wanted to say."

I nodded and couldn't think of any way to fill the silence that went from the diner past the paper bells on out into the snow. It was heavy now. I thought I'd better wait for the sand trucks before starting home.

"Thanks, Roberta."

"Sure."

"Did I tell you? My mother, she never did stop dancing."

"Yes. You told me. And mine, she never got well." Roberta lifted her hands from the table top and covered her face with her palms. When she took them away she really was crying. "Oh shit, Twyla. Shit, shit, shit. What the hell happened to Maggie?"

Questions for discussion

1. Does the author tell readers the racial identity of the two girls in the story? Do you know who is white and who is the colored? Why?
2. Why does the story end the way it does? Do you think Twyla and Roberta will ever see each other again?
3. What do you think this story says about friendship? About memories?

文学术语(Definition of Literary Terms)

Magic realism or magical realism is a genre where magic elements are a natural part in an otherwise mundane, realistic environment. The term is broadly descriptive rather than critically rigorous: Professor Matthew Strecher defines magic realism as "what happens when a highly detailed, realistic setting is invaded by something too strange to believe."

Section B Cultural Notes

Before You Read

1. Try to search the Internet or in the library about Harlem Renaissance and its influences on Toni Morrison. Give a 3-minute classroom presentation.
2. Do you know Martin Luther King and the Civil Rights Movement? Briefly summarize his life.

Start to Read

Harlem Renaissance

The Harlem Renaissance① was a cultural movement that spanned the 1920s. At the time, it was known as the "New Negro Movement," named after the 1925 anthology by Alain Locke. The Movement also included the new African-American cultural expressions across the urban areas in the Northeast and Midwest United States affected by the Great Migration (African American), of which Harlem was the largest. Though it was centered in the Harlem neighborhood of the borough② of Manhattan in New York City, in addition, many francophone③ black writers from African and Caribbean colonies who lived in Paris were also influenced by the Harlem Renaissance.

Until the end of the Civil War, the majority of African Americans had been enslaved and lived in the South. After the end of slavery, the emancipated African Americans, freed men, began to strive for civic participation, political equality and economic and cultural self-determination. Soon after the end of the Civil War the Ku Klux Klan Act of 1871 gave rise to speeches by African-American Congressmen addressing this Bill. By 1875 sixteen blacks had been elected and served in Congress and gave numerous speeches with their newfound civil empowerment. The Ku Klux Klan Act of 1871 was renounced by black Congressmen and resulted in the passage of Civil Rights Act of 1875, part of Reconstruction legislation by Republicans. By the late 1870s, Democratic whites managed to regain power in the South. From 1890 to 1908 they proceeded to pass legislation that disenfranchised most Negros and many poor whites, trapping them without representation. They established white supremacist④ regimes of Jim Crow segregation in the South and one-party block voting behind southern Democrats. The Democratic whites denied African Americans their exercise of civil and political rights by terrorizing black communities with lynch mobs and other forms of vigilante violence as well as by instituting a convict labor system that forced many thousands of African Americans back into unpaid labor in mines, on plantations, and on public works projects such as roads and levees. Convict laborers were typically subject to brutal forms of corporal punishment, overwork, and disease from unsanitary conditions. Death rates were extraordinarily high. While a small number of blacks were able to acquire land shortly after the Civil War, most were exploited as sharecroppers⑤. As life in the South became increasingly difficult, African Americans began to migrate north in great numbers.

---

① Harlem Renaissance：哈莱姆文艺复兴
② borough：自治市镇，行政区
③ francophone：说法语的
④ supremacist：种族优越论者
⑤ sharecroppers：佃农

Most of the African-American literary movement arose from a generation that had lived through the gains and losses of Reconstruction after the American Civil War. Sometimes their parents or grandparents had been slaves. Their ancestors had sometimes benefited by paternal investment in cultural capital, including better-than-average education. Many in the Harlem Renaissance were part of the Great Migration out of the South into the Negro neighborhoods of the North and Midwest. African-Americans sought a better standard of living and relief from the institutionalized racism in the South. Others were people of African descent from racially stratified① communities in the Caribbean who came to the United States hoping for a better life. Uniting most of them was their convergence in Harlem.

The Harlem Renaissance was successful in that it brought the Black experience clearly within the corpus of American cultural history. Not only through an explosion of culture, but on a sociological level, the legacy of the Harlem Renaissance redefined how America, and the world, viewed African-Americans. The migration of southern Blacks to the north changed the image of the African-American from rural, undereducated peasants to one of urban, cosmopolitan sophistication. This new identity led to a greater social consciousness, and African-Americans became players on the world stage, expanding intellectual and social contacts internationally.

The progress—both symbolic and real—during this period became a point of reference from which the African-American community gained a spirit of self-determination that provided a growing sense of both Black urbanity and Black militancy, as well as a foundation for the community to build upon for the Civil Rights struggles in the 1950s and 1960s.

The urban setting of rapidly developing Harlem provided a venue for African-Americans of all backgrounds to appreciate the variety of Black life and culture. Through this expression, the Harlem Renaissance encouraged the new appreciation of folk roots and culture. For instance, folk materials and spirituals provided a rich source for the artistic and intellectual imagination, which freed Blacks from the establishment of past condition. Through sharing in these cultural experiences, a consciousness sprung forth in the form of a united racial identity.

Many critics point out that the Harlem Renaissance could not escape its history and culture in its attempt to create a new one, or sufficiently separate from the foundational elements of White, European culture. Often Harlem intellectuals, while proclaiming a new racial consciousness, resorted to mimicry of their white counterparts by adopting their clothing, sophisticated manners and etiquette. This "mimicry②" may also be called assimilation, as that is typically what minority members of any social construct must do in order to fit social norms created by that construct's majority. This could be seen as a

---

① stratify: 分层
② mimicry: 模仿

reason that the artistic and cultural products of the Harlem Renaissance did not overcome the presence of White-American values, and did not reject these values. In this regard, the creation of the "New Negro" as the Harlem intellectuals sought, was considered a success.

After You Read

I. Discuss the following questions based on the text.
1. What kind movement was the Harlem Renaissance?
2. Why did African Americans begin to migrate north in great numbers after the Civil War?
3. Why was Harlem Renaissance successful?
4. What kind of new identity have the Black people acquired by means of Harlem Renaissance?
5. What provided a venue for African-Americans of all backgrounds to appreciate the variety of Black life and culture?
6. Why did many critics point out that the Harlem Renaissance could not escape its history and culture to create a new one?

II. True or false
1. The Harlem Renaissance also included the new African-American cultural expressions across the urban areas in the Northeast and Midwest United States affected by the Great Migration, of which Harlem was the second largest.   (   )
2. In the movement, lots of white writers from Caribbean colonies are influenced. (   )
3. After the end of slavery, the emancipated African Americans, freedmen, began to strive for civic participation, political equality and economic and cultural self-determination.   (   )
4. After the Civil War, a large number of blacks were able to acquire land.   (   )
5. The Harlem Renaissance supplied a foundation for the community to build upon for the Civil Rights struggles in the 1950s and 1960s.   (   )
6. The Harlem Renaissance encouraged the new appreciation of folk roots and culture. For instance, folk materials and spirituals provided a rich source for the artistic and intellectual imagination, which freed Blacks from the establishment of past condition.   (   )

For Fun

I. Movies to see

Beloved (1998): It is a 1998 film based on the novel by the American writer Toni Morrison. Set after the American Civil War (1861–1865), it is inspired by the story of an African-American slave, Margaret Garner, who escaped slavery in Kentucky late

January 1856 by fleeing to Ohio, a free state.

II. Websites to visit

1. http://womenshistory.about.com/od/tonimorrison/p/toni_morrison.htm
2. http://global.britannica.com/EBchecked/topic/255397/Harlem-Renaissance
3. http://en.wikipedia.org/wiki/Harlem_Renaissance

III. Writing

More and more companies tend to employ equal numbers of male and female workers. Do you think it is negative or positive for social development? Discuss both of opinions and present your opinion within 250 words.

Chapter 19

John Updike (1932-2009)
约翰·厄普代克

Section A Literary Focus

作者简介(About the Author)

【生平】 约翰·厄普代克,美国作家、诗人,生于美国宾夕法尼亚州雷丁。父亲是高中数学教师,母亲是一名作家,热爱写作,一度是《纽约客》的撰稿人。厄普代克年少时,常常看到母亲坐在打字机前敲敲打打。厄普代克小时有口吃的毛病,又患牛皮癣。从小嗜读推理小说,喜欢的作家有阿加莎·克里斯蒂,后来在母亲的鼓励下尝试写作。1950年在哈佛大学攻读英文系,并曾在英国牛津大学留学一年。返美后成为《纽约客》杂志(The New Yorker)"城中话题"(Talk of the Town)专栏作家,辞去《纽约客》工作后专事写作。为了解决经济压力,他养成了每天必写5页纸的习惯,并长年定居新英格兰区(New England)。一生发表了大量体裁多样的作品,包括系列小说"兔子四部曲"、"贝克三部曲"以及一些短篇小说集、诗集和评论集等。其中,《兔子富了》和《兔子歇了》使他分别于1982年和1991年两度获得普利策小说奖。厄普代克被公认为美国最优秀的小说家之一,他的文风对许多作家产生了巨大影响。2009年1月27日,因肺癌在马萨诸塞州去世,终年77岁。

【主要作品】《兔子,快跑》(Rabbit, Run, 1960),《兔子归来》(Rabbit Redux, 1971),《兔子富了》(Rabbit Is Rich, 1981),《兔子歇了》(Rabbit at Rest, 1990),短篇小说集《早期故事》(The Early Stories: 1953-1975, 2003)等。

作品选读(Selected Writings)

《A&P》是美国小说作家约翰·厄普代克的"奥林格故事"之一,创作于1963年,正是《兔子跑了》(1961)的时代。作家以一古老小镇中央的A&P食品超级市场为背景,借19岁的店员萨米之口,讲述了一个篇幅不长但含义深刻的故事。厄普代克在一次同记者的谈话中谈过小说题目的深刻含义,从大西洋到太平洋,正是美国本土的地理位置,因而是整个美国的象征。

A & P

　　In walks these three girls in nothing but bathing suits. I'm in the third check-out slot, with my back to the door, so I don't see them until they're over by the bread. The one that caught my eye first was the one in the plaid green two-piece. She was a chunky kid, with a good tan and a sweet broad soft-looking can with those two crescents of white just under it, where the sun never seems to hit, at the top of the backs of her legs. I stood there with my hand on a box of HiHo crackers trying to remember if I rang it up or not. I ring it up again and the customer starts giving me hell. She's one of these cash-register-watchers, a witch about fifty with rouge① on her cheekbones and no eyebrows, and I know it made her day to trip me up. She'd been watching cash registers forty years and probably never seen a mistake before.

　　By the time I got her feathers smoothed and her goodies into a bag—she gives me a little snort in passing, if she'd been born at the right time they would have burned her over in Salem—by the time I get her on her way the girls had circled around the bread and were coming back, without a pushcart, back my way along the counters, in the aisle between the check-outs and the Special bins. They didn't even have shoes on. There was this chunky one, with the two-piece—it was bright green and the seams on the bra were still sharp and her belly was still pretty pale so I guessed she just got it (the suit)—there was this one, with one of those chubby② berry-faces, the lips all bunched together under her nose, this one, and a tall one, with black hair that hadn't quite frizzed right, and one of these sunburns right across under the eyes, and a chin that was too long—you know, the kind of girl other girls think is very "striking" and "attractive" but never quite makes it, as they very well know, which is why they like her so much—and then the third one, that wasn't quite so tall. She was the queen. She kind of led them, the other two peeking around and making their shoulders round. She didn't look around, not this queen, she just walked straight on slowly, on these long white prima donna legs. She came down a little hard on her heels, as if she didn't walk in her bare feet that much, putting down her heels and then letting the weight move along to her toes as if she was testing the floor with every step, putting a little deliberate extra action into it. You never know for sure how girls' minds work (do you really think it's a mind in there or just a little buzz like a bee in a glass jar?) but you got the idea she had talked the other two into coming in here with her, and now she was showing them how to do it, walk slow and hold yourself straight.

　　She had on a kind of dirty-pink—beige③ maybe, I don't know—bathing suit with a

---

① rouge：胭脂
② chubby：圆胖的
③ beige：米黄色

little nubble all over it and, what got me, the straps were down. They were off her shoulders looped loose around the cool tops of her arms, and I guess as a result the suit had slipped a little on her, so all around the top of the cloth there was this shining rim. If it hadn't been there you wouldn't have known there could have been anything whiter than those shoulders. With the straps pushed off, there was nothing between the top of the suit and the top of her head except just her, this clean bare plane of the top of her chest down from the shoulder bones like a dented sheet of metal tilted in the light. I mean, it was more than pretty.

She had sort of oaky hair that the sun and salt had bleached, done up in a bun that was unravelling①, and a kind of prim face. Walking into the A & P with your straps down, I suppose it's the only kind of face you can have. She held her head so high her neck, coming up out of those white shoulders, looked kind of stretched, but I didn't mind. The longer her neck was, the more of her there was.

She must have felt in the corner of her eye me and over my shoulder Stokesie in the second slot watching, but she didn't tip. Not this queen. She kept her eyes moving across the racks, and stopped, and turned so slow it made my stomach rub the inside of my apron, and buzzed to the other two, who kind of huddled against her for relief, and they all three of them went up the cat-and-dog-food-breakfast-cereal-macaroni-rice-raisins-seasonings-spreads-spaghetti-soft-drinks-rackers-and-cookies aisle. From the third slot I look straight up this aisle to the meat counter, and I watched them all the way. The fat one with the tan sort of fumbled with the cookies, but on second thought she put the packages back. The sheep pushing their carts down the aisle—the girls were walking against the usual traffic (not that we have one-way signs or anything)—were pretty hilarious. You could see them, when Queenie's white shoulders dawned on them, kind of jerk, or hop, or hiccup, but their eyes snapped back to their own baskets and on they pushed. I bet you could set off dynamite in an A & P and the people would by and large keep reaching and checking oatmeal off their lists and muttering "Let me see, there was a third thing, began with A, asparagus, no, ah, yes, apple sauce!" or whatever it is they do mutter. But there was no doubt, this jiggled② them. A few house-slaves in pin curlers even looked around after pushing their carts past to make sure what they had seen was correct.

You know, it's one thing to have a girl in a bathing suit down on the beach, where what with the glare nobody can look at each other much anyway, and another thing in the cool of the A & P, under the fluorescent lights, against all those stacked packages, with her feet paddling along naked over our checkerboard green-and-cream rubber-tile floor.

"Oh Daddy," Stokesie said beside me. "I feel so faint."

---

① unraveling: 松散的

② jiggle: 轻摇

"Darling," I said. "Hold me tight." Stokesie's married, with two babies chalked up on his fuselage① already, but as far as I can tell that's the only difference. He's twenty-two, and I was nineteen this April.

"Is it done?" he asks, the responsible married man finding his voice. I forgot to say he thinks he's going to be manager some sunny day, maybe in 1990 when it's called the Great Alexandrov and Petrooshki Tea Company or something.

What he meant was, our town is five miles from a beach, with a big summer colony out on the Point, but we're right in the middle of town, and the women generally put on a shirt or shorts or something before they get out of the car into the street. And anyway these are usually women with six children and varicose veins② mapping their legs and nobody, including them, could care less. As I say, we're right in the middle of town, and if you stand at our front doors you can see two banks and the Congregational church and the newspaper store and three real-estate offices and about twenty-seven old free-loaders tearing up Central Street because the sewer broke again. It's not as if we're on the Cape; we're north of Boston and there's people in this town haven't seen the ocean for twenty years.

The girls had reached the meat counter and were asking McMahon something. He pointed, they pointed, and they shuffled out of sight behind a pyramid of Diet Delight peaches. All that was left for us to see was old McMahon patting his mouth and looking after them sizing up their joints. Poor kids, I began to feel sorry for them, they couldn't help it.

Now here comes the sad part of the story, at least my family says it's sad but I don't think it's sad myself. The store's pretty empty, it being Thursday afternoon, so there was nothing much to do except lean on the register and wait for the girls to show up again. The whole store was like a pinball machine and I didn't know which tunnel they'd come out of. After a while they come around out of the far aisle, around the light bulbs, records at discount of the Caribbean Six or Tony Martin Sings or some such gunk you wonder they waste the wax on, six packs of candy bars, and plastic toys done up in cellophane that fall apart when a kid looks at them anyway. Around they come, Queenie still leading the way, and holding a little gray jar in her hand. Slots Three through Seven are unmanned and I could see her wondering between Stokes and me, but Stokesie with his usual luck draws an old party in baggy gray pants who stumbles up with four giant cans of pineapple juice (what do these bums do with all that pineapple juice I've often asked myself) so the girls come to me. Queenie puts down the jar and I take it into my fingers icy cold. Kingfish Fancy Herring Snacks in Pure Sour Cream: 49¢. Now her hands are empty, not a ring or a bracelet, bare as God made them, and I wonder where the money's coming from. Still with that prim look she lifts a folded dollar bill out of the

---

① fuselage：机身

② varicose vein：静脉曲张

hollow at the center of her nubbled pink top. The jar went heavy in my hand. Really, I thought that was so cute.

Then everybody's luck begins to run out. Lengel comes in from haggling① with a truck full of cabbages on the lot and is about to scuttle into that door marked **MANAGER** behind which he hides all day when the girls touch his eye. Lengel's pretty dreary, teaches Sunday school and the rest, but he doesn't miss that much. He comes over and says, "Girls, this isn't the beach."

Queenie blushes, though maybe it's just a brush of sunburn I was noticing for the first time, now that she was so close. "My mother asked me to pick up a jar of herring snacks." Her voice kind of startled me, the way voices do when you see the people first, coming out so flat and dumb yet kind of tony, too, the way it ticked over "pick up" and "snacks." All of a sudden I slid right down her voice into her living room. Her father and the other men were standing around in ice-cream coats and bow ties and the women were in sandals picking up herring snacks on toothpicks off a big plate and they were all holding drinks the color of water with olives and sprigs of mint in them. When my parents have somebody over they get lemonade and if it's a real racy affair Schlitz in tall glasses with "They'll Do It Every Time" cartoons stenciled② on.

"That's all right," Lengel said. "But this isn't the beach." His repeating this struck me as funny, as if it had just occurred to him, and he had been thinking all these years the A & P was a great big dune and he was the head lifeguard. He didn't like my smiling—as I say he doesn't miss much—but he concentrates on giving the girls that sad Sunday-school-superintendent stare.

Queenie's blush is no sunburn now, and the plump one in plaid, that I liked better from the back—a really sweet can—pipes up, "We weren't doing any shopping. We just came in for the one thing."

"That makes no difference," Lengel tells her, and I could see from the way his eyes went that he hadn't noticed she was wearing a two-piece before. "We want you decently dressed when you come in here."

"We are decent," Queenie says suddenly, her lower lip pushing, getting sore now that she remembers her place, a place from which the crowd that runs the A & P must look pretty crummy③. Fancy Herring Snacks flashed in her very blue eyes.

"Girls, I don't want to argue with you. After this come in here with your shoulders covered. It's our policy." He turns his back. That's policy for you. Policy is what the kingpins want. What the others want is juvenile delinquency④.

All this while, the customers had been showing up with their carts but, you know,

---

① haggle：讨价还价，争论
② stenciled：用模板印刷
③ crummy：寒酸的
④ delinquency：行为不良，违法犯罪

sheep, seeing a scene, they had all bunched up on Stokesie, who shook open a paper bag as gently as peeling a peach, not wanting to miss a word. I could feel in the silence everybody getting nervous, most of all Lengel, who asks me, "Sammy, have you rung up this purchase?"

I thought and said "No" but it wasn't about that I was thinking. I go through the punches, 4, 9, GROC, TOT—it's more complicated than you think, and after you do it often enough, it begins to make a little song, that you hear words to, in my case "Hello (bing) there, you (gung) hap-py pee-pul (splat)"—the splat being the drawer flying out. I uncrease the bill, tenderly as you may imagine, it just having come from between the two smoothest scoops of vanilla I had ever known were there, and pass a half and a penny into her narrow pink palm, and nestle the herrings in a bag and twist its neck and hand it over, all the time thinking.

The girls, and who'd blame them, are in a hurry to get out, so I say "I quit" to Lengel quick enough for them to hear, hoping they'll stop and watch me, their unsuspected hero. They keep right on going, into the electric eye; the door flies open and they flicker across the lot to their car, Queenie and Plaid and Big Tall Goony-Goony (not that as raw material she was so bad), leaving me with Lengel and a kink[①] in his eyebrow.

"Did you say something, Sammy?"

"I said I quit."

"I thought you did."

"You didn't have to embarrass them."

"It was they who were embarrassing us."

I started to say something that came out "Fiddle-de-doo." It's a saying of my grandmother's, and I know she would have been pleased.

"I don't think you know what you're saying," Lengel said.

"I know you don't," I said. "But I do." I pull the bow at the back of my apron and start shrugging it off my shoulders. A couple customers that had been heading for my slot begin to knock against each other, like scared pigs in a chute.

Lengel sighs and begins to look very patient and old and gray. He's been a friend of my parents for years. "Sammy, you don't want to do this to your Mom and Dad," he tells me. It's true, I don't. But it seems to me that once you begin a gesture it's fatal not to go through with it. I fold the apron, "Sammy" stitched in red on the pocket, and put it on the counter, and drop the bow tie on top of it. The bow tie is theirs, if you've ever wondered. "You'll feel this for the rest of your life," Lengel says, and I know that's true, too, but remembering how he made that pretty girl blush makes me so scrunchy[②] inside I punch the No Sale tab and the machine whirs "pee-pul" and the drawer splats

---

① kink: 弯曲
② scrunchy: 揪心

out. One advantage to this scene taking place in summer, I can follow this up with a clean exit, there's no fumbling around getting your coat and galoshes, I just saunter① into the electric eye in my white shirt that my mother ironed the night before, and the door heaves itself open, and outside the sunshine is skating around on the asphalt.

I look around for my girls, but they're gone, of course. There wasn't anybody but some young married screaming with her children about some candy they didn't get by the door of a powder-blue Falcon station wagon. Looking back in the big windows, over the bags of peat moss and aluminum lawn furniture stacked on the pavement, I could see Lengel in my place in the slot, checking the sheep through. His face was dark gray and his back stiff, as if he'd just had an injection of iron, and my stomach kind of fell as I felt how hard the world was going to be to me hereafter.

Questions for discussion
1. What rules and conventions are customers expected to follow in a supermarket? How does the behavior of Queenie and her friends violate these conventions?
2. Given what you learn about Sammy in the story, what do you see as his primary motivation for quitting his job?

文学术语(Definition of Literary Terms)

Tetralogy is a compound work that is made up of four distinct works. The typical example is John Updike's *Rabbit Series* (*Rabbit, Run*; *Rabbit Redux*; *Rabbit is Rich*; *Rabbit at Rest*). There is also (*Rabbit Remembered*), the fifth part of the series.

Section B Cultural Notes

Before You Read

1. Try to search on the Internet or in the library about the Vietnam War and the related information. Give a 3-minute classroom presentation.
2. Do you know The Vietnam War? Share your knowledge with your classmates.

Start to Read

The Vietnam War

The Vietnam War, also known as the Second Indochina② War, and known in

---

① saunter: 漫步
② Indochina: 印度支那

Vietnam as the Resistance War against America or simply the American War, was a Cold War-era proxy war that occurred in Vietnam, Laos, and Cambodia from 1 November 1955 to the fall of Saigon on 30 April 1975. This war followed the First Indochina War (1946-1954) and was fought between North Vietnam—supported by the Soviet Union, China and other communist allies—and the government of South Vietnam—supported by the United States and other anti-communist allies. The Viet Cong (also known as the National Liberation Front, or NLF), a lightly armed South Vietnamese communist common front aided by the North, fought a guerrilla① war against anti-communist forces in the region. The People's Army of Vietnam (aka the North Vietnamese Army) engaged in a more conventional war, at times committing large units into battle.

As the war wore on, the part of the Viet Cong in the fighting decreased as the role of the NVA grew. U.S. and South Vietnamese forces relied on air superiority and overwhelming firepower to conduct search and destroy operations, involving ground forces, artillery, and airstrikes. In the course of the war, the U.S. conducted a large-scale strategic bombing campaign against North Vietnam, and over time the North Vietnamese airspace became the most heavily defended airspace of any in the world.

The U.S. government viewed American involvement in the war as a way to prevent a Communist takeover of South Vietnam. This was part of a wider containment strategy, with the stated aim of stopping the spread of communism. According to the U.S. domino theory, if one state went Communist, other states in the region would follow, and U.S. policy thus held that accommodation to the spread of Communist rule across all of Vietnam was unacceptable. The North Vietnamese government and the Viet Cong were fighting to reunify Vietnam under communist rule. They viewed the conflict as a colonial war, fought initially against forces from France and then America, as France was backed by the U.S., and later against South Vietnam, which it regarded as a U.S. puppet state②.

Beginning in 1950, American military advisors arrived in what was then French Indochina. U.S. involvement escalated in the early 1960s, with troop levels tripling in 1961 and again in 1962. U.S. involvement escalated further following the 1964 Gulf of Tonkin incident, in which a U.S. destroyer clashed with North Vietnamese fast attack craft, which was followed by the Gulf of Tonkin Resolution, which gave the U.S. president authorization to increase U.S. military presence. Regular U.S. combat units were deployed beginning in 1965. Operations crossed international borders: bordering areas of Laos and Cambodia were heavily bombed by U.S. forces as American involvement in the war peaked in 1968, the same year that the Communist side launched the Tet Offensive. The Tet Offensive failed in its goal of overthrowing the South

---

① guerrilla：游击队
② puppet state：傀儡政权

Vietnamese government but became the turning point in the war, as it persuaded a large segment of the United States population that its government's claims of progress toward winning the war were illusory despite many years of massive U.S. military aid to South Vietnam.

Disillusionment with the war by the U.S. led to the gradual withdrawal of U.S. ground forces as part of a policy known as Vietnamization, which aimed to end American involvement in the war while transferring the task of fighting the Communists to the South Vietnamese themselves. Despite the *Paris Peace Accord*, which was signed by all parties in January 1973, the fighting continued.

In the U.S. and the Western world, a large anti-Vietnam War movement developed. This movement was part of a larger Counterculture of the 1960s which fed into it.

Direct U.S. military involvement ended on 15 August 1973 as a result of the Case-Church Amendment passed by the U.S. Congress. The capture of Saigon at the hands of the North Vietnamese Army in April 1975 marked the end of the war, and North and South Vietnam were reunified the following year. The war exacted a huge human cost in terms of fatalities. Estimates of the number of Vietnamese service members and civilians killed vary from 800,000 to 3.1 million. Some 200,000-300,000 Cambodians, 20,000-200,000 Laotians, and 58,220 U.S. service members also died in the conflict.

After You Read

I. Questions for discussion

1. How many years did the Vietnam War last?
2. What were the two main forces involved in the Vietnam War?
3. What was the intention of American's fight in the Vietnam War?
4. Why was the Ted Offensive the turning point of the war?
5. What was the aim of Vietnamization?
6. How many U.S. service members died in the war?

II. True or False

1. The Vietnam War, also known as the Second Indochina War, and known in Vietnam as the Resistance War against America or simply the American War, was a Cold War-era proxy war that occurred in Vietnam, Laos, and China from 1 November 1955 to the fall of Saigon on 30 April 1975. ( )
2. In the course of the war, the U.S. conducted a large-scale strategic bombing campaign against South Vietnam. ( )
3. The North Vietnamese government and the Viet Cong viewed the conflict as a colonial war, fought initially against forces from France and then America. ( )
4. Regular U.S. combat units were deployed beginning in 1965. ( )

5. In 1966, American involvement in the war began to decline, so bordering areas of Laos and Cambodia were heavily bombed by France forces. (   )
6. The Tet Offensive aimed to overthrow the South Vietnamese government, but it failed. (   )

For Fun

I. Websites to visit

1. http://www.nybooks.com/contributors/john-updike/
2. http://history1900s.about.com/od/vietnamwar/a/vietnamwar.htm
3. http://en.wikipedia.org/wiki/Vietnam_War

II. Writing

Some people think the government should act to decide how people live in order to make a healthier life. Others think individual should decide their own lifestyle. Discuss both views, and write down your opinion about 300 words.

参考文献

江宁康.美国文学经典教程.南京:东南大学出版社,2010.
刘存波.文学导论.北京:高等教育出版社,2007.
马浩岚.美国语文.北京:中国妇女出版社,2008.
陶洁.美国文学选读(第三版).北京:高等教育出版社,2011.
王守仁,刘玉红,赵宇.英美短篇小说.南京:南京大学出版社,2012.
虞建华.英语短篇小说教程.北京:高等教育出版社,2010.
张冲.美国文学选读.上海:复旦大学出版社,2008.

Baym, Nina. et al ed. *The Norton Anthology of American Literature*, Vol. 1 and Vol. 2, Sixth Edition. New York: W.W. Norton, 2003.

Beach, Christopher. *Introduction to Twentieth-Century American Poetry*. Cambridge: Cambridge UP, 2003.

Hart, James D, ed. *The Oxford Companion to American Literature*, Fifth Edition. Oxford University Press & Beijing: Foreign Language Teaching and Research Press, 1993.

http://assets.cambridge.org/97805217/90895/excerpt/9780521790895_excerpt.pdf
http://www.emersoncentral.com/selfreliance.htm
http://www.english.illinois.edu/maps/poets/g_l/hd/helen.htm)
http://www.freepatentsonline.com/article/College-Literature/211454294.html
http://www.history.com
http://www.learner.org/amerpass/unit04/authors-5.html
http://www.newrepublic.com/article
http://plato.stanford.edu/entries/transcendentalism
http://sfs.scnu.edu.cn/hhzhang/webcourse2/kcln/13/5.htm
http://thoreau.library.ucsb.edu/thoreau_life.html
http://en.wikipedia.org/wiki

图书在版编目(CIP)数据

美国文学与文化：英文 / 朱丽田主编. — 南京：南京大学出版社，2015.10
(高校英语选修课系列教材)
ISBN 978-7-305-15814-8

Ⅰ. ①美… Ⅱ. ①朱… Ⅲ. ①英语－阅读教学－高等学校－教材 ②文学史－美国－高等学校－教材 ③文化史－美国－高等学校－教材 Ⅳ. ①H319.4

中国版本图书馆 CIP 数据核字(2015)第 202066 号

出版发行	南京大学出版社
社　　址	南京市汉口路 22 号　　邮　编　210093
出 版 人	金鑫荣
丛 书 名	高校英语选修课系列教材
书　　名	美国文学与文化
主　　编	朱丽田
责任编辑	董　颖　　　　　编辑热线　025-83592655
照　　排	南京南琳图文制作有限公司
印　　刷	南京玉河印刷厂
开　　本	787×1092　1/16　印张 16.5　字数 412 千
版　　次	2015 年 10 月第 1 版　2015 年 10 月第 1 次印刷
ISBN	978-7-305-15814-8
定　　价	40.00 元

网址：http://www.njupco.com
官方微博：http://weibo.com/njupco
官方微信号：njupress
销售咨询热线：(025) 83594756

* 版权所有，侵权必究
* 凡购买南大版图书，如有印装质量问题，请与所购图书销售部门联系调换